"Fast enough to see a lot, slow enough to touch it all: travel by bicycle is unique"

Andy Shackleton

The author, setting out.

Crossing the Tay Bridge.

Arctic Cycle

Two Wheels, Ice and Fire

Andy Shackleton

Kennedy & Boyd

Published by
Kennedy and Boyd
an imprint of
Zeticula
57 St Vincent Crescent
Glasgow
G3 8NQ

http://www.kennedyandboyd.co.uk
admin@kennedyandboyd.co.uk

ISBN 1-904999-33-6 Paperback

Dedication

To my uncle, whose memory was the catalyst for this journey.
And my wife, who suggested that it might be thus.

Contents

Dedication   5
List of maps and illustrations   8
Prologue   13
Cold comfort   15
Sorted   18
Memories   19
All at sea   22
All points north   31
With a little help   51
On the buses   78
A hitchhiker's ride to   96
Tourist   102
Capital   119
Day tripper   130
On tenterhooks and tyres   138
'Caps and 'bergs and contemplation   146
Thank you   153
Proceeding in an easterly direction   159
On fjords   164
Decompression   172
Next   180
On small islands   184
Reflections   199
Towards life in the fast lane   215
Journey on   225
And a little culture   231
It's all over, now   244
Appendix   253
Acknowledgements   257
About the Author   259
Index   261

List of maps and illustrations:

The author, setting out. 2
Crossing the Tay Bridge. 2
Northern Europe. 10
Iceland. 11
Faroe Islands. 12
First of many punctures. 24
Lerwick. 24
First Sight of Iceland. 30
Approaching Seyðisfjörður. 30
Seyðisfjörður. 34
The long and winding road. 34
Hot brakes, two tumbles ..... and a couple of punctures. Wouldn't miss
it for the world. 41
Vopnafjörður. And a lupin or two. 41
Vopnafjörður ..... the sort of church where a fairy princess might
marry the lonely woodman. 44
Home alone. Cold running water available ..... near Bakkafjörður. 44
Mighty driftwood blown ashore has long been regarded as a building
material in coastal regions. 47
Þorshöfn. 47
Look out 50
Decades' worth of ancient rusting hulks and skeletons of agricultural
machinery had assumed character, art form. 50
Námaskarð. Underfoot was warm, hot even, to touch 60
..... and pools of hot, grey mud plopped, spouted, boiled. 60
I camped close to clear blue water at a wonderful site in Reykjahlid. 63
Mývatn is an island infested lake that covers an area of 37 square kilometres. 63
Akureyri ..... a thriving university city and commercial centre. 70
Bordeyri ..... looked like it would be the first to succumb to any rise
in sea level. 70
Stykkishólmur. 85
Ísafjörður ..... contrasting with the harsh landscape left behind, a
breathtaking combination of mountain and water. 85
Reykjavik ..... a thoroughly modern cityscape, complete with all the trappings. 103
Reykjavik ..... What charmed me was the near-universal vista of sea
and mountain as a backdrop. 103
Hvolfjörður ..... its dark water reflecting rolling moorland. 107
Deep beyond imagination, crystal clear water filled a volcanic ravine. 107
Þingvellir ..... Parliament Plains. 112
Strokkur ..... a foaming jet of near-boiling water that spouts to a
height of 20 metres. 112
Gullfoss ..... where the river Hvita (white river) tumbles 32 metres in
two spectacular falls. 117
Reykjavik ..... suburbs built on volcanic lava. 117
Reykjavik ..... Lake Tjornin, backdrop to many of the municipal buildings. 124
Reykjavik ..... Gardens, open parkland, water, and well proportioned buildings. 124
Reykjavik ..... In a country renowned neither for its sand or its castles,
an imported beach. 125
Reykjavik's suburbs ..... autonomous regions spread out over vast areas. 125

Leaving Reykjavik ..... At ten o'clock, I set out amongst the Saturday evening traffic. 127

At 3.00am a dozen horses dashed past in the opposite direction. Nothing seemed odd any more. 127

Seljalandsfoss ..... For company, only noisy waterfalls that tumbled down huge rocky cliffs. 133

Here would live Trolls. A magical ravine where shafts of sunlight cut through the shadows. 133

With bike lifted over my head, that day I waded through a dozen or more rivers. 135

Seljalandsfoss ..... landing in the most delightful ice cold pool. 135

Vik ..... Iceland's most southerly village. 141

Eating the meal I had cooked at a table in a car park close to a river. 141

Just one of the enormous timber decked concrete and steel bridges that went on for ever. 144

Morsárjökull ..... glacier & lagoon. 144

Jökulsárlón ..... camped within a stone's throw of so much beauty. 149

Cliffs of ice, shimmering, near luminescent under the surface sank from view. 149

Jökulsárlón ..... the shapes, the colours, the cold raw impact of ice towering above. 151

From cliffs to cartoon characters. All these and more. 151

Housing estate ..... Icelandic style. 163

Djúpivogur ..... just the second fishing harbour I had come across on the south coast. 163

A night in close company with gently breaking surf. 170

Fáskrúðsfjörður ..... once home to 5000 French people, with street names to match. 170

Mablik Endar ..... where surfaced roads run into the gravel. And more! 174

Just when it looked impossible, we swept sharply northwards through a steep mountain pass. 174

Back to Seyðisfjörður. 181

Tórshavn ..... capital city, Faroe Islands. 181

Tórshavn harbour. 189

Beyond Toftir ..... the combination of mountain and water so perfect. 189

Leirvik ..... Brightly coloured craft of all shapes and sizes filled the harbour. 198

Towards Klaksvik ..... together, we willed our ferry through a confusion of water. 198

Firmly clamped in position by the neck, most had plainly decided to keep it simple. 205

One poor creature had found it all too much and with all four legs bound together, lay grumbling. 205

Climbing away from Funningsfjørdur on gradients so steep the front wheel lifted with each stroke of the pedals. 209

Gjögv ..... home to just sixty. Narrow streets, Old world charm. 209

A well mannered stream. 209

Jarlshof ..... Shetland Isles. Where I had to leave travel mode for a while. 221

Arrival in Stromness (Orkneys) ..... a town huddled together for warmth. 221

Thurso ..... The surfers had all left. 243

Caledonian Canal, Inverness ..... couldn't have been more different. 243

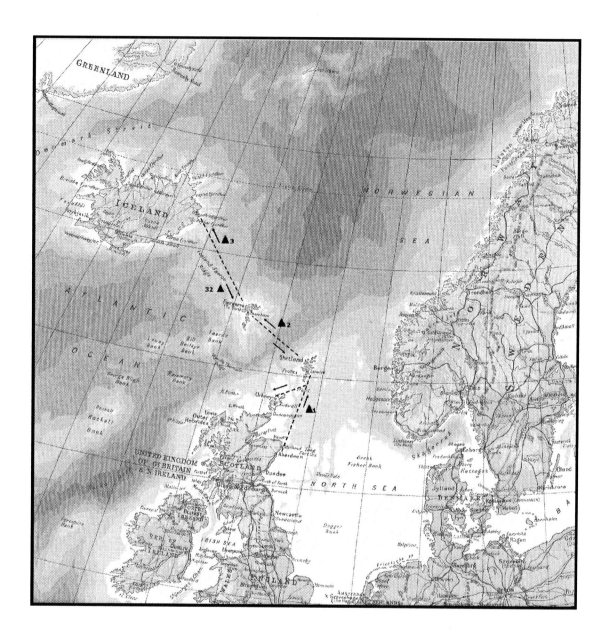

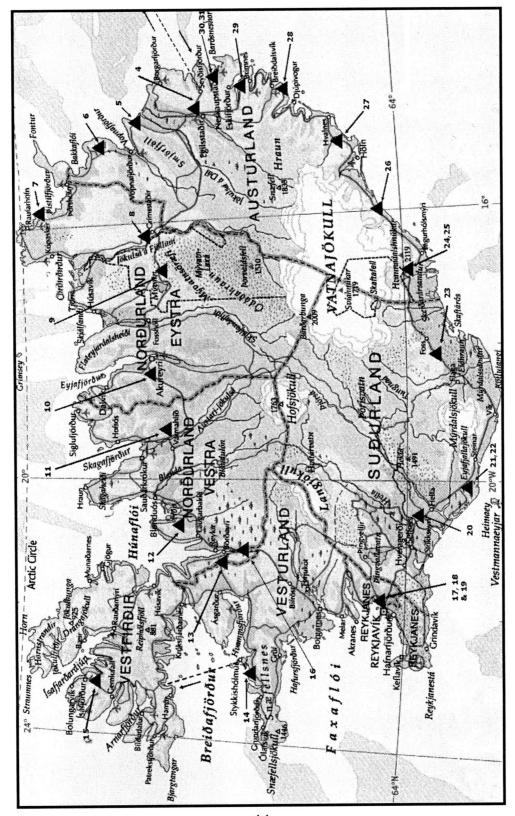

Iceland

11

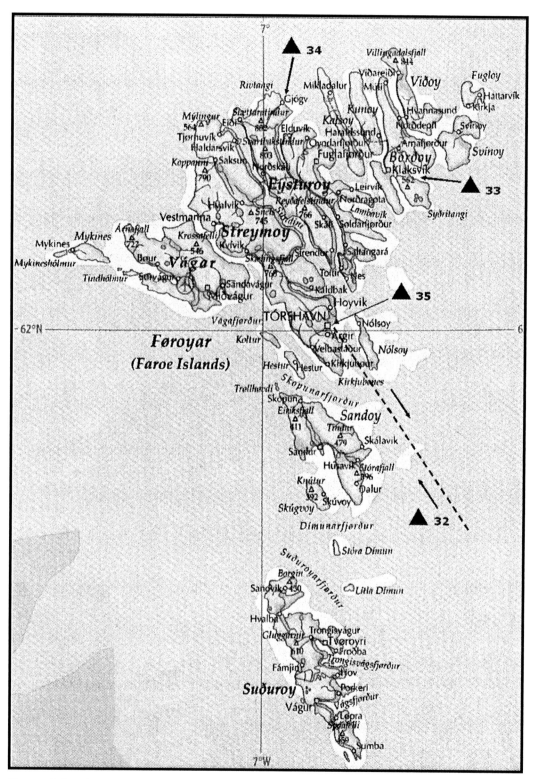

Faroe Islands

Prologue

The horizon is alternately disappearing, to re-appear a shining mass of watery sunlit swell. I am on the ferry, *Norrona,* nine hours out from Lerwick, on my way to Iceland, a country I've wanted to visit for years. Below, on the car deck, is my bicycle: transport for the next few weeks.

Several years ago I cycled from Bergen to Narvik, beyond the Arctic Circle in Norway. Riding North the landscape became ever more barren, the coastline stark, rocky, spectacular. It developed from there. The feeling that Iceland would be a natural sequel. And whim became "must do".

Early retirement, a part time business, a little relief teaching. For the first time in my life I could decide what to do and, more importantly, when to do it. The catalyst was a small legacy from an elderly relative. I wanted to do something with it that would always be there. My wife suggested that it would go a long way towards funding the Iceland trip. And memories are for ever. Outside the mid-summer period, roads there are often closed by snow. With a six-week time slot in June, July or August lined up and a decision to travel by ferry, my schedule would also include The Shetland, Faroe and Orkney Islands.

Cold comfort

"For sheer excitement it was hard to beat. Only a steamy night in the arms of some exotic new lover could have come near."

Floating on water so deep in colour as to defy belief, there they were. Cold, raw cliffs shimmering high above deep luminescent turquoise. Icebergs. Most pure white, others streaked with black volcanic debris scraped out in an on-going ice age. Imagination fashioned the rest. Cartoon characters, caterpillars, cacti. Animals, shells ..... and mushrooms where the water had undercut. All these and more, together with tiny floaters not unlike those you'd find in the iced water jug. And beyond that spectacle, the glacier that spawned all of this. Full of crevasses ..... a river of ice pushing, creaking, ever downward from the permanent ice-cap above at a rate of up to a metre per day. Only to have great chunks, some as big as houses, factories even, float away in the lake to finally melt and join that incredibly short river to the sea beyond.

Wisps of cloud settled over the icecap. Evening sun picking out snow covered peaks. The quiet, for even the wind had died off, broken randomly by great splashes as lumps of ice melted off and tumbled into the lake. All of this right outside my tent, set up on grass at the top of the embankment not a stone's throw away from such splendour. Memories that will be with me for all time. Surely a place to contemplate one's soul. The sense of space, of nature in the raw, nature in charge, crept in the more I looked on the scene. Every shade of turquoise reflected in the fading light, cobalt blues and near-greens melded, their gently rippling colours mirrored on giant white forms above.

My imagination was still hard at work as I crept into my sleeping bag for a disturbed, if relaxing night. For sheer excitement it was hard to beat. Only a steamy night in the arms of some exotic new lover could have come near. But that is the stuff of dreams. Back down to earth, quite alone in the calm of that half-lit northern night, drifting between sleep and what passed for being awake, I dreamt of shapes. Of *gruyère* cheese, tail of a plane, pulled teeth and more. Yet sharply conscious of ice noisily crashing into the water beside me.

Back to my sojourn by the breakfast table. It was here in the ferry port of Seyðisfjörður that my journey round Iceland had started all those weeks ago. Outside, mountains mirrored on the fjord rippling gently in the morning sun. Inside, the book simply had leapt out from the shelves, asked to be opened. *Landscapes - Images of Iceland* ..... amazing images provoking instant recall and a powerful rush of emotions. It's how Alice must have felt. Delving further into memories of my journey I, too, was in Wonderland and risked a flood of tears. Looking back over the trip, feelings about it had changed almost by the minute ..... an emotional roller coaster at the mercy of challenging landscape and weather alike, yet rewarding beyond imagination for all of that. To say that I was on high emotional alert is to understate my feelings.

The night by icebergs had to be a highlight. But what of the others, the people, amusing incidents, trips down memory lane? And the low points. For without them no reflection would be complete. In no particular order a whole bunch of images flashed before me. In moments I was back making preparations for the journey. Then it was the train trip north, the sea crossings, stopovers, and snapshots of just what a body is capable of doing, given opportunity and determination. I had ridden on roads that thought they were river beds, waded through fast flowing real ones with bike aloft, crossed fearsome sand desert, battled with tearing winds and pedalled through the night to avoid them. In more than 1200 miles of riding I had wrecked tyres, buckled wheels and carried out endless roadside repairs. But I got to walk amongst hot mud pools, spouting geysers and glaciers, drink in Reykjavik's bars, and bathe in the world famous Blue Lagoon. Engaging with countless travellers and local people alike, souls had been bared, doubts, disappointments aired, thrills and humour shared. The region's colourful past had unfolded as the lid lifted on ancient democracies and medieval soaps that are the Icelandic sagas.

The beauty and majesty of what I had seen brought to mind so many images from the past it was difficult to know where to start. But returning to the present, the important issue of considering what was to follow came next. Tomorrow I would sail on to The Faroes, an eighteen island nation of 46,000 set in the North Atlantic Ocean half way between Iceland and Norway. Complete with its own language and currency, the country has a reputation for spectacular green slopes sweeping down on deep water, turf roofed buildings, fishing, fishing, and fishing. And weather. But that aside, using fine roads, ferries and tunnels I planned to see much of what was on offer. Then for dessert there would be the Shetland and Orkney Islands. And a little ancient culture.

But enough of anticipating the end. That would be then. This was now. And there was a whole lot of mileage left in the tank. Time to get the show back on the road.

Sorted

"It left just four days for all my preparations."

A single phone call to Aberdeen was all it took. Booked on the overnight crossing to Lerwick, Shetland Isles. In one week's time. That was my preparation to date. Plus a determination that wells up inside when a decision has been made. As a school boy, homework was always left till the last possible moment. I functioned better under pressure then. And nothing's changed. The weekend away with my wife had been arranged for some time. It left just four days for all my preparations.

My mountain bike had taken me all over the world. But, having bought "The Lonely Planet" guide book twelve months earlier I knew it would be in for the ride of its life. I had also learned that repair facilities were to be found in only two places on my intended route. Forgotten until preparation for Iceland got under way, the freewheel (the bit that clicks when you stop pedalling) had been giving notice for some time. Then I remembered it slipped occasionally, made the most frightful noises. That was a starting point. And it went on from there ..... winding up as a costly exercise that saw wheels re-built, new brakes, tyres, and more. Water had been a problem on my last ride, the more so when rough-camping away from sites. A third bottle, mounted under the frame, would give more flexibility. Three days to go and decisions about what clothes to take. Two days to go, and waterproofing everything in sight.

Guide books are fine, but people so much more assuring. Concerned about all sorts of issues, I phoned the Icelandic embassy. They answered queries concerning how much food it would be wise to carry, water supplies, weather, camping restrictions, insect problems, language and the like. Now, with one day to go, it was time to make final decisions on exactly what to take with me. From initial wish list, it filtered down to very little. For obvious security reasons, important items such as camera, palm top computer, travel documents, films, batteries, would travel in my backpack. Tent, sleeping bag and mat were secured to the rear rack with bungee cords, and plastic wrapped against the weather. Everything else packed in two rear panniers or the handlebar mounted carrier, on top of which sat my map, making it easy to follow while on the move. A test run, fully laden, proved I could make it go. Which was just as well since my train would be arriving in Aberdeen at roughly the same time next day.

Memories

"Such is the power of memories: I was at the start of an experience that would create a whole bunch of new ones."

1

After a turn, arm in arm round the garden, a little emotional in the cool of an early summer dawn, my wife drove me to Skipton station. A photograph, a tearful goodbye hug, a wave. This was it. For six weeks it would be just me, my bicycle ..... and an exceedingly small tent.

For me large railway stations possess a unique aura. A heady mix of people who want to be somewhere else. A special kind of urgency as anxious faces check departure boards, companions are met, last minute purchases are made, and garbled announcements ring out. Out of nowhere, as I joined the early morning crowds dashing through Leeds city station, memories of childhood holiday journeys flooded back. Taxis, suitcases, steam, smoke ..... a word with the driver picked out in the glow from the firebox as he and his fireman made final checks on all those brass-rimmed gauges. For a moment I was back there trailing along behind my parents, bucket and spade in hand. Such is the power of memories. And I was at the start of an experience that would create a whole bunch of new ones.

The East Coast main line has a reputation for spectacular views along the Northumberland coast, north of Newcastle. With this in mind, and a window seat facing forwards, I would make the most of the journey to Aberdeen, almost 350 miles away. The woman with seat reservation slips came round soon after that. And my spot would be required from York onwards. The pair who joined me there had left their wives in charge of respective business commitments and were off to St Andrews for a short golfing break. Together, we put the world to rights as the countryside flashed by in a blur ..... coffee and biscuits close at hand. The stop at Newcastle added a fourth member to the team. Of an age, that age when the rule book says perm, the style police in her area were plainly tightening up. The four of us, now, wrestled with world crises and our family stories. A fine way to spend a journey ..... and so different to the isolation engendered by motoring.

The Northumberland coast did not disappoint. On past Holy Island, before pausing in peaceful Berwick on Tweed, firmly fixed in England now, scene of many a battle for power in times past. Over the Royal Border bridge and into Scotland, up through Edinburgh and beyond. Then the Forth bridge, monumental in scale as it strides across the sea, a symbol of Britain's engineering greatness since 1890. And Dundee, after crossing the Tay estuary on the two-mile-long, gracefully curving, bridge ..... scene of the 1879 collapse. Seventy-five people died when their train plunged into the water on a stormy December evening witnessed, still, by the stumps of Thomas Bouch's ill fated structure. We continued to hug the coast spectacularly, passing through places the names of which I had not heard since times spent quietly as a small boy, while my father listened to the football results on Saturday tea times. He only rarely did the pools, yet each week sat gravely taking in the scores of teams up and down the country, delivered in unique monotone with predictable inflection as results were announced. Thus, childhood images of Arbroath, Montrose, and more, turned into places with stations. Just how Partick Thistle had made out that week flashed through my mind. That's the power of travel, for Scottish League or, indeed, any results hadn't crossed my mind in more than forty years. And I still had no idea where Partick was.

My golfing companions left the train at Cupar, to complete their journey by taxi. Despite its fame St. Andrews, like so much of the country, is no longer accessible by rail. I said goodbye to my other companion as we drew into Aberdeen. Although continuing north on a connecting train she, too, would complete her journey by road. As the demand for travel continues to increase, the state of a once-complete rail network saddens me. Ever-increasing traffic congestion on our roads is testimony to decades of short term political decisions on transport needs.

Arriving at a busy city station after a long journey is an exciting travel experience. If you like that sort of thing. Negotiating roughly a thousand steps, laden with a bicycle and all I needed for six weeks travelling was less so. Alone amongst a sea of people who clearly knew exactly where they were going, done it many times before. At last, the feeling that my journey had begun.

My ferry did not leave for hours, but anxious to collect tickets, make sure all was in order for the onward journey, I wobbled out amongst the city traffic. Ports have an air of expectancy about them. Cranes, warehouses, vessels of all shapes and sizes. Cars, trucks, buses. And their occupants ..... who want to leave the country just as soon as possible. Starting the next phase of a journey is a good feeling. Glancing down at the schedules on the tickets, part of me was at sea already. Back out to reality, and a flat tyre, it wasn't long before the couple approached. Colourful lycra on middle aged bodies had marked them out as cyclists on the train. Now they were here, booked on the same ferry to Lerwick on the Shetland Islands. My French is poor, their English worse. Despite this, the fellow set to and showed me how to repair a puncture. That I might have done this sort of thing before didn't appear to concern him as the pair told of home in Paris, careers. And this ..... their first cycling holiday.

Described as the biggest granite hole in Europe, just a little to the north is a quarry. For over two hundred years it has provided building material for Aberdeen, the Granite City, where a third of the working population is employed in oil-related industries, and an air of prosperity dominates the area. I ought to have spent time in any one of the museums and galleries to be found there but, anxious about leaving possessions locked to a lamp post, contented myself with a little sightseeing amongst rather grand buildings.

Travel provokes all sorts of feelings. Here, I was transported back to Dunedin, on the east coast of New Zealand's South Island; eleven years ago I had been reminded of Aberdeen, Scotland. A year-long exchange had found me teaching in Tasmania, Australia's island state. Along with my wife and son we had swapped jobs, homes, cars, cats even. A two week break in September saw us two thousand miles away, travelling extensively on both New Zealand's North and South Islands in a large, hired motor-home. What we packed in was amazing: skiing, swimming in naturally heated pools, helicopter and jet boat rides. Plus sights that send shivers down my spine yet. What we saw there might be responsible in some small way for the Iceland trip I was embarking on. Visions of hot streams, plopping mud and mighty geysers made a serious impression then. I hoped to see more. Another flashback featured quite different surroundings. Aberdeen harbour, Hong Kong, was awash with sampans and houseboats, surrounded by skyscrapers when I was there, a tourist amongst it all some years ago. Memories. Experiences. They are for ever.

All at sea

"Time for reflection, time for anticipation. Time to get my head round what lay ahead. "

For check-in procedure a bike is regarded as a vehicle. But that said, along with motor-cycles, they are kept waiting until all other vehicles are on board. In unbelievably poor French I found myself chatting to Monsieur et Madame Puncturepair. They had been shopping, and dangled all over their bikes were the plastic bags to prove it. Near impossible to ride, but clearly they were going to eat well.

On board at last, my bicycle tied to the loops provided at the side of the vehicle deck. The ramps were raised and huge doors closing by the time I made my way up to my cabin, deep within the bowels of the ship. That's where budget travellers find themselves. And basic describes accommodation like this. Bunk beds for four, a sink, a noisy fan. Stuffy. Not a place to linger.

Up on deck people everywhere with a sense of purpose that is exclusive to travel. Land receded as piers and jetties were left behind. The North Eastern coast of Scotland drifted by, remaining in sight until late on a beautiful, if cool, summer evening. And final gasps of daylight fell on what had to be the Orkney Islands ..... on my itinerary for the return journey. A turn on deck before going to bed had me puzzled for a moment or two. Out at sea a whole bunch of lights. But this was the North Sea. Not half a mile away were oil rigs. And between them, more lights. That, on paying close attention, turned out to be attached to small boats moving between rigs. North Sea oil. It's been helping the UK economy for years. And here it was, right beside me. Seeing this sort of thing on film is one thing. But realising that hundreds of folks were hard at work way out at sea, late at night, made me think about my career as a teacher. And it couldn't have been more different.

2

My cabin companions had been on deck. Conscious of an ever present rumble and the vibration of diesel engines, their note changing as we rode the swell ..... in an American accent I learned of land on both sides, our approach to Lerwick. And the fact that we would be docking soon. On deck in that early morning it was cold, damp, blustery. And very grey. If I'd just opened the flap of my tent, I would have closed it again and crept back inside my sleeping bag. That sort of day. This was Bressay Sound. With mainland Shetland to port and Bressay, the island, to starboard. Low, white painted buildings crept out of a grey dawn. And somewhere in there, the feeling that this was a film set ..... that nothing but scaffolding lay behind the fronts. But fifteen inhabited islands, amongst the archipelago of one hundred-plus that make up The Shetlands, are home to twenty-three thousand people, a relatively stable population now, since oil related industries reversed a trend toward migration, which saw only seventeen thousand living here forty years ago.

Lerwick's wet stone buildings huddled round deserted streets. Despite breakfasting on porridge, a bacon butty and coffee, a feeling of emptiness washed over me. Not yet into travel mode, familiar routines filled my mind, still. Alone amongst hundreds of people an undercurrent, a feeling of "do I really want to do this" swirled through my mind, invaded my thoughts. But it is the challenge of the unknown that drives travellers on. This would soon click in, I knew. If it didn't I was in a fix. "Will all drivers return to their vehicles" rang out, as though the speaker had fingers clasped tightly over his nose. Not unlike the "cabin crews cross-check all doors" routine, I smiled to myself, as flights to exciting places flashing up on some kind of memory scan. With that I hurriedly collected belongings from my cabin and spent a few moments exchanging plans with the American. There is always someone doing that bit more. And here he was. Like me he was travelling to Iceland. After meeting up with friends in Lerwick. Who had crossed the North Sea from Norway in a thirty-five foot sailing vessel. Together they would take on the North Atlantic. Recalling conditions just a dozen miles off Cornwall several years past when I had crewed on a similar sized vessel, my proposal to cycle round Iceland paled. But in fairness, he seemed impressed with my plans too.

First of many punctures.

Lerwick.

Right in front of the harbour is the Shetland Hotel. With all the charisma of a young tower block it came a close second to the moored barges that are home to hundreds of oil workers. Together they reflected the weather. And my feelings at the time. My ferry to Iceland did not leave until two o'clock the following morning, and though it was still early I followed signs to the town centre. Riding past folks on foot, overtaken by cars, trucks, buses, the feeling that everyone else knew exactly what they were doing, where they were going, done it hundreds of times before. My world had shrunk to a bicycle. And what I could carry on it.

Like the ones that clicked every time the wheel went round, the ones I used as a schoolboy, my cycle computer records distance covered. This being the twenty-first century, not content with mere distance, tiny modern equivalents have a mode for everything. They tell you the time, time spent riding, actual and average speed as well. Only a mode that tells how much your wife spent on clothes and what to have for tea is missing. In my pocket for security on the ferry, riding into town mine did none of this, its screen remaining quite blank. A Virgo, a perfectionist, a fusspot some would say ..... and about to set out on my biggest bicycle challenge ever. To say that I was unamused is to understate my feelings. Yet less than five minutes from the harbour, a garage doubling up as supermarket and, I could scarcely believe, a cycle shop. One that sold cycle computers. Out there in the blustery rain, tool kit unleashed for its first (of many, but happily I didn't know that at the time) engagement, the new gadget fitted. And order restored.

Eighteen hours before continuing my journey, yet I had no specific plans apart from the need to see something of Shetland. A short ride into town found me, typically, at the small boats harbour admiring the craft, which included a reproduction Viking longship, and wondering if the American had met up with his companions. Here was a place that plainly looked to the sea for a living. The wealth and variety of shipping made that clear. Clearly an important shopping area, surfaced not in tarmacadam or quaint cobbles but large stone flags, one block back from the sea front is Commercial Street. This narrow, winding street provided a fascinating introduction to the town. Old world, yet up to the minute amongst the solid charm of stone. At the Northern end is Harbour Street, the sort of name you'd expect in a place like this, but then St.

Magnus, St. Olaf, and King Harald Streets. Odd ..... until considering the fact that Bergen, in Norway, is closer than Aberdeen. Vikings settled here over a thousand years ago. Shetland was effectively part of Scandinavia, and handed over to Scotland in 1468 as part of the marriage dowry for Margaret, daughter of the King of Norway, Denmark and Sweden, on her marriage to King James III of Scotland.

Warm, dry, and comfortably seated in the library, I caught up with my notes and sought advice on must-sees within a half day ride. Scalloway. That was the place to go. Nice ride, not too steep, interesting harbour, castle. That sort of thing. So, with wind and rain in my face, that's where I ended up. Moorland with spectacular views of the sea might best describe the route. But what did strike me is the excellent state of the infrastructure. Shetland Council receives an income from all oil brought ashore. It has plainly impacted, for even in tiny Scalloway is a thoroughly modern Leisure Centre. The roads are excellent, the buses frequent and near-new.

Lunch of fish and chips found me chatting to a bunch of boys from the local secondary school. Quite contented with their lot in life, long journeys from scattered communities included. But not to be trusted with the salt and pepper pots, it seemed, for "would I return them to the counter if I left before them?" Everyone waved to me, it seemed. Just like home videos where it's compulsory. After a quick look at the castle, complete with its modern windows, I took the road for Burra. Heading south on a string of tiny islands now joined by bridges the coastal vistas were amazing. Turquoise sea broke over white sand in the watery sunlight, while the wind desperately tried to push me back where I had come from. But then it made riding back the easier.

My ferry didn't leave till early next morning but it was too cold to sit around outside, and could prove expensive holed up in the pub. In the event I wound up at Lerwick's stunning Youth Hostel. Where, after a shower and a meal I was able to relax in the lounge. And learn a little of Shetland life. The day had seen a roller-coaster of feelings and emotions. But the evening was truly mine. Time for reflection. Time for anticipation. Time to get my head round what lay ahead. A whirlwind of activity the week before had left no time for any of this. Now, with doubts dispelled and body alerted to huge demands that would be made upon it, I was ready for anything and busting to get on with the journey, if truth be told.

Evidently about to leave, on the same ferry, was a party of schoolchildren from The Faroe islands. They had been staying at the hostel for a week on some kind of cultural visit. Tearfully hugging one another and their Shetland hosts, plainly put about by their imminent departure, they were unquestionably drunk on excitement. And more. I did not envy their teachers.

Riding towards the harbour at midnight, it was not quite dark. There was a calm I could feel as much as see. Exciting, relaxing, reassuring at the same time ..... the journey had begun to wash over me. Travel mode at last. Everyday life behind me. With boarding pass sorted I sat in the departure lounge amongst languages that were literally foreign to me. Guessing that they were Danish, Faroese, Icelandic, the only certainty was they were unfamiliar. In foreign parts one's native language stands out. And Alicia spoke perfect English. Having lived in Iceland on an exchange scheme some years previously, she was travelling down Memory Lane and planned to visit her hosts there. Smiling knowingly when told of my plans, she filled me in on detail, gave a little low-down on places to see. Alan & Margaret were to visit friends there as well. Over the tannoy came an announcement. "Would Mr Shackleton report to vehicle check-in immediately as boarding is commencing." After rushing through passport control I was told to join a couple of other cyclists near the ramps and await instructions. Together, we waited almost an hour while all the vehicles boarded. This, despite the fact that we could see exactly where to put our bikes. They would be tied to the loops, clearly visible at the side of the vehicle deck. Jorn and his new wife were using bikes that the postman might have rejected forty years ago. Together with bulky kit roughly tied on, they planned to cycle in The Faroes for a week, sail on to Iceland and after riding there, abandon the bikes and fly back to their home in the USA. Some honeymoon!

Aboard at last, my berth was shared with a bunch of young Norwegian men on a drinking holiday. They had plainly taken their brief seriously and were still hard at work after crossing the North Sea from Bergen. By the time I joined them, my five companions had covered the entire floor with bottles, glasses and cans. All in a terribly civilised fashion, for one by one they quietly fell into a drunken stupor, leaving me to arrange myself round their debris. Too late to be early, after claiming my bunk I sat in the bar with several large, smooth, whiskys for company. On this layer a few couples danced to live music in the dusky dawn. But what were they up to on the one below? And the one below that? Descending social order. Or what? People. Asleep, cleaning their teeth, reading, having a pee, sex even! Then the cars. My bike. And engines thudding away. The question occupied my thoughts for all of two nanoseconds. It's an odd concept if you think about it as we floated across the ocean. At times like this being alone is a state of mind as much as anything else. For here I was late at night amongst a sea of couples, with only thoughts for company. Out on deck before turning in, the lights of Shetland still flickering over the stern ..... our creamy wake picked out in the moonlight. The beat of the engines felt, as much as heard, together with that of the music indoors.

3

Next morning, clearly hung over, my Norwegian companions spoke in low tones and breakfasted on Coke. Leaving them to it for coffee and a sticky bun, the horizon of my world shifted gently with the swell. Time, now, to spend getting to grips with my plan to ride right round Iceland. Alicia had confirmed that the ring road, Route 1, was the way to do it ..... a "standard" trip being around fourteen hundred kilometres, just short of nine hundred miles. But I've always been attracted to the idea of going to the extreme limits of places. The furthest east, the highest point. That kind of thing.   It came as no surprise then ..... a final decision to see the North Eastern tip of Iceland. A route that would take me over mountain passes on minor roads only recently opened after winter closure. Wind, it seemed, was unpredictable. Having spoken to several people who had been to Iceland before, they appeared to be evenly split on which direction to go round. I would ride north first, go anti-clockwise. If only to avoid having half a road between me and the sea on coastal stretches. That was a final decision on the matter. The rest, I would work out as I progressed.

Arriving by boat is another of those unforgettable travel experiences. Docking in Tórshavn, capital of The Faroes, an archipelago of eighteen islands, total population 46,000, was no exception. From specks on the horizon they grew, until we were sailing close to vibrant green hills with houses nestling at their base. It being a pleasant, if cool, afternoon, most of the passengers, it seemed, were on deck for arrival. It's the sort of thing you do if, like me, you've never been there before, an opportunity to get a fix on a place, its buildings, people, even. Scandinavia for sure. A city brimming with those delightful coloured timber buildings, seemingly cascading down steep hillsides and views to die for. A city plainly looking to the sea for support. Homeward bound (now sober) school children waved demurely to parents, visitors gawped, sailors threw ropes to harbour crew, vehicle ramps clanked on concrete.

Alicia was spending a week here before sailing on to Iceland. Alan, Margaret and I had three hours and waited until the crowds had cleared before collecting landing cards. My (still vertical) cabin companions walked down the gang-plank, carrying yet more duty-free. They were in with a chance, I thought, if it's some kind of alcohol consumption event they've been practicing for. And there was me, thinking they were just a bunch of drunks.

A short walk through Tórshavn's prosperous looking streets aimlessly looking at the prices of things, comparing them with those at home, took us high above the city amongst traditional housing, some with turf roofs. And all within sight of the sea. I would have a four day stopover here on the return journey, so collected maps and tourist information on the way back to our ferry. Re-joining ship for the final stage of my journey to Iceland felt very expeditionary.

With the cabin to myself now, I had three sacks of empty bottles and cans removed by cleaning staff before, exhausted, taking an early night that promised rough weather. Waking around midnight, a huge sea threatened to throw me out of my bunk. Dressed again, I sat by a window in the bar. In the half light of a northern summer night, we ploughed through waves I guessed to be in excess of thirty feet. One moment riding high, the next thumping down, a wall of water tumbling over the vessel. Gulls raced alongside, skimmed the wave tops, soared high above, then back through or round the spray to re-emerge, surprisingly, then repeating the game time and time again. Transfixed for almost two hours, witnessing what these creatures were capable of made me feel almost inadequate. Pure theatre outside. Inside, a bunch of hardy drinkers who, together with the bar staff, plainly had more pressing things on their minds. With soft music playing, tables and chairs skidding we lurched through the waves.

First Sight of Iceland.

Approaching Seyðisfjörður.

All points north

"What I needed to do was to get my head round the task ahead, my mind half way up there, going for the summit."

4

Waking early to a still-strong swell, washing was a problem. To the extent that one moment the water splashed over me in the time honoured fashion that one comes to expect of a shower ..... the next, the umpire called "wide", we rolled through the waves. Already five hours behind schedule, and sailing directly into a force seven head wind, arrival time in Iceland would be early afternoon.

But one of the pleasures of a sea crossing is the company of fellow travellers. And with language the common denominator, it took just a couple of Canadians, a pair of ex-pats now living in sunny Greece, and myself to sort out politics and education. But a fellow away from home travelling for six weeks must "do something". That out of the way we went on to tackle the thorny problem of waste ..... at international level. Societies, we agreed, started with little in the way of possessions ..... almost all waste being re-cycled. So called development involves the acquisition of more, leading to increased waste that is often disposed of pretty randomly. Only when further development takes place do societies begin to take in the bigger picture, disposing, re-cycling, and generally considering their environment. Together we got it all sorted, in extra time, on our North Atlantic crossing.

Right at the start of my voyage, I had been reminded that people take on all sorts of challenges. Crossing the North Atlantic in a small sailing craft is something I would not consider. Catherine was travelling with her partner to Iceland to do some sea kayaking. A number of years ago, a couple of friends suggested I try some. "Camp on Anglesey," they said. "Go through the Menai Straits at slack water." And that's exactly what we set out to do. Only slack is not the word that exactly springs to mind. Starting just a short distance out of Conway we paddled along the coast in a gentle swell. Beyond Bangor and past the point of no return it was clear that rough water lay ahead. "Keep paddling, fast as you can," they shouted, "or the back end'll swing round with the current and you'll be in." The Swellies, for that's what it is called, beneath Thomas Telford's magnificent suspension bridge, built in 1826, lived up to its name. Never so terrified, yet exhilarated in all my life. Stopper waves and cross currents, whirl pools that opened up spontaneously threatened to swing my bow sideways lest I should slack off paddling. But I lived to tell the tale. And make the return trip next day. Memories of this made me all the more intrigued by a disabled woman who would take this sort of thing on board. And more. Just how much more, I learned as she told me of a recent trip. She had pedalled round Japan on her hand powered trike, hauling a trailer containing camping gear and wheelchair. And, as she went on to describe her ride in Iceland some years before that, I was left in no doubt about the strength of this woman. As I said earlier, there's always someone who's done that bit more. But that's something of an understatement. Having spent time talking to someone who took challenges so seriously, almost too soon Iceland was in sight. From speck on the horizon that might have been cloud, it took on form, grew into a country of majestic snow capped peaks and deep fjords. Rapidly becoming more than just a dot, Seyðisfjörður, at the end of the sixteen kilometre fjord of that name turned into the small, temporarily bustling port. Disembarkation was informal. No one asked for my passport, the authorities being more concerned about food ..... and was I bringing any meat or fresh fruit into the country? A short consideration on the status of dried food found me ashore in foreign parts.

I had said goodbye to my travelling companions earlier. They had partners, plans, schedules, reservations, vehicles. Alone now with nothing more than a bicycle for company, amongst a boat load of folks who plainly knew exactly what they were going to do next ..... and who they were going to do it with. What I needed was somewhere to chill out ..... somewhere to get used to the idea that I make all the decisions from now onwards. In truth, with only one route out of Seyðisfjörður there wasn't much to decide, though I did feel the need to get dug in. I don't dislike the uncertainty of a situation such as this, but have friends who will not leave home without bookings, reservations, firmed up plans made months in advance. Fine, if you're on a "proper" holiday; planes, hotels, hire cars, and the like. Been there, do that when I travel with my wife. But the rules of engagement are different on a venture like this. And travelling by bike is an uncertain means when you don't know the terrain. Wind, steep hills, poor roads, simply being off form. All these, and more, can turn the best laid plans on their head. Little more than a week since that final decision to travel, and here I was at the start of a major challenge that would take me amongst sights I had only imagined.

At the supermarket, over (free, would you believe) coffee, a first meaningful look at my map before selecting food. Prepared for an exchange in sign and nod, the entire transaction was conducted in perfect English, learned, the young cashier explained, at school she had recently left. Only with difficulty would visions of a similar scenario at my local supermarket come to mind. With all three water bottles full, and food for several days on board, I would be independent, could stop anywhere. It's a good feeling. I guess snails must feel much the same ..... what with carrying their homes around, travelling, eating where they like. And there'd not be much in it as far as speed was concerned either. It had been a long time since I'd ridden any distance at all.

Established in the mid-nineteenth century as a trading centre and herring fishery, Seyðisfjörður developed into East Iceland's largest community. Norwegian settlers later that century were responsible for many of the delightful timber buildings, some imported in kit form, that give the town its unique appeal today. With a current population of around 900 it was plain that many still look to the sea for a living. In the cool afternoon sun I rode gently round the streets, drinking in the mountains on three sides, their flanks a mass of snow melt streams dashing for the sea. High level snow accentuated their stratified appearance before giving way to bare rock. Lower down still, traces of vegetation as grass, brightly coloured wild flowers, and finally scrubby trees, battled to survive harsh conditions. Crystal clear water lapped the shore, boats of all shapes and sizes in the harbour completing the picture postcard as the ferry loaded for her return voyage to The Faroes and Denmark, where the week-long summertime cycle would begin all over again.

Leaving was hard in more ways than one. Gently undulating amongst pastureland with a fast flowing river for company, riding inland the wind was behind me. This was to be a pattern that would repeat itself time and time again. The valley narrowed, the road becoming steeper and winding to gain height. Now repeatedly tumbling amongst the rocky terrain, ever faster, louder with its load of melted snow, the river providing an

Seyðisfjörður.

The long and winding road.

unforgettable introduction to the delights of Iceland. Observed earlier from below before setting out, the changes in vegetation were now close at hand as I climbed through them. Patchy at first, snow randomly concealed the river, now turquoise against brilliant white, with a lacework of ice at the edges. Later a small ski area ..... a simple affair, just a shed or two and a couple of lifts. Early June, almost mid summer, yet only a week or two earlier it would have still been open. Parts of the six-mile climb were amazingly steep. Stop for rests. Maybe. But I will not push. Stubborn, stupid, call it what you like ..... one of my principles is that I ride all hills. The road now cut through snow a metre and a half deep, and the river had disappeared from sight by the time I finally reached the plateau, to realise just how cold it was.

The large hut was set back from the road. It was crudely equipped with bunks and a stove. One of many set up in places where the weather can catch travellers out, I first came across this sort of thing cycling in Northern Norway. Placed in similar situations they, too, are open to travellers; in complete contrast, the one I stopped at to cook a meal was complete luxury, with furniture and polished floor to match. Rapidly moving on in the gathering cold, my reward for pedalling through that white desolation in blustery conditions was a rapid, if cold, nine mile twisting descent, to approach Egilsstaðir through low woodland. Exciting new landscapes opened up as a taste of things to come. Snow capped mountains as far as the eye could see, barren heath land dotted with small snowmelt lakes, a river in the valley below.

Egilsstaðir is situated at a crossing point on the river and lake chain that extends from Vatnajökull, Iceland's largest ice cap (and world's third largest!). Situated close to icy-green Lake Lögurinn (The Smooth One), the town is a concrete place with a population of around 1600. With all one would expect of a service town, the main attraction for me was a comfortable camp site and, just a short walk away, the naturally heated public swimming pool and Jacuzzi complex. Relaxing in my tent after eating a first camp meal, I phoned home to assure my wife that all was well. Describing my spectacular surroundings and experiences to date, home, in reality less than a thousand miles away might have been on another planet. Later, in the sulphur smelling hot water of the Jacuzzi I reflected on my venture. It was, I considered, privilege indeed. Then, back in the warmth of my tent I planned next day's ride, insofar as that was possible.

5

It was almost ten o'clock before climbing out of my sleeping bag, to follow what had become routine on previous trips. The domestic quarters of my tent are so small that it is impossible to sit up properly. That said, the storage area accommodates all my kit. Included in this is a Trangia stove. A large base, allied to the fact that the pans sit low inside, makes it virtually impossible to tip over. Fuelled by clean, non-explosive methylated spirits, cooking under cover becomes an option ..... vital on a trip like this ..... cool and windy weather being the norm.

The camp site water smelled a little sulphurous. It is plain common sense here, bearing in mind that folks simply drill a hole in the ground and hey presto, out pops hot water. Plainly it's not that simple in reality, but it does mean that heating costs in a country renowned for the severity of its weather can be kept under control. Water at 70 degrees C is piped into town from hot springs several kilometres away and used for communal heating purposes.

It took an hour and a half from waking to getting on the road. Clearly out of practice, packing stove, plates, cutlery and food, followed by sleeping mat and bag all took time. That done, the tent has to come down. It's an odd feeling. And one I'm always conscious of. The security of a place you can call home, if only for a few hours. There one minute ..... a crumpled heap on the grass, the next. Then until the evening it's an outdoor life, no matter what the weather.

My plan was to head for the coast, then follow it as closely as possible, taking in the far North Eastern peninsula before heading west for Húsavík and Akureyri. Weather information and forecasts are displayed at official camp sites and tourist information centres. Staff told me that a snowstorm had blocked my proposed high level route the day before but it was now reported passable again. With this in mind I rode north on Route 1, the ring road. Traffic near nil, terrain uninteresting, dull even. Roughly it might be described as low level moorland extending as far as the eye could see. A little over ten miles and already it was decision time. Head for the North Eastern Raufarhöfn peninsula and ride within a whisker of the Arctic Circle. Ride those extra one hundred and twenty miles on second class coastal and mountain roads that might just be blocked. Or follow the main road? I wrestled with the decision for all of half a second and set off on unsurfaced Route 917. Having crossed it on a mighty bridge I followed the Jökulsá á Dal, another river and lake chain making its way from ice to gravely estuary. So often turning out to be nothing more than a single farm, signs for places came and went, a collection of dead four wheel drives being the common denominator. Finding somewhere sheltered to eat lunch was a problem. There were no trees. In fact nothing vertical but telegraph poles. Standing amongst spectacular desolation as I pedalled into the wind, crossing endless rivers full to bursting as they dashed down steep gullies from the snow on the mountain range to my left, before sweeping through wide valleys and heading for the sea. Smjörfjöll (Butter Mountain) is reputed by locals to be the home of Father Christmas. They've got it wrong. Everyone knows it's Number 1, Snow Street, Fairyland. It was this range that my route north would cross ..... a high level pass within sight of the sea. My map showed surfaced roads in red, unsurfaced ones yellow. Shown in white, the road over the pass was described as a Highland Track, only passable in summer, and not suitable for normal passenger vehicles.

"Folks like us don't do that kind of thing", my parents would tell my sister and I when we had ideas beyond our station. As to why: "well, we just don't." Anything, from expensive toys to holidays abroad, could be covered by this universal clause. Quite why that phrase popped into my mind at that moment never became clear. But what it did highlight was the fact that my family had been neither poverty stricken nor wealthy. And it must have been a state of mind. That's the way I look at it now. Insert a simple clause in so many of life's decisions. That you can do it, you will do it, that folks like me really can do this sort of thing and you're half way there. It is the difference between a perception that the glass is half empty and the reality that it is half full. And as I pedalled into the wilderness, thoughts concerning what folks like me did not do evaporated.

One of my "must dos" is to put both hands in the sea, river or lake at strategic points on my trips. It's a ritual that confirms arrival, departure, being at one with the elements. Or something. Sounds daft. Is daft. But I like it. And now, for the first time since leaving Seyðisfjörður, I was within a whisker of the sea. Not just any old sea but the North Atlantic crashing noisily on to a deserted gravel beach. Getting there meant crossing the sediment-laden glacial river that I had followed for miles. I would ride through it, keep my feet dry. But, having tumbled several times, I thought better of the plan. Mystic placing of hands would have to wait.

What I needed to do was to get my head round the task ahead, my mind half way up there ..... then mentally image being at the summit, and riding all the way. Niels was on his way to the summit, too. Slowly making my way round the hairpin bends, the motor cycle was rapidly catching up. The spaceman stopped, beamed, laughed loudly, then introduced himself. A Danish student, we exchanged travel experiences the world over. On some kind of course in tourism, fluency in English and German was a requirement. Less than half my age, he had no concept of why I would want to do something like this. Packing things in while I still could, challenging myself, male pride, the sheer exhilaration of tackling a solo journey in spectacular, inhospitable regions. All had an airing. But I still don't know whether I got to the bottom of what makes me do these things, let alone explain it to this eager young man.

This was to be the first of many encounters with fellow travellers. It became so natural to stop, speak, discuss experiences, routes, must sees, must avoids ..... that sort of thing. The transient nature of these encounters was brought into sharp focus quite recently by a friend of mine. She, too, has undertaken some spectacular journeys. Deep and meaningful exchanges, mutual histories shared with complete strangers at the roadside, hundreds, thousands of miles away from home. These, it seems, are not uncommon. Not unlike a party, and finding ourselves talking to all sorts of people, recalling experiences and generally trying to impress them with our prowess at work, sport, or indeed anything that comes to mind as the drinks flow. Only here, there's no need. The fact that you, too, want to travel is a great leveller. It revokes so many taboos ..... age, gender, race, religion, wealth, and many more. So, half way up a mountain pass in spectacular surroundings, I spent half an hour in increasingly weighty conversation before realising that I was simply frozen.

I did ride all the way, the road cutting through deep snow as, together, we gained height. My reward was a view that opened up to read like a large scale map, with sea, mountain, river, estuary, beach and barren lake strewn tundra all easily visible in the cool sunlight. It had got to that time. The time when I start to consider where I will spend the night. Although it was still bright in a land of permanent summer daylight, my stomach reminded me it was time to stop. But just where to camp? I toyed with the idea of setting my tent up on the snow. Done that before. But cold though it was, in the fierce wind, pegs might pull out of the frozen snow. The alternative was to keep going and ride off the mountain.

But, as though placed there just for me, set back from the road, there it was. Surrounded by deep snow, and anchored to the ground with steel cables, with a wooden platform outside, the unlocked door invited me to look inside. Measuring no more than two metres by two and a half, it was roughly divided into sleeping and cooking areas. Equipped with foam mattresses, a gas bottle and cooking platform, double glazed windows framed a view of surrounding mountains picked out in the golden evening sunlight. Now I'm a law abiding fellow, and wasn't sure of the rules of engagement here. Having said that, the wording on the sign pointing to the hut did not make sense. It didn't feature on my map as an emergency hut for use, I knew from my reading, only in life threatening situations. So with no threat to my life, simply no desire to cycle further that day, I manhandled my bike through deep snow to play house for the night. Beans, mashed potatoes and cold ham never tasted so good and washing up afterwards with frozen snow was something of a novelty. A whisky would have completed the picture, I reflected, settling down for the night, with bright sun still a blaze of orange on the snow. Unremarkable you might say, bedding down before it's gone dark. But Iceland goes one better. For the whole of the summer months it never quite goes quite dark. The reason. Proximity to the Arctic Circle ..... an imaginary line drawn at a latitude of 66° 33'. Missing Melrakkaslétta, Iceland's north eastern peninsula by a whisker, it passes through the offshore island of Grimsey. North of this line the sun never sets for at least one day per year and in winter fails to rise above the horizon. So close to that line, I would not see darkness for several weeks.

6

It didn't snow in the night. I wasn't blocked in by it. And after freshening up with the stuff then melting more for breakfast, it was with a little sadness that I left my haven in the hills, though not before signing the little-used guest book. I have told several people of that wonderful night on the mountain. "Weren't you afraid?" was a common, if somewhat sad response. Iceland is one of the safest places in the world, I guess. And just what sort of person would go to the top of a 700 metre snow covered mountain pass on the off chance that someone up there needed getting?

On across the plateau between cliffs of snow, and yet more climbing to another craggy summit. In danger of wobbling off the edge, so steep was the final ascent, but still I would not push. But with Vopnafjörður adding a third dimension to the scene, the view before starting that long descent took my breath away. The road wound down through all of this and below the snow line. Through my spy glass I could follow it running beside the sea into (the town of) Vopnafjörður, some fifteen miles away. In Australia they are described as unsealed roads. Over a period of time ridges develop across them and gravel is shunted into central heaps or at the edges, the more so on sharp corners or steep sections. Maintenance involves scraping the surface flat again using hefty machines that go on to redistribute the gravel evenly. I've driven thousands of miles on them. Go too slowly and the vehicle thumps into every ridge and hollow. Widely known in foreign parts, the technique is to drive fast enough to glide over the surface, allowing the suspension to accommodate undulations. I've cycled there as well and can tell you that Icelandic mountain roads are in a league of their own. Closed for winter under ice and snow, surfaced roads are not an option. Only recently opened for the summer season, my route plainly still featured on the "to do" list for maintenance crews. Picking my way down the steep, loose surface I tumbled off more than once, the front wheel simply sliding away on gravel. Another first was the puncture ..... not a proper puncture. No nails. In fact nothing at all. So hot had the rims become with heavy braking that the glue on previous repairs came unstuck not once, but twice.

Following that amazing descent, stunning coastal vistas opened up with every twist and turn, the whiff of seaweed never far away as the sea lapped round jagged volcanic rock. Snow-covered mountains soared above green meadowland that gave way to scrub, then bare rock. Pedalling close to the shore contrasted so beautifully with earlier experiences, despite the fact that my heavily laden bike slammed into the rutted road no matter how carefully I picked the route. Simple things mean a lot on this kind of venture. And the surfaced road after joining the route from the West was quite simply heaven. Approaching in bright sunshine, the roadside was awash with wild lupins, bright blue almost down to the water's edge Vopnafjörður, at the head of a wide fjord that shares its name, is a village, small town even, with its toes dabbling in the sea. Brightly coloured buildings clustered round the working harbour. Boats tugged at moorings in a brisk wind that would dash them on any

Hot brakes, two tumbles ..... and a couple of punctures. Wouldn't miss it for the world.

Vopnafjörður. And a lupin or two.

one of the rocky outcrops and tiny islands that completed the postcard scene. The church would make another. White painted, timber built, a pointy spire, red corrugated metal roof. It is the sort that a fairy princess might choose when marrying the lonely woodman, to live happily ever afterwards. Lunchtime found me in the first of many filling station cafés that are all things to all people in the smaller communities. With a view to die for I ploughed through a freezer full of burger and chips. Not my kind of food but on this sort of trip energy burns up almost as fast as it can be taken on board. The ice cream would have fed half a dozen. The girl just kept piling on the soft whipped stuff that came to resemble Dusty Springfield's bee-hive hairdo of the 'sixties. Light beer, relatively cheap in a country where folks need a bank loan for a night out on the tiles, rounded off a near-perfect experience while people popped in for a chat, drink, snack. It might have been a TV soap where they all do it. "Iced Enders", perhaps? Here were videos for hire. With titles that included Harry Enfield's Kevin & Perry and (American) Friends. All would be watched and understood without subtitles.

On my way out of town I came across Jonas. Or rather, I came across his bicycle. It was the sort of bicycle one could hardly miss. Large, ancient and bright yellow, it was parked at the roadside on a hefty stand, a trailer not far behind. Panniers, water containers, tent, and sleeping bags the size of a small elephant clung to the combination. Jonas, an older gentleman addressed me in Icelandic ..... that much I gathered. My reply confirmed that his English was limited, though infinitely better than my German. But having shaken hands like long lost brothers we sat together in the sun and using word, gesticulation, drawings even, exchanged plans and experiences. Particularly rewarding for me was the fact that he regarded me as young. I am young. On the inside. But to be told that I am so is encouragement indeed. He was spending three months in Iceland ..... on holiday from home in Switzerland. And has done this for the past eighteen years. In his younger days, like me, he set out to cover a lot of ground, see as much as possible. Now, however, with three week's worth of food on board he planned to stay in the same spot for longer stretches, draw a little, then move on, perhaps 5km, to repeat the scene. With Icelandic friends to call on, it sounded like an excellent way to spend the summer months. Looking more Alpine mountaineer than cyclist, he rides level and downhill stretches. And with waist-mounted harness to ease the burden he hauls his bike up hills and returns for the trailer.

Leaving was hard. It would have been so easy to cop out and spend a night in that lovely setting. But after topping up on food supplies I pedalled into the wind for another twenty miles, the latter part on gravel surfaces that many would describe as off-road riding. Despite continual jolting that threatened the welfare of my bike, I was hanging in there very well indeed. On previous rides saddle soreness has been a major problem. Years ago on a trip over the Pyrenées into France I bought a new saddle in an effort to ease a desperate situation. I did the same in Hobart, Tasmania, and applied creams and gel pads as well, in addition to using cycling shorts with built in padding. In New Zealand I put my bike on the bus from Auckland to The Bay of Islands and rested there for two days before being able to carry on, such was the pain. Experiences like that dampen spirits, sap energy, and make progress near impossible at times. Returning from my trip down under, I determined to get to the bottom, so to speak, of the problem. And here I was, comfortable still, amongst Iceland's finest, fully appreciating the seat post with a spring inside it and expensive saddle with a hole at the vital point, designed for those with little to absorb the jarring.

The fellow from Leipzig was doing it in the opposite direction. Stopping amongst splendid desolation, chatting to someone simply because he, too, was a cyclist seemed so normal. He had ridden 1200 miles before arriving in Iceland, had done a similar distance here and would do more before leaving the country. We discussed routes, sights, kit, aspirations, thoughts about Iceland, and agreed that it made a wonderful challenge. With patches of snow at the roadside, and soaring mountains beyond endless rolling tundra, my route disappeared into the haze as I pedalled on into an empty vastness that threatened to creep inside my head.

I had planned to camp at Bakkafjörður, a fishing settlement tucked away in the Southern corner of Bakkaflói . Then cool clear water cruising cheerfully over a gravel bed, and neatly contained between heather covered banks invited me to stay for the night. Where, after a seriously cold wash in the river, and a meal, I spent the rest of the evening catching up with my notes. Reading is something of a luxury on cycling ventures. Books are heavy, bulky. Instead, I settle down with my palm top computer, committing thoughts, experiences and feelings to record. It rounds off a day's activity, is some kind of a seal of approval that purges what has gone before. And from the homely shelter of my tent that is what I did, while no more than six feet away the river rippled by,

Vopnafjörður ..... the sort of church where a fairy princess might marry the lonely woodman.

Home alone. Cold running water available ..... near Bakkafjörður.

sun shining on the hills beyond.   Having covered only a little over 100 miles to date, I came to the conclusion that I would have to be more disciplined. And yes, tomorrow I would get round that Northern tip.

7

The early start I'd promised myself didn't happen, but with washing dangling off the back to dry in the wind, before long was riding on a sealed road. This, I had learned from experience, meant that I was near a town. But just yards beyond the junction for Bakkafjörður came the sign I had come to dread. *Mablik Endar*, it said, and showed the surfaced section ending. At the top of one of the many steep hills, amongst the vastness that had become so normal, was another junction. The sign made it clear that unauthorised persons were not to be admitted as a radiation hazard existed at this NATO radar installation. It went on to warn against making visual contact with the reflector or guide horn during periods of transmission, and told of danger to pacemakers. Reflectors. Easy. Bowl shaped and shiny. But a guide horn in the act of transmission. Sounds positively racy. Just the sort of thing any God fearing soul would wish to avert his eyes from. If only he knew what not to look at. Now that's a tough cookie. So, feeling not a little unwelcome, I left this heart stopping attraction behind ..... a stark reminder, amongst empty splendour, of what people are capable of doing to one another, it took the edge off the moment. For most of that day I rode on bone jarring gravel. As desolate a spot as you'd find anywhere, I began to wonder why I was there, until looking to my right. There it was again. The sea, with a backdrop of snow capped mountains. Even now, mid June, in sheltered gullies it was possible to see an odd patch of snow right next to the sea. So strong was the wind that I rode across bridges in the centre of the road, for fear of being blown over the low guard rails into icy water below.

Birds were much in evidence. Crossing yet another fast flowing river about to join the sea, Concorde-like geese flew in, surfing to a halt gracefully while (plainly territorial, and concerned for their young) swallow-like Arctic Terns swooped down close. Trees, I thought. They'd have no need for all this angst, this defending of nests on the ground. But that's for another country. Here, anything more than a metre high and they call it a forest. Not a bit of good for a young couple with an egg or two to raise. Sitting on grass at the edge of a pebble beach the Atlantic rolled in so powerfully that, in addition to pulverising the seaweed it had brought a healthy trade in driftwood for someone. Piled at the roadside were what looked like complete tree trunks. Goodness only knows where they floated in from. It isn't Iceland, that's for sure. Some were still drying out. Others were sawn ready for collection.

Shorelines are notorious for all kinds of debris. Sure enough, miles from anywhere in the world, there you'll find them. Like carrots when someone's been sick. And with not a dairy in sight, here they were. Milk crates, that is. Together with the usual selection of oil drums, shoes, plastic bottles and yes ..... the disposable nappy. It's as though some organisation exists to provide these amenities in remote areas. Shoreline Trash International, perhaps? Whose advertisement might read something like: "You tell us what and where. We do the rest. Condoms, crates, cans: anything messy. You make the decisions: we'll trash the beauty spot of your choice. One call to S.H.T.I. and it's a done deal. Distance no object. All areas covered. Discretion assured." Who knows? Demand might be high enough for the business to be floated. The developed world. Where would we be without it?

Up then and over the hills to Þorshöfn, it was a rocky ride on unsealed roads ..... with a strong wind in my face all the way. Despite the fact that it was Sunday there was activity amongst the fishing fleet. Yesterday, Jonas had told me about Sailors' Day. From rowing contests to tugs of war and rescue demonstrations, events and awards take place in coastal towns all round the country. And here the boats were all decked out with bunting to prove it. Having just missed them, it seemed, boat rides for the families were all I got to see. Setting off two hours later, yet another flat tyre demanded attention. The cause, would you believe: heat from the sun had increased pressure in the already rock hard rear tyre and blown off yet another patch!

I must have looked foreign, or was it simply that only foreigners would be daft enough to cycle here. Jörgen, pronounced Jurgen on account of two dots over the "o", approached, and in perfect English enquired where I came from, what I was doing. And why? He really couldn't get his head round the fact that I wanted to do it at all and plainly concluded that I might well be a couple of ships short of a task force. I learned that cod and haddock, plus a little tourism, keep this little town and its population of 430 afloat. But sadly not Jörgen, sea

Mighty driftwood blown ashore has long been regarded as a building material in coastal regions.

Þorshöfn.

sickness confining him to work in the fish factory. Whose manager was disappearing out of the harbour in a small boat. "Gone fishing", it was pointed out. As if working in the industry, week in, week out, was not enough.

A bread crisis found me in the filling station. Sure enough, on this festive occasion, while some mournful, quietly seated diners were filling, others waited patiently ..... as though their train was about to leave. Picture a meal sitting opposite your partner. With whom you've just had an almighty row ..... cutlery is clanking audibly through the hefty silence. You have it in one.

Leaving this merry band with half a loaf, that being all I could carry, I noted that the services on offer here included tyre repair. No prizes for guessing why. On a sealed road with the wind behind I raced along heading for Raufarhöfn, a little over forty miles away. Sheer exhilaration took over as I sped northwards. It was here that I came across the first of many steaming beaches and mudflats. Fascinated by a fellow with the palms of his hands on the ground to detect temperature rise, a tractor driver stopped to check on my sanity. Assured that all was well he went on to tell me that it was quite normal to see clouds of water vapour gently rising from the ground, to be caught in the wind and disappear. "Thin earth's crust", he explained in broken English, "was the cause."

A route through the mountains heading west would cut off sixty-five miles. And the far north. It would be decision time again at the junction, with the prospect of another night at high altitude on the mountain pass if I chose the shorter route. Then all too soon the surface ran out and favourable wind became a distant memory. Still dithering as to which way to choose even as I approached the junction, the idea of some steep climbing and camping amongst snow at the top had its appeal. But simply knowing that I had been to the far North Eastern tip of Iceland also appealed. In the event, there was no decision to make. The route through the mountains had not been opened following winter snow. And after toying briefly with the thought that it might be passable with a bike I rode north. With Arctic Terns for company, their calls repetitive and irritating, by late evening I was passing the airport. Deserted, and less than obvious, facilities were confined to a simple shed at the side of a short, empty runway beside the road ..... surfaced, now, as some sort of gesture to the extra traffic. The camp site, within a whisker of the sea, right next to the leisure centre in Raufarhöfn was sheltered on three sides by large, purpose built grassed banks. A simple hut provided facilities for me, its sole resident. In overwhelming need of a beer, I rode into town to a smart hotel. Smart, that is, on the inside. Outside, it might have been another port warehouse. Here, again, were all the signs of a vibrant fishing industry. That said, the only customer in the beautifully appointed bar, I sat amongst scrumptious Scandinavian furnishings with my ridiculously expensive Carlsberg. Black and white photographs of the town in times past cast their emotive images down. Faces peered out of the frames, inviting me to step into a world of sail and steam. And to reflect on the harsh conditions faced by generations of people here as they looked to the sea for a living. Another beer would have gone down well, a meal there, the more so. But my wallet would not have appreciated the experience.

Small populations cannot support specialist shops. Distances between centres mean that local shops carry a huge variety of stock and are effectively small supermarkets selling almost anything. The light (low alcohol) beer cost 70 kronor (50p). My Carlsberg had cost 500. The difference, the woman in the shop explained, is a tax regime designed to counter alcohol abuse, not uncommon in this land of near permanent winter darkness.

A little over 70 miles that day, three quarters of it on gravel roads. Better progress. And yes; tomorrow I would get round the Northern tip.

Look out .....

Decades' worth of ancient rusting hulks and skeletons of agricultural machinery had assumed character, art form.

"Thus I rode on through mist, wind and rain, with a mental image of Charlie striding out beside me, an encouragement; just as all those years past as a small boy."

8

Heavy rain eased off sufficiently for a late start. With the wind behind I set off in the certain knowledge that soon I would be as far North as it is possible to be on mainland Iceland and within a stone's throw of the Arctic Circle. The intention was to take it gently, see where I ended up that day. That said, events were to catch up with me and turn that decision on its head. The sign warned to beware of birds. Something of an understatement, they swooped down close shrieking loudly, dive bombed my head for intrusion on their patch. Scenes from "The Birds" flashed through my mind, a real life version being played out all around me. With helmet and protective glasses this entertainment did, to an extent, compensate for what was otherwise unremarkable riding close to the sea on a gravel surfaced level road.

I had grown used to the collection of dead vehicles that surround so many of the outlying farms. It appears no big deal to leave them where they drop. The cost of removing them for recycling is clearly prohibitive in this sparsely populated country. But nothing prepared me for the mechanical graveyard right next to the sea. Accidentally, yet beautifully juxtaposed as they lay on the salt blown grass, decades' worth of ancient, rusting hulks and skeletons of agricultural machinery had assumed character, art form. Custodians for the gallery were a couple of scrap yard sentinels, their ragged clothing blowing wildly. And testament to their windswept home.

Round the Northern tip, travelling south for the first time and into a powerful wind it had been hard riding. The smell of fresh coffee had been too much. Stepping inside the filling station shop in Kópasker to top up on food supplies, it had caught me off guard. And it had been good to sit down on a chair. But back outside after the warmth and comfort it all felt very threatening. Close to the sea for mile after mile, scrubby grass and black rock gave way to equally black volcanic sand. Given half a chance, a playful, raw wind would have had me swimming in icy cold water beneath any one of endless timber built bridges striding across gravelly estuaries that disappeared amongst powerful surf.

The lamb was bleating pitifully. With mother on one side of the fence, it was hurtling up and down the other, occasionally charging headlong into it. Panic struck, the creature was still doing it when I came out of the church that had attracted me there in the first place. A simple white painted structure with small rectangular windows, roofed in red corrugated metal, topped with a chimney like spire and simple cross. Inside, an aura of peace and tranquillity ..... to the extent that, amongst other thoughts, I found myself seated in a simple pew and offering thanks for so many of the privileges that make it possible for me to undertake ventures like this one. In a country with no trees, here, miles from anywhere was a timber building, fitted out and furnished in the same material. Ever the practical sort, I speculated on the practicalities of building in isolated places before the age of good road transport. Resourcefulness is not a recent phenomenon. I learned later that mighty driftwood blown ashore has long been regarded as a building material in coastal regions. Outside again, cornered and lifted bodily over the fence, the terrified lamb had soiled my clothing before making a vigorous reunion with its mother.

The excitement of a surfaced road was short lived. A couple of miles further on, my plan to ride right round the coast came unstuck too. Here at the junction was a tourist authority information board that told of the Jökulsárgljúfur National Park. At no time had this been on my agenda, but here was the opportunity for a ride on second class interior roads that would take me past Dettifoss. 35 miles to the next settlement. So what. I had lots of food, could stop anywhere then go on to see Mývatn (Midge Lake) ..... one of the country's top tourist attractions. Húsavík, the largest settlement in North East Iceland, with a population of 2500, would have to wait until next time, along with the whale watching for which, amongst other attractions, the town is famous.

Patrick and Michelle had started their ride from Keflavik, Reykjavik's international airport. They were doing much the same as me but in the opposite direction. Four days into my ride, the Swiss couple were just the third cyclists (and first female) I had come across. Such is the reputation of this country. Once again it was so natural to stop and exchange experiences with perfect strangers, the only thing in common, that we were cyclists. They told of glaciers, empty vastness and spectacular sights that defied description. The pair had spent all day riding from Grímsstaðir. Late in the evening, having covered sixty miles already I set off, about to discover just why the natives regard cycling as a form of masochism. Soft sandy surfaces made for difficult riding. If you've ever tried cycling on a beach, you'll have some idea of what I mean. The sign warned of poor road surface for the next 43 kilometres. What it didn't say was that the road was about to degenerate into something akin to a dry(ish) river bed, amply provisioned with the full range of effects from soft mud to loose gravel and small boulders. The wind got stronger, the rain more intense ..... as though it really meant business this time. Climbing steeply amongst boulder-strewn tundra, the mist rolled in. Higher still, vegetation had all but given up the unequal struggle for life, now limited to straggling willow that crept along rather than upwards in an effort to survive the torments of the climate. Thus, with wind ripping through my clothing, I toiled upwards passing summit after summit, each one raising hopes that it would be the last, and my route would level out, descend even.

With elastic bands securing plastic bags over sopping wet gloves in an effort to maintain contact with numbing hands and wearing just about all the clothes I carried, roadside maintenance was the last thing on a list of priorities. But occasional creaks had turned into a persistent groan that synchronised with my pedalling. My head simply wanted to ignore the problem, hope it would go away. It's odd what goes through one's mind in a crisis. For I remembered a story told by one of my sister's boyfriends when I was just a child. Making small talk as the whole family passed judgement on the fellow while we sat round the dining table, he told of his philosophy on motoring. "Unusual noises", he said, "should be ignored. They will either go away or get worse until such a time as the offending item drops off. Either way, the noise disappears". Ever practical, all sorts of explanations flashed across the scene as images of cracked frame or buckled wheel about to collapse refused to go away. The mindless optimist in me really didn't want to know what the problem was if it was going to be that serious. The mechanic in me was much more pragmatic. Together we agreed to stop. Spending the night in this moonscape would have been a real problem, the ground soft and sandy with not trace of vegetation or shelter of any kind. A huge walk out would have been the only option. It was with some trepidation that I approached the casualty: not unlike the way we are told to approach an accident victim if back injury is suspected. Close inspection of the entire frame and its welds revealed no damage. Rotating the pedals indicated no bearing break up. No spokes were broken, the wheels ran true. Yet riding still produced that unnerving creak-cum-rattle. Stopped again, more puzzled than worried this time and shaking the bike from side to side, a couple of turns with an Allen key were all they required. Despite securing all fittings with thread lock (glue for bolts) before leaving, bolts securing the luggage rack had worked loose.

Now thoroughly cold in the tearing wind and rain, I had to work hard to get warm again. And it was getting late. In most parts of the world, this would have added another dimension to my predicament. But in Iceland it does not go dark in summer. Thus I rode on into the so-called night, the simple solution to what might have been a major problem with my bike still on my mind. All sorts of "what ifs" had an airing along the way. OK, I'd had spare bolts in the tool kit, but to catch them in time before they were lost in the road ..... good fortune, coincidence, simply being systematic in my investigation. Or, was there another explanation? Many years ago someone told me that I was being looked after. Not the minder thing. More of a feeling, a presence. Robbie Williams sings of angels, and here I did have that spine tingling feeling that the loose bolts had been no chance discovery. More the result of a helping hand to keep me on the move in extreme circumstances.

I never knew my Grandparents. Three of them died before I was born and all I have is a hazy image of an ailing old lady who wore glasses. More real were the elderly couple next door. They had no children of their own, and as a child I spent a huge amounts of time with them. Including walks in the countryside, and train trips to the seaside. Everything I made, be it Meccano model or cardboard boat had to be ooh'd and aah'd over by Charlie and Mrs Taylor, for that is how my family knew them. Quite why I, too, was allowed to use an adult's first name in this one instance still baffles me. In an age when children referred to all adults as Mr, Mrs, Miss, here was my seventy-something-year-old neighbour-cum-acting grandfather who had a name. His wife, forever "Mrs" did not. I'll never forget the furore, the one and only time I referred to a friend's father by his first name. I did not make that mistake again. Charlie had fought in the trenches, come through the entire First World war intact, and had a piece of shrapnel on display next to the radio if ever he needed reminding. Handling this shred of desperate times past was almost ritual, sitting at the oil cloth covered table in their kitchen, the black kettle singing gently on the ledge in front of the fire. Here was a home locked in the 'thirties. Maybe earlier. Monday was wash day. And wash days meant just that. A full day event, equipment included a metal tub rather like a beer barrel and mangle that clamped to the dining table. Extra oil cloth was tied round its legs for the duration. A successful encounter would last all day and, in winter, see the kitchen festooned in damp clothes for days afterwards. By Wednesday it was sometimes possible to see across the room again. Only then could my cranes be tested, for that involved a long winding string being passed over one of the empty kitchen washing lines and attached to a bundle of newspaper. Each new construction was examined, then subjected to this test. Only when the load was raised to the full height of the line was my work deemed a success, a Bobby Dazzler.

Charlie had been a keen cyclist in his time. Years later I would admire the faded Dursley Pedersen machine he had kept in his spare bedroom workshop, its flat tyres dry and crumbling. Manufactured in Dursley between 1893 and 1922, by Mikael Pedersen, a Dane, they had an unusual frame design that resembled a cantilever bridge, its rider comfortably seated on a hammock like saddle. Radical, lightweight, and regarded by many as the Bentley of bicycles, the design has been resurrected, to be re-manufactured in Denmark and marketed internationally.

No job too small. My father ever the academic, but Charlie had tools for everything. Drilling, soldering, bending, cutting, and more. Model railways, bikes, boats ..... everything a small boy could desire. Every child should have one. Always asked for, never paid, "That'll be ninepence", his cheerful goodbye. It was only reasonable that he should be there with me to offer a helping hand in difficult circumstances. Thus I rode on through mist, wind and rain, with a mental image of Charlie striding out beside me, an encouragement, just as all those years past. A delight to handle and use to this day, those tools are now mine. Charlie left them to me. The tears well up in my eyes.

The tourist police would take a dim view. But it was snowing hard by the time I passed the sign for Dettifoss, Europe's most powerful waterfall. I ought to have taken time out to go and see it, but with no indication of distance, had visions of still worse roads going on for miles before getting there. The thought uppermost in my mind was simply to get somewhere to shelter and spend the night, for it was late into the evening by then. "Missed the sign", I would say, in an effort to avoid being marched back from the ferry port, banned from leaving the country until I'd seen it. It's odd what goes through one's mind in a crisis. "They might just buy that", I conjectured, smiling through a snow and ice encrusted beard at the thought of this zany concern. And keeping my head down and legs busy, I ground on through a moonscape of fractured black rock, sand and boulders for, by now, not a shred of vegetation braved the climate. Boulders do not have much to say for themselves. Here, they clearly had a rough time of it, but nevertheless took their role as sentinels on my route seriously. As though guardians of the region, with a presence felt as much as seen I found myself addressing them, thanking them for seeing me through safely. There is more to stones than meets the eye. I found them heartening to touch. Just the once or twice, mind. A daft thought, when you're sitting warm and comfortable in an armchair, with not a care in the world. Less so when stones and desperate weather are all you have for company.   Thus, I rode on through the worst of the weather, pedalling downhill now past hints of vegetation again, that included the ubiquitous horizontal willow and pampas-like grass. Well into the night I investigated several potential camping sites, but dismissed them as nowhere was the ground stable enough for tent pegs. A large steaming lake loomed out of the mist. Hundreds of birds taking advantage of the facility called eerily through the wind, plainly unaware that it was way past their bedtime. Lower down were odd bunches of sheep, again unaware of the time. Twenty four hour grazing plainly does nothing for their manners. Addressed with a cheery "good morning" they steadfastly ignored me, preferring their dingy grass.

Grímsstaðir is a tiny place even by Icelandic standards. Guidebooks describe it as a farm, but the attraction for me was the fact that it has a camp site. A camp site that, as it happened, was closed, its facilities locked. It was after midnight when I made the disappointing discovery. After a difficult ride of almost ninety-five miles I settled for a wash in the river. Nonetheless I did spend what was left of the night there. A meal cooked in the shelter of my tent at one o'clock on a wet, half lit morning was exceedingly cosy, a sort of two fingers up to the weather that had done its worst. Made it, hung in there to tell the tale. Thanks to a bunch of rocks. And my childhood next door neighbour.

9

In Reykjavik, heads would be rolling. The planning department would be in uproar, the press would be having a field day. Somewhere in Iceland, no one would admit where, would be a road where there ought to have been a new river. That was the only explanation. The plans had got mixed up. Here, where Route 1 should have been, part of the well publicised busy ring road, a new river was under construction. Was nearing completion it seemed, for the boulders, stones, sand, gravel and mud were already in place. And water already being directed along it. The trouble was that no one had told the road engineers to divert the not inconsiderable (for Iceland) traffic round the new feature, devoid of workmen for its entire length, while the administrative nightmare was sorted out.

I really ought to have stayed at home. The dour woman at the farm had let me use the facilities there, before I scuttled back to my tent in the vain hope that the weather would improve. Later, after it hadn't, picking my way through those ten miles of incredible road works lacked even the remotest element of entertainment as tearing wind slammed rain and sleet in my face, threatening to blow me into the ditch. Lunch, in that moonscape, crouched behind an enormous boulder provided a little respite but only later, in the afternoon, came a break in the weather.

Guardians, beacons to us travellers, the line of large rocks and boulders continued to follow the road. As on other occasions, in the absence of anything more appreciative I found myself addressing them. Not complicated stuff, you understand. Struggling on, more a "hi, how are you?" or "get this weather straightened out, you bastards." These, unsurprisingly one-sided, conversations were complementary to tirades of abuse shouted at those in charge of the weather. But as if on cue the construction site gave way to a surface of hard packed mud, then a sealed road. Moments later the sun came out and it stopped raining. Someone was listening. Stones have ears. Perhaps?

Travelling with a partner or group one is part of a unit, a corporate decision making body. To an extent, that unit can operate independently of outside agencies. A common language in a sea of foreigners is the norm. The moral support of companions can be very reassuring in unfamiliar situations. Solo travel, on the other hand, is a unique experience. Thoughts become your major companion, closely followed by personal items that take on an enhanced roles. My bike became part of the plot. Together we would decide which route to take. Together we would complain about the road, the weather, the hills. And together we would whiz down those same slopes. We were mates on an adventure. Together. In the absence of someone to share the day's experiences with, my palm top computer assumed a role way beyond its station, somewhere I could report high and low points. And those in between as well. In my tent, in cafés, at the roadside. It made no difference. I could say what I wanted, and no answering back. As a breed, we humans are a naturally gregarious bunch. Fulfilling the need for companionship is one of life's delights. So familiar, now, with the fact that here cyclists stop to exchange stories, the three Americans riding in the opposite direction caught me on the back foot. A couple of words shared with the chap out in front: his slower companions found it almost too much trouble to speak. The encounter left me feeling not a little perplexed. Here was I, spoken to few people in days. They ..... full time travelling companions, a unit. Paranoia? Or expecting too much from strangers who, like me, were working hard in challenging circumstances and, perhaps, fresh out of time for pleasantries with foreigners?

That no cloud is complete without its silver lining is a fact well known to optimists. Difficult to locate sometimes, but after two especially hard days here it was. Not so much silver, just boring old white. Thing was though, those in charge had got it wrong again. Those folks in Reykjavik. Can't they get anything right? Any school boy will tell you that clouds belong up there, in the sky. But there was no mistaking this lot ..... seen them from miles back, and they were coming out of the ground. If I'd not seen it with my own eyes, I'd never have believed it.

Four-letter words have an aura, a life form of their own. Applied sparingly they pack a real punch. Liberally daubed, they provide a mindless prefix for a wealth of otherwise pedestrian adjectives. That just one of them could even begin to describe the scene has changed my perspective on them for ever. "Hver", the simple sign at the roadside read. Translated, it means hot spring or fumarole: an opening near a volcano through which hot vapours emerge. In the shadow of the Námafjall ridge, just a little short of Mývatn, is Námaskarð. Here the full spectacle revealed itself, the terrain resembling a rock strewn dried lake bed. But no ordinary dry lake bed: a grey landscape stained multicoloured with sulphurous deposits. Underfoot was warm, hot even, to touch ..... the result of thin earth's crust. Countless noisy jets of steam issued from the ground. Pools of hot, grey mud plopped, spouted, boiled. Pressure cooker on heat, porridge on the boil, kettle at full tilt. Place in a natural bowl, surround with mountain peaks. Add an all embracing smell of sulphur and a sprinkling of (stirred) tourists. Get the picture?

Like me, the pair would return home with exciting tales of spectacular sights. Only, their situation couldn't have been more different. Three hours from London, internal flights, pre booked hotels, rented car. That's how they were travelling, on a whistle stop tour of Iceland's tourist hotspots, so to speak. Eight days since leaving home, thoroughly immersed in the travel thing, it had become my mission, my *raison d'être*. I had even begun thinking in a funny accent. This was my first real conversation for days. The two women were English ..... that much was clear. A postal vote had been the only way. Unable to pick up any information on my radio, I had been busting to know the result for days. The General Election had been held on the day I sailed from the UK. A (second) landslide victory for Labour. And the Tories in disarray after another splendid defeat: their leader, William Hague resigned. A just verdict for the nation, we agreed, before moving on to the Brits on holiday thing ..... the bit where we tell each other where we live and isn't it just wonderful. Mutual use of each other's cameras for photographs next to a mud pool sealed the brief encounter before moving on.

The steep climb on my route out revealed a view of mountains dotted with steaming fissures as far as the eye could see. But to the South, a scene that contrasted with everything I had experienced so far. Mývatn is a shallow, island infested lake that covers an area of 37 square kilometres, and at the heart of a region that has a reputation for being the driest in the country. Bright green grass, wild flowers, scrubby trees, sunshine, a gentle breeze. I camped close to clear blue water at a wonderful site in Reykjahlíð, on the North Eastern shore of the lake. The region is steeped in geo-thermal activity, past and present. My geography teacher would have had a field day. Moraines, lava flows, volcanoes, and pseudo-craters would have kept him talking for days. Nearby is Krafla power station, making full use of the natural energy on offer as well as being another tourist attraction.

Houses have four windows, a door in the middle, a pointed roof, and a chimney on top with a pig's tail spiral of smoke. Ask any small child to draw one and that's what you get. Ask them to draw a volcano, and

Námaskarð. Underfoot was warm, hot even, to touch .....

..... and pools of hot, grey mud plopped, spouted, boiled.

you get Hverfell. That was the view from my tent, and it couldn't have been more realistic. 2500 years old, over 500 feet high, with a 3,000 foot crater, the result of a huge eruption, it dominates the area east of the lake. To an extent, this classic sums up the region. A further sweep with my spy glass brought the pseudo-craters, particularly around the Southern end of the lake into focus. Lava flows from the East ran into the lake. Water trapped beneath the lava boiled forcing steam through it, to form the instantly recognisable small mound and crater islands dotted throughout the modern lake and its shores. A can of beer made good company, taking in the scene, relaxing in the sun on lawn like grass next to my tent. Truly, this was a land of contrasts, I reflected.

Still breathing in the scene hours later, sitting at a table by the cook tent window with the meal I had just prepared, details infilled. Earlier I had showered, and changed into lightweight trousers and tee shirt, then strolled in warm sunshine to the shop wearing flip flop sandals. I had relaxed with another beer, and made a meal standing up. My perspective on the whole venture was being challenged.

The fondue that they insisted I share was wonderful. Seared fresh meat dipped in a cheese sauce compares very favourably with convenience camping food. Like me, Itzhak and Reuven had left their wives at home, Iceland not being quite their scene. Freelance touring in their rented four-wheel-drive was going as planned, but accommodation had been a problem. They had been aware of Iceland's reputation for being pricey, but the reality was worse. Like they were buying the hotels, not just paying to stay there. What with down-payments on several hotels not being an option they had researched the alternatives and bought sleeping bags, a stove, crockery and cutlery. This was enabling them to use sleeping bag accommodation, a rung or two up from my in my tent, yet affordable at roughly £10.00 per night each. Offering a basic room with bed(s) in it, many provide cooking facilities as well, saving the cost of eating out. Down on cooking facilities at their accommodation, they had been recommended to try "my" site, only to find that pans were not provided. Sharing the meal they prepared in my pans, they told of life on a kibbutz close to the Lebanon border. Out of the media spotlight life goes on, despite the desperate situation concerning Palestine, they went on. I desperately wanted to quiz them further, get true feelings on this issue, but feared for the can of worms it might open on a transitory friendship with fellow travellers. Insisting that we swap addresses and that I visit them one day, we shook hands and said goodbye, though as it turned out "au revoir" might have been more appropriate.

10

Part of me really did not want to leave this oasis. Besides, the brochures told of countless activities for tourists. Walks, coach tours, cycle rental perhaps - for those fit enough. Now, there's an idea Take a short ride. Make a change from all those long ones. But cynicism apart, it was plain that there were an awful lot of reasons to hang around this spot for a day or two. If only to get my washing dry. But, less than a quarter of the way round my planned route, I was booked on the ferry in three weeks time. The show had to go on.

Cycling meant that each day I saw more than tourists travelling by car or coach might see in a month. Not the business of rushing from one tourist hotspot, train-spotter-like, to the next. More the fact that in some small way I feel at one with the countryside. Most travellers see things through glass. I heard them, smelled them, was outside with them in their world, communed with them. I could see the different grasses, hear them rustling in the wind, stop on a whim to examine things closely. With so much packed into each day, so much to reflect on, many of the things that your average tourist demands become superfluous, as I settle down each night in my tent. Fast enough to see a lot; slow enough to see it all. That's long-distance cycling.

Bright sun had seen off the early morning frost long before I dragged myself away from that lovely place. One last ride round the village brought me to the church. The original survived a massive volcanic eruption in 1729, the lava flow parting to pass, some say miraculously, either side. The current building of 1972 stands on the same site, lava each side still witness to events almost three hundred years past.

Riding close to the lake, with frequent stops to take in the volcanic landscape, made for slow progress. Mývatn (Midge Lake) gave an indication of its true colours as morning sun raised the temperature. Clouds of the little buggers took to the air, plainly appreciating the fact that I was sweating in the warmth. Stuck to clothing, in my ears, up my nose, behind sunglasses. And stopped to admire the view, worse. Much worse. The lake is centrefold for a magazine, its pages turning with every twist in the road south, to reveal a backdrop of huge volcanic cones, their

I camped close to clear blue water at a wonderful site in Reykjahlíð.

Mývatn is an island infested lake that covers an area of 37 square kilometres.

crater tops plainly visible. Set amongst lava they sternly overlooked smaller ones, themselves the focal points of a myriad of grassed islands and peninsulas in a watery scene that is quite unforgettable. A track through low forest lead down to the shore. In the shade of young trees, the midges still dormant in the cool, I spent some time, able to appreciate fully the sights and sounds of my surroundings.

Itzhak and Reuven greeted me as a long lost friend. Passing on the road they had waved madly. Now, like me, they had taken the track that lead from Skútustaðir, a tiny village at the southern end of the lake. It took us to the tip of a long extinct crater that, complete with tourist information in several languages, served as a viewpoint for the area. Another tick on the "been there, seen that" sheet. A reminder that I was just another tourist. But doing it the hard way, as if to justify myself.

As a foreign tourist it's always wise to visit a museum or two. And keep the ticket as proof of your visit. This one looked closed. I would have got away with it, pleaded that at least I'd tried ..... if the elderly curator hadn't caught me sniffing round the place. Despite my protestations, still wearing his slippers he shuffled back to his home for the keys and gave me a personal guided tour. With displays and photographs that catalogued the region from the time of the first settler in 1912, it might be described as a cottage museum. Together with my guide's constant address, the occasional English written information provided, and my own practical common sense, I viewed the exhibits. Despite not having a word in common, I managed to pick up a feel of the place in times past. Farming and fishing was the basis for the region's economy, it was heavily represented in exhibits that also included home interiors, costume and domestic equipment. What summed it up for me was the snowmobile. American made in 1942, awash with chains, belts and levers, I couldn't work out whether it was the first in Iceland or simply the first in the region. But it did mark a line in the snow, so to speak, for land transport. From October to May the lake is frozen; and much of the winter here is spent in near darkness. These snippets of information plus my guide's intonation and gesticulation told their own tale of hard times past. Back outside to reality, a team of telephone engineers was busy and, with good reason, were clad in full head nets. Pleased to leave them behind, despite the fact that they are an important part of the food chain that keeps the region's fish and wildlife alive and kicking, I wondered how locals, past and present coped with the midges.

I needed a photograph of Goðafoss. It was vital to have evidence of visiting at least one giant waterfall. Thorgeir, the lawmaker is responsible for its name. Riding home to nearby Ljósavatn after the ruling at the government assembly that Iceland should adopt Christianity he threw away his pagan idols there. Thus, in the year 999 it became Waterfall of the Gods. A long, fast descent had brought me there after an undulating, if unspectacular route from Mývatn. Awesome is, perhaps, the only word that can adequately describe the cliff of glacial water that crashes downwards, a mass of foaming white picked out in the sunlight before rushing, turquoise blue in a deep chasm beneath the original road bridge and brave new concrete replacement that leap the gap. As for statistics: I haven't a clue. Big. Bloody big. Big enough to contemplate the power of nature in the raw. Fuel for the soul. I spent a satisfying hour in its company, walked both banks, peeped cautiously from safe places, took photographs ..... and sat in the café drinking coffee out of the wind.

If looks were anything to go by, the three ought to have been drinking Iron Bru: the one made from girders. With equipment laden roof rack, tyres so fat they almost met in the middle, extra lamps sprouting everywhere and a radio antenna the BBC would be proud of, they would be fighting over whose turn it was to drive. It looked as though it would eat Land Rovers for dinner and drive over them for fun. With visions of expeditions, of exciting new discoveries ..... I had to ask them. Something of an anti-climax, the reality was much more mundane as they explained that they were a power cable maintenance team, this was the works van ..... and right now it was their tea break. American built for their armed forces, this 6.5 litre Hummer go-anywhere vehicle looked unstoppable. Just the ticket in a country with terrain like this. And weather to match. Time was when every small boy wanted to be a train driver. If power cable maintenance teams the world over drove vehicles like this, there would be a queue of small boys outside the offices of electricity companies waiting to enlist.

On then through wide, sweeping countryside. Cold, clear water in the adjacent fast flowing river danced cheerfully over gravel, singing encouragement to me. Together with a lake or two, my route shared its grassy valley: always a backdrop of snow capped mountains, their flanks a mass of fast flowing streams tumbling, as tradition dictates, downwards. Besides, it just wouldn't sound right. Just imagine a myriad of streams racing uphill as they dash for the clouds. Better to stick with boring old downwards. For now. Wind direction remained unpredictable, and I developed a sort of guessing game. Looking ahead at the terrain, the rules said I had to work out whether I would be blown along, back, or off. Wrong on almost every occasion, such is the fickle nature of wind in these mountainous regions, by late afternoon it was still behind. Blowing alongside the river for mile after mile on a good road, pedalling furiously in an outburst of schoolboy enthusiasm, I raced the water on our downhill journeys.

The short cut would save miles ..... cut out an enormous loop in the main road. But signs at the junction were at variance with my map. A wrong road late in the day is the last thing a cyclist needs. The couple who had pulled up there told of a steep, rocky route that was hard to find. And waited several miles further along the road to make sure I did not miss the minor route that would take me over the mountain. Such is the nature of people.

Steep, yes, rocky, yes. But the views were to die for as I made my way up hairpin bends and beyond the snow line. It's a wonderful feeling at the top of a mountain, the landscape below set out like a map. Features on the map turned into mountains, valleys, settlements, roads, rivers. But transfixed by my first glimpse of the sea for days, Eyjafjörður lay shining in the hazy evening sun. At the head of the fjord on the Eastern shore, still out of sight lay Akureyri, Iceland's second largest city ..... my destination that day, and no more than five miles across the fjord. Yet three times that distance to cycle. The ride down was exhilarating, the views amazing. Like descents in a plane, blobs became ships, dots became buildings, lines became roads, pinpricks became cars. The largest blob turned into a cruise ship sailing down the fjord out to sea ..... its passengers travellers, like me. But what a contrast, I speculated, picturing a conveyor belt of meals followed by turns round the deck to burn them off. And wallet sapping shore leave to justify it all. Riding ever faster, gaining confidence on my fully laden bike, it was a thrilling descent on rough tracks. My seat post (the bit that the saddle fits on) with a spring inside it appreciated the experience less, came apart and needed roadside surgery amongst the snow to lock it back together. A proper repair would need the services of a cycle shop. Seventy miles after leaving Mývatn, finally crossing the causeway into town, the wind was huge. Coming straight up the fjord from the open sea, it threatened to blow me off my bike. It felt odd to be amongst people, buildings, traffic. And traffic lights, even.

Here, for a change I would use the Youth Hostel, sleep in a bed, eat at a table. Evidently recently revamped with acres of pine cladding, floors and furniture it might have been a luxury hotel. Only sleeping bags and shared rooms hinted of hostel. And, at £10, I could still afford to eat. My room mate was on his sixth cycle trip to Iceland from home in Belgium. Having lived off camping food for the last week, the meal at a nearby Italian restaurant was heaven. £15 for three courses and a beer was never better spent. Common interest kept us talking over the dinner table as we shared experiences, one of which is the fact that our wives do not care to be included on these energetic trips. Pierre, a shop fittings salesman in his forties, has taken solo cycling holidays for the past fifteen years. His biggest, a 7,000 kilometre ride from Brussels to the North Cape – the bit where Norway borders with Russia – and back, in a month. I was impressed. We had both tried hard, it seemed, and between us, got much of the (developed) world covered, so to speak. Back to Iceland, it seemed that I had got off lightly so far, as I learned of winds so strong that it was impossible to stand, let alone ride, of blinding sandstorms, of river crossings without bridges. But more of those later. Yet still, the country draws him back, time and time again. Such is the majesty, an element of nature untamed, in your face, spectacular beyond imagination, challenging all the senses. And I hadn't seen the half of it yet. Together, we put crosses, must sees, on my map. Names on paper, descriptions to titillate. The reality would have to wait. Spending the remainder of the evening sitting comfortably in front of the television, many of the programmes were broadcast in English. It becomes a little less surprising that so many, in all walks of life, speak the language. They hear it almost daily.

11

To wake up in a bed, in a room, take a shower, sit at a table eating breakfast was luxury indeed. Contrasting with a tent so small I have to lie down in order to pull my trousers on, all of this served to remind of just how much we in the West take for granted. In the convivial atmosphere of the communal kitchen guests prepared food, shared plans for journeys, visits, walks. Travel is a great leveller for all age groups that crosses so many taboos. Here in this international kitchen was proof. Such was the air of anticipation, it might have been the departure lounge at an airport. Most people were using buses, others had rented cars. A few relied on their thumb for travel arrangements. Two fingers were sufficient to count the cyclists.

My bicycle appreciated the town enormously as well. For here, a feature in my guidebook told of one of few dedicated repair facilities outside of the capital, Reykjavik. In the reassuring setting of the Youth Hostel I dismantled the ailing seat post, to find that all it needed was a long reach Allen key. Nothing lost or broken ..... simply worked loose on unbelievable roads. I carried only short Allen keys, and with this in mind wound up at the nearby cycle dealer. Using the equipment he willingly provided I fixed the problem myself while the shopkeeper attended to his other customers. We managed the small talk easily enough: travelling, interests, and life back home. But a request for thread lock (glue to prevent the thing loosening again) needed drawings of toothpaste-like tubes, of nuts, bolts. And mime. Bicycles were not the whole story. Making a living out of them here might just be a problem out of the summer season when masochists like me take to the hills. The nearby ski area on Mt. Hlíðarfjall plainly provided an extra source of income and displays of glossy equipment demanded my full attention. Now with customers sorted, having refused payment for helping out, in words and gesticulation, Vidar told of the slopes there. They sounded to have much in common with those I take so much pleasure from in Scotland, ice in my beard included.

Walking back to the Hostel, having triumphed over loose parts, I came upon a bunch of young people busily engaged in gardening, tidying up public areas. Roundabouts, central reservations, verges, and more were all being spruced up. Curious, I spoke to a group of girls aged about fourteen, and hard at work, wearing high visibility waistcoats ..... to learn that it is common for school children to do this for obvious cash. It also engenders a sense of pride in the community. Besides being something to do in the holidays.

Situated next to the sea in bright clear air, a trading station since 1602, Akureyri is a thriving university city. A centre for commerce, communication and services, shipyards, fishing, agriculture, and now tourism ..... all contribute to its economy. With a population of 15,000, it has a mixture of delightful coloured timber buildings set round narrow pedestrianised areas, together with some imaginative modern concrete ones sporting a surprising amount of glass in this cold region. Together with student maintained flower beds, shrubs, trees and lawned areas, and empty (for a city) roads that Le Corbusier would have been proud of, the city has a wonderful aura. Notwithstanding, pastel colours failed to disguise housing blocks on the outskirts. Purely utilitarian, an economic necessity in a growing economy but, like those of cities the world over, endowed with similar aesthetic appeal.

Pierre introduced me to the delights of eating at Icelandic bakeries. Having fixed my bike, exchanged addresses, and done the photograph thing before going our separate ways, we took lunch together. For just a little over £4, an enormous hunk of pizza, followed by cakes of similar proportion and endless free refills of excellent coffee. As ever, a last slow ride round the city, posting the cards. As one does. With their amazing pictures of waterfalls, geysers, and glaciers, all taken on cloudless summer days ..... and sporting my accounts of weather, roads and washing in rivers on the reverse side. Would recipients ooh and aah, wish they were there, vow to visit one day, as tradition demands. Or pity the poor bugger who was daft enough not to go somewhere warm on a fly drive? What I didn't see were the museums, galleries, Botanic gardens. Neither did I walk in the woods, play golf, or visit the swimming pool with its sauna and Jacuzzi. I ought to have made time, I really ought, but it was early days yet, with an awful long way to go. And we've been into all of that before. Besides, I was saving it all for Reykjavik. Where I would chill out for a while. But it was early afternoon by the time I finally left Akureyri.

Widely spaced, Scandinavian in style, yet true to the ethos of suburb construction the world over, was the ubiquitous DIY supermarket. The traffic strewn road out west ran alongside the fjord, taking in, reasonably enough for a modern city, a mixture of housing, industrial and service buildings. With the sea left behind, the now-standard issue fast flowing river twisted and turned and danced alongside, providing music as I worked at the pedals. This road would take me high through the mountains before hitting the coast again at Blönduós, ninety miles away. With no particular destination in mind, to an extent, the terrain would dictate where I spent the night. With several day's worth of food, all three water carriers full, and a whole river-full to myself as well, it didn't matter a jot. And following a whole lot of deliberating and sniffing at the garage to make sure it was the right stuff, the new bottle of stove fuel meant a cosy tent too. The valley got narrower, "my" river faster,

Akureyri ..... a thriving university city, and commercial centre.

Bordeyri ..... looked like it would be the first to succumb to any rise in sea level.

splashing, tumbling now as the road steepened between rocky crags, broken only by dashing streams that had cut their own routes downwards at all angles before joining forces and heading for the sea. Climbing steadily with the wind still, unbelievably, behind me, a final push past the sign warning motorists to put (tyre) chains on, found my stove and I sheltering behind some sort of a buzzing building with masts and things sticking out of it, and firmly held in place against the wind by enormous cables anchored in concrete blocks. Zapped by electrons or blown away in the wind. The choice was simple as I relaxed with a hot drink and chocolate bar, satisfied with my efforts, pleased at the delicious prospect of riding downhill for miles with a following wind.

Breathtaking, towering, craggy, barren, almost frighteningly empty, lacking any signs of life. For fifteen miles the valley slowly unfolded, metamorphosed, bringing yet another variation on the grassy valley and wide gravely river theme. Battling with the wind, now shifted in direction and blasting straight in my face, grey clouds scuttled overhead, rain threatened. The anticipated exciting long descent that I had worked so hard for evaporated in a 180 degree wind shift at the summit. Pedalling downhill in squally conditions, the desolation began to creep inside my head. Worse, nagging doubts about the state of my tyres began to surface after stopping to investigate unexplained wobbles with each turn of the wheels. No rim damage, no broken spokes. Yet the tyres were out of true.

The campsite at Varmahlíð was awash with people. A coach load of people were setting up their tents. My normal reaction would have been to keep as far away from others as possible but this time, feeling a little low, decided that company was just the ticket. I might as well not have bothered: my theory on insularity, of self sufficiency, of being unapproachable played out right alongside. And I couldn't even step outside for a pee because it wouldn't be going dark. That said, getting the tent set up after a gruelling day was like arriving home after a bad day at work. Out of the wind, echoes of domesticity in a familiar, if rather small personal space. In moments, the world was a better place. Security, warmth. Dry. And a mobile phone to unload events on to an unsuspecting wife! A picture of home, its thick stone walls, its English country garden, the tall herbaceous plants, trees, and gravel paths. To hear of domestic life proceeding without me. The power of a telephone. Back to reality, and a queue for the shower. Worse, the hot tub – OK, jacuzzi – was out of action: simply too hot to use. Back in my tent, mashed potato, tinned tuna and vegetables followed by crushed pineapple and cuppa soup. With nothing more than my palmtop computer and stove for company I spent the rest of the evening catching up with my notes. In these circumstances writing is a form of therapy. To an extent it draws a veil over events. A form of exorcism ..... low points are purged, highs committed to memory. It is like having a companion to share experiences with. Wind and hills always featured. They were major issues ..... controlling factors around which each day revolved. If only the rest of our lives was so simple.

12

Queues before breakfast are what you get when there are only two toilet and shower facilities for a coach load of campers. And facing adversity together people talk to each other. Like when their train is late. Or the supermarket cashier has a problem with the till. In no time I learned that the happy campers were Canadian architectural students involved with a project in Reykjavik. After working hard for some time, a bus ride round Iceland accompanied by their lecturers, and sleeping in confined spaces, was their reward. Their visiting lecturer was on tour with them. A well known Englishman, they said. But couldn't quite recall his name. Marked out by a grander tent, despite the fact that we were expats in foreign parts he gave little away. As for "well known", I guess that he'd being flinging his charges a line, told them his name was Brunel or something - and didn't want me to blow the whistle on him. In the event I settled for "possible maybe" regarding an entry in the notoriety charts, excused myself and hastened back to the security of my own tent. More pressing things needing attention before leaving ..... I removed the rear tyre and re seated it on the rim yet again in an effort to get it to spin true. Bought new for the trip, the heavy duty mountain bike tyres were having a hard time. This was just the start of my tyre and wheel problems. But thankfully I didn't know it at the time.

The smell of coffee and displays of sticky buns were more than a fellow could endure. So, sitting in the supermarket café, writing cards amongst a sea of American coach travellers on a "comfort break", the real world of cool wind was kept at bay for a few moments longer. Shopping for cycle camping is an experience on its own. The supermarket run, a car heaped with pre packed this, boxes of that, not to mention two-for-the-price-of-one offers on the other. None of this applies. The questions of weight, where it will be carried, if it can be cooked on a small stove, and the all important business of energy demands. These are the issues. So, what do I eat? Powdered mashed potato, pasta, tins of tuna, vegetables, beans, stew, and dried sauce bases, plus fruit, chocolate, dehydrated desserts. With variations on a theme these formed the basic evening meals. Luxuries like cakes or pastries might find their way on to the menu when they leapt out and insisted they come along for the ride, despite the fact that they would be crushed beyond recognition before being eaten. Muesli, a banana, coffee for breakfast ..... ham or cheese in bread rolls, followed by fruit and chocolate for picnic lunch, with a hot drink made on the spot. Nuts, and yet more chocolate were treats allowed at the start of major challenges like enormous hills or, later, river crossings. Or in reality, just any time. Not knowing the protocol can be a problem. It almost caused an international incident. Packing purchases at the checkout, the cashier threw a couple of plastic carrier bags in my direction. The angry man behind snatched them out of my hand before I could make use of them. Customers, it seems, buy them here. His face said all that. And more. I did not make that mistake again.

It had been one hell of a ride. The Esso café in Blönduós was a safe harbour, having been nearly wrecked at sea. The wind had been behind at first, lulling me into a false sense of security. But at the top of the climb from Varmahlíð it changed: first in my face, then from the right, and threatening to blow me into traffic or right off the road. Only by leaning heavily over to the side to compensate was progress was possible. Sometimes it was simply too dangerous to ride.

Everyone pops into these service stations. Including teenagers who meet and talk on their mobile phones. The young woman came in wearing a skimpy crop top and trousers she might have been poured into. Sunnies worn on top of her head casually complemented the outfit. All male eyes, and some female as well, were in her direction as, draped over the bar she engaged in animated conversation with one of the girls working there. It was plainly the place to be seen but not, perhaps, quite so much of it, for everyone else was clothed against the weather. My mother had an expression to cover situations like this "Thuss naught ne funnier ne folk." Translated from Yorkshire dialect: "there is nothing stranger than people". From the point of view of a foreigner looking in,

I reckon that would have it covered. The light beer and doughnut went down very well, then temptation got in the way. Not tight pants and the like, but burger and chips being served up to other customers. Normally very much a "proper food" fellow, if I were to call it my evening meal and ride further instead of spending the night there ..... well, it might be all right.

Thoroughly pigged out, the decision to ride that extra thirty miles towards Hvammstangi had been out of my hands. That huge wind would now be right behind if it didn't change. It's hard to turn down an opportunity like that. In the event I never got to Hvammstangi. After being blown along at a fine pace, the last part of the ride would have been an out and back trip anyway. It had got to late in the evening and the wind, finally shifted, was doing its best to blow me off my bike again. Yet half an hour later, in a (relatively) sheltered hollow next to a bridge overlooking a fjord, just two thicknesses of fine textile had brought instant security, warmth and comfort.

The next day it would be make your mind up time as regards seeing the Western Fjords. A massive three hundred mile detour would need some re-scheduling. But that was not the only item on the agenda. That afternoon I had stopped to investigate a worsening wheel wobble. Badly mis-shapen, the rear tyre had taken quite a beating and it was now clearly only a matter of time before having to make use of the lightweight spare, leaving me without that vital safety net. The extra strain created on the rest of the bike, plus contempt for things that don't work properly, gave cause for extra concern in the knowledge that the nearest replacements were in Reykjavik, 150 miles away by the shortest route. On the other hand, being a lightweight fellow the tyre might just hang in there long enough. It was a good line to cling to anyway and a convenient point to wind up the debate. The meeting almost over, AOB concerned privileges ..... sticky buns and coffee, coastal vistas, stunning mountains, the open road, a beer at half time. And more. Much much more. But somewhere in there, the feeling that I needed to do more than simply ride. Then the stove ran out of fuel. Perhaps answers would have bubbled to the surface by morning?

13

Making breakfast from the deceptive warmth of my sleeping bag, with the tent open just a tad, the weather did not appear to be too awful. In a moment of madness a short debate on the possibility of giving my shorts their first outing. The fleeting thought lasted only as long as it took to get my head outside, where it became clear that a cold wind was still blowing. Back out in the open, once again that odd feeling as the tent came down. Despite the following wind, a desperately dull ride found me in low spirits and questioning just why I was doing this. And worse, the possibility that my plan to ride right round the island might be approaching madness. In no time I was feeling windswept and dishevelled. Only coffee and sticky buns could save the situation.

After riding South on eastern shore of Hrútafjörður I would cross the bridge at Bru to hug the opposite coast, heading north, and straight into the wind blasting off the open sea. Ísafjörður: the largest settlement in the Western Fjords. One way or another, I would get to this North West tip and re-schedule the rest of my ride if it became necessary. I had not made a decision. It had simply happened, crept up on me when I wasn't looking. Low spirits, it seemed, could well have been part of that process.

Everything came with chips at the roadside café-cum-post-office, shop, filling station and tourist office. Sticky bun and chips did not appeal. Besides, it had been eighteen hours since my last proper meal and I needed something substantial. Someone translated the menu. I settled on tourist information and chips with chicken. Then it all got a bit muddled what with me still windblown, and more than a little disorientated in this world of people, tables, chairs. That was the easy bit. Getting my meal on the table less so. Order food at counter, get chitty, pay at checkout, wait for your number to be called out in Icelandic, collect meal. Everyone else knew exactly what to do. But at least it wasn't windy in there.

Remember pub meals in UK not so long ago? Chicken and chips served in a plastic basket with a garnish of limp lettuce. Not a trace of proper vegetables. Before coming good on food. Before drink / drive law made them look for other means of earning their keep. Nevertheless, three free coffee refills delayed going back outside for as long as was decent ..... and a little beyond. The photographs on display were part of this ploy. Faces, typically frozen in time by long exposures, peered out. The only means of transport in this region, when most of the rest of Europe was fast developing an infrastructure of railways, one dated 1898, showed pack ponies at work. Like criminals with ball and chain – useful when there are no trees – tethering stones prevented ponies from wandering off. Many of these stones remain to this day, reputedly put there by Trolls, who plainly get about a bit. For the last time I came across them was in Norway where they are held responsible for all kinds of ill-disciplined activity.

Almost as though it was meant to happen, there was a bus going north tomorrow. A connection would complete the journey. The following day, another would link up with the ferry, enabling me to pick up the ring road more or less where I left it. The Tourist Information staff gave assurances that my bike would not be a problem on the buses. I could be in Ísafjörður, more than two hundred miles away, by tea time next day, a Sunday. It would buy some time ..... and keep me out of the wind for a while. Yet it hurt. I would be giving in. But my original plan to ride the ring road would remain intact. As would my schedules. My conscience might just about hack this one. I had till lunch time next day to decide.

By the junction at Bru it had become a plan. One that called for food from the shop there. The assistant had a bus timetable and together we confirmed the 1-00 pm arrival time next day. Paying for my goods took some time. The poor girl had no idea how to use the new electronic till, she said. A full ten minutes went by before she had totalled my bill. Time to eat the ice cream ..... not your average scoop. More a whole cart load that filled the flat bottomed cone, to spiral of out of control.

Bru translates to bridge. The settlement was little else. One other building supplemented the roadside filling station / shop / café that served as staging post and junction for bus services between Reykjavik, Akureyri, and Ísafjörður. In the UK it would have been an old Coaching Inn, with echoes of horse shoes on cobbles and, if the film industry is to be believed, frothing tankards of porter heartily flung down on bar room tables by busty maids in mob caps. Others would be endlessly scurrying around with pitchers of hot water, while fending off amorous travellers with rebuffs like "Ooh, Sir" or "You are a tease." These days it's real ale, expensive wine with menus and ankle deep carpets to match: the place awash with waiters. Or owned by a conglomerate and serving meals from the freezer, the fact heavily disguised by eloquent descriptions an Estate Agent would be proud of. Here, I wondered just how an empty place like this, out in the middle of nowhere and entirely at the mercy of travellers, stayed afloat.

Borðeyri, the next village, was less than ten miles away. I would camp there before catching the bus next day. The tiny, near deserted settlement set, postcard like, on a spit of land jutting out from the Western shore of Hrútafjörður looked like it would be the first to succumb to any rise in sea level. In the breezy summer sunshine it took little imagination to feel the icy winds that would be sure to whistle down the fjord in winter. Despite evidence of a current fishing industry, this looked like a village past its sell by date. Observed at close quarters, many of its well proportioned coloured buildings with corrugated metal roofs were in awful shape.

The pagoda-style hut provided basic camp site facilities. But they did allow me to catch up on my washing. Then I spent ages truing up buckled wheels. The rear tyre was in desperate shape, its sidewalls badly damaged, bulging and close to failure. Swapping them round, back to front might delay the inevitable. The longer I could put off using my spare tyre, the better chance of making it to Reykjavik. By this time it was getting cool, and that feeling of being quite alone in this otherwise deserted spot right next to the fjord began to drop in again. But back in my tent, on the right side of a meal, with my stove for company the world, once again, seemed a better place as I caught up with my notes. Little things get to mean a lot in this kind of situation. It really was time to make a final decision as regards the Ísafjörður peninsula. Try as I might, it wasn't going to be possible for me to do all I intended: Iceland was simply too hard for that. But using the bus, assuming the plan worked, I would get to see the North Western tip next day. Back south to the ferry across Breiðafjörður the day after that, I would be back on the ring road again by Tuesday, heading for Reykjavik. And replacement tyres.

On the buses

"Our descent from the summit was amazing: amazing, that is for the fact that the bus reached new speeds, the noise a new crescendo as we tore downwards on the rubble road."

14

Waking next day feeling utterly relaxed, a firm decision at last. It was to be the North West peninsula. I don't normally get on with buses. And back home will go to the ends of the earth to avoid using them. Trains, boats and planes are fine but, for me, buses have never lost that stale cigarette and diesel fumes aura. A hangover, perhaps, from school days and seven years catching the eight o'clock bus. A fifty-three seater double-deck half-cab, open at the rear, enabling latecomers like me to leap aboard after it had set off. Often so full, seats only available upstairs amongst the smokers ..... a merry band, we lurched and bounced for nine miles. And back. Sometimes taking time out after school to look round the shops in Burnley, feeling terribly grown up I would take coffee in the Atlantis café and hope that no girls came and sat at my table. Trouble with girls ..... they make you come over all embarrassed, bright red and stuck for words. Until you're old enough. Not even buses were safe from embarrassment. Catching the later one increased the risk of the tired fellow sitting next to me falling asleep. And if lurching round the corners didn't shift him I had to keep pushing his head off my shoulder. Yet now I was all keyed up, excited even, about a bus ride that, admittedly, would take me to an area whose reputation for splendour goes before it. Effectively it would buy time that would put the North West tip in the frame without upsetting my original plans. The best of all worlds.

This morning, for a change, I did not have to get on the road as quickly as possible. Outside, it was cool, sunny, windy. Again. Inside, on the right side of a relaxed Sunday breakfast, Rod Stewart and his contemporaries played softly on the radio. With map spread out on the tent floor, in so far as it was possible I worked out an agenda for the journey to Reykjavik, included the 300 mile detour by bus and a ferry crossing as well. Thoroughly appreciating a lazy morning, I marked each day's ride on the map and reflected on the journey so far. Lest I should forget. Could I ever? 1000 miles from home, it might as well have been the moon. Once again, images of "is it the right decision?" flashed up on the screen and, still in reflective mode, I got to considering if this was what I really wanted. Whether this whole thing was what I wanted. Would an open return date have helped? Was it the pressure to perform that fuelled those doubts? All of this in contrast to Jonas, the fellow I had met at the start of my journey, who would be riding an odd mile or two to set up camp, draw a little, then move on as the mood took him. But I had wanted to do this trip for so long now.

This was all about challenges. Drawing on inner strength. I tried a little relaxing, meditating perhaps, colours, images of harmony between man and machine. Then, to get the most from my body, I gave thanks to my legs in particular for their splendid work so far, and issued a warning of demands to come. It simply seemed the right thing to do. All the essentials of my trip received a round of thanks. From sleeping bag, stove and tent that together kept me warm, dry and fed. To palm top computer with whom, mistress like, I consorted, made confessions before going to sleep each evening. As you would expect, my bike and its ailing tyres came in for a special thought. Those who know a thing or two about meditation and its allies would have fallen about to witness my feeble efforts. But I do have a sense of being at one with the technology I use, whatever its nature. And firmly, naïvely perhaps, believe that it may be persuaded to serve us better if we operate in harmony, with some kind of understanding, empathy. Call it blind faith in inanimate objects, but they have all seen the hand of mankind from conception to construction, and earth is the source of all raw materials. I feel a need to know my machines and expect them to perform accordingly. The teacher in me recognises the mutual trust that comes from long-term learning relationships. For me, machines are more than things to be traded in when the initial gloss has worn off. My bike has served two generations of the family. Together we have seen the world. I keep my cars for years, nursing them through all their ailments. I service and repair most of the household mechanical possessions, and am not happy using things until I know how they work. They come to be more than just machines. I believe them to be the more trusting and reliable for it. Back from mechanical musings, it was scarcely believable that my miniature home from home, the familiar things that have accompanied me on journeys before, would ever pack down again.

I had been to the North East, would go North West, and never mind the consequences. Reykjavik is extreme South West. Seyðisfjörður, where I would re join the ferry, is extreme East. That was it then. My plan was taking shape. And like the lecturer back in Varmahlíð had said. It was approaching madness. Images of the garden back at home swept across my mind again, its trees, herbaceous plants and lawns contrasting with the scene before me ..... scrubby grass right down to the rocky shore of Hrútafjörður. Opposite, moorland swept up above the water as far as the eye could see, interrupted only by Route 1 cutting northwards towards Hvammstangi, the road I had used only the day before. Inside my tent was warm, sheltered. Out there it looked fine and bright. But a cold wind continued to blow. I imagined it would be rather like this inside a television ..... an artificial world where almost anything can happen. A haven from which the real world could be safely observed. But not for long because my bus was due in less than two hours. If I had got it right. Spirits were rising. On the move again soon. Peaks and troughs. That's travelling. For this was no holiday. More, a crusade to salve something inside.

The best laid plans can come unstuck. Climbing the hill to the main road the bus went past. Twenty minutes early. I could scarcely believe what I had seen. The build up to that journey, having compromised my principles to accommodate it. And now this. Not a little deflated, the optimist tried to believe the one that went by was a charter and the service bus would be along shortly. The philosopher said that it just wasn't meant to happen, that something else would happen along. The realist found me still at the roadside an hour later ..... the next bus going north in two days time. It might come early. But two days early was asking too much. I had to do better than that. And with map laid out on the grass, I searched for alternatives. Homing in on the ferry route I had planned to use the following day it occurred to me that the tour might work in reverse. The guide book confirmed this, and with that in mind I took the moorland track west that led to the café in Búðardalur, at the head of Hvammsfjörður. For twenty five miles the low level pass climbed away from Hrútafjörður. From the summit the fast flowing river Laxa visibly grew as, together, we headed for Hvammsfjörður. Then it would be the coastal road to the ferry port of Stykkishólmur.

I had tried to find a different sort of place to eat, but this being tea time on a Sunday at the height of the short tourist season ..... best to close! So, out of the rain and wind for another respite, I wound up in yet another filling station café. And eating healthier for a change, courtesy of a passing bus driver who translated the menu for me. Norah Batty once complained that the trouble with folks going abroad was that they came home with funny ideas about what's to go in salads. She'd have had a thing or two to say about mine, for its contents went far beyond limp lettuce and a shred of tomato. Saladt, it was called in Icelandic. A mighty heap that included mushrooms, egg, tomatoes, cucumber, cheese, lettuce, plus, of course, chips, for there was no option on anything else.   Mountainous helpings like this might go some way towards explaining why there were so many big folks about. And I mean big. In all directions. It was reassuring to know that these fellows weren't on the other end of a battle axe. For to meet your average Viking thus must have been a frightening experience for ancient Britons like me. It is at these places that a fellow wearing a baseball cap rolls up in a twin cab Tonka truck, pops in for a burger, does a bit of shopping, fills up with gas, and away into the wind. It was more like the USA than any Europe I have seen.   At least half the vehicles are full-blown Tonkas or four-wheel-drive derivatives of Japanese hatchbacks found all over the world. I guess they need them here in winter. Again, I was reminded of tales of coaching inns when they were an exchange point for all sorts of activities and people. Similarly, anything worth taking place did so here, it appeared.

Back by the sea again, a long ride lay ahead if I was to make it next day.   Research at the café cum staging post revealed that a ferry left Stykkishólmur at ten o clock the following morning for the 40 mile crossing of Breiðafjörður. A bus would meet it at Brjánslækur, on the Northern shore for the journey to Ísafjörður. The following day I would take a bus south, down the winding road that followed the Western fjords, to pick up the ring road again at Bru. All was well in the world again. High on caffeine after a third re fill of coffee, I left Búðardalur at seven o'clock in the evening for the 55 mile journey to Stykkishólmur. Back on schedule if my plan worked, a lot depended on that evening ride.

Towering mountains, their vast scree runs threatening the road one side, lazy inlets of the sea nibbling at scrubby grass the other. Not a soul in sight. The fjord. Open sea beyond. Islands, reputedly a thousand of them. And golden sunshine radiating down between the clouds. The wind behind me all the way. Despite the fact that ninety per cent was unsealed gravel the road was a joy to ride. Ailing tyres forgotten under a rash of exuberance, the mountain bike came into its own, enabling downhill stretches to be taken very quickly. I stopped several times simply to soak up the atmosphere. Utter quiet, broken only by the calling of birds and, just for a change, that favourable wind. The stuff that memories are made of.

Picking up the route from Reykjavik for the last few miles, the volume of traffic at well past midnight made me speculate on the possibility that there might be a night crossing. That being the case I could get ahead of the game, make up for lost time, sleep on the ferry. In the golden sunlit still of early morning I rode through the silent streets and wound up at the harbour. On some kind of high after my fifty-five mile ride next to the fjord, earlier disappointments forgotten, plans locked together again. Exciting places, harbours. This one the more so at one o'clock in the morning, having made it there against the odds. Climbing the steep grassy hill that sheltered it, a vision to make up for any amount of hardship. Out to sea the most glorious golden sunset, or maybe sunrise, hung over glittering water. Below, safely tucked up for the night, fishing boats, ferries and small craft nodded gently in the early morning light. Trucks, cars and cranes waited on jetties. Like a stage set without actors. And beyond, set to a distant backdrop of white peaks, a town that looked like a town. It would have been wonderful to spend the night up there, and I momentarily toyed with the idea of lugging all my gear to the summit. But that was as far as the notion got. Stykkishólmur, a fishing port and administrative centre, the largest settlement on the narrow Snæfellsnes peninsula, with a population of 1200, appeared to be built on a series of grassy hillocks. Typical timber-built homes with coloured roofs were approached via roads that crept every which way for access. Beautifully proportioned and presented timber buildings lined the streets.

Plainly, there was no night ferry, but the security fellow who found me snooping around the booking offices for information pointed out that it would be leaving at nine the following morning, not ten as I thought. Still less sleep. But who cares? At the camp site, I turned in very quietly, but still high on adrenalin and coffee, couldn't settle. Back in the driving seat, in charge of events again, not simply responding to them. On track once more it all seemed worthwhile.

15

Waiting in a ferry queue, no matter where, there is always that sense of anticipation. There amongst the cars, buses and trucks, with nothing better to do it is easy to fantasise. On the possibility that the young woman in the Toyota might fancy me. Or the pity she must feel for the fool out in the rain who can't afford a car. The reality is the distinct possibility that she hasn't noticed me at all.

I would have liked to have spent more time in Stykkishólmur, but when travelling the show must go on. Eighty miles the day before and four hours sleep, I went below deck for the coffee and bun thing. Catching up with my notes, happy to be inside again, I did feel to be conducting my life entirely outdoors. It had poured with rain during the night and was still pelting down next morning. The sort when I really didn't want to get the tent packed down. But at the eleventh hour it had come fine. Who knew what today would bring. It all depended on schedules now. And whether the bus driver would be prepared to take my bike. It was an odd feeling, being dependent on the whims and timetables of others. Peaks and troughs. Life's full of them. Cycle touring, the more so. The site office had been closed. A notice told campers to pay at the sports centre down the road. Which, being a straightforward sort, is exactly what I did. Honest Jo, that's me. Although I expect the same in return. It's my belief that life is full of consequences.

Up on deck again, we crossed Breiðafjörður, threading the myriad of tiny islands I had seen from my ride along the shore only a few hours before. Ferries are a fabulous way to travel. Itzhak and Reuven were making the crossing too. The standard issue round Iceland thing. That's what we were about, so to some extent it became less surprising that we kept coming across each other. Like long lost friends, again we followed the "did you see?" routine. Two and a half hours out from Stykkishólmur we called at Flatey; tiny, yet the largest island in Breiðafjörður. With a name that tells much about its terrain, Flatey has seen a monastery, been a cultural centre, but is now largely deserted apart from summer, when some of the houses are occupied and tourists wonder if they ought to have chosen ten records to bring with them. Martin was travelling round Iceland on a two week bus pass. He had spent the night camped on Flatey, having travelled from Reykjavik the previous day and taken the afternoon ferry from Stykkishólmur. Half my age, a fellow cyclist, it turned out, we had much in common and spent the rest of the crossing exchanging travel experiences the world over. Unable to take more than two weeks off work, for this journey he'd had no option but to travel by bus in order to see as much of Iceland as possible in the time. Weather, hills, roads, breakdowns ..... they were familiar stories for both of us. But all travel is fun, thought provoking. And a great privilege. We were in no doubt on that one. Then I got to wondering about the bus on the other side (of the fjord ..... not the other other side!), and speculating on the power of willing something to happen. Martin's timetable confirmed the connection. But could I get my bike on that bus. Uncertainty was creeping in. But if it was meant to be ..... I'm that kind of person.

Sure enough the bus was there, but before departing for Ísafjörður, it would take a return trip to the extreme Western tip of Iceland at Bjargtangar and back. I could have gone, but jibbed at further spending, being already committed to the expensive trip north. Neither did I feel like riding far after 80 miles the day before and only 4 hours sleep. Too late I discovered that the ferry did a second crossing, to meet the bus for its departure north. More sleep and exploring Stykkishólmur. It would have been the better option. But with seven hours to spare, I ambled a little way round the shore and, with nothing but sea birds for company set up my stove and made a meal. A comfortable hollow in the grass, a place to watch the sea gently lapping the rocky shore. Time to contemplate the journey so far, to consider expectations for what was to follow, to watch the ferry silently disappear between distant islands on its return journey.

The rain woke me up. Drinks at the hotel just a short ride round the bay provided cover for a bunch of postcards that needed writing. Conveying the essentials of a pedal-powered journey to those unfamiliar with the ethos was reduced to practicals like "been there, did this, that, the other." Real issues like feelings and emotions generated by the experience were left blank for recipients to fill in as appropriate. Some, I knew, would conjure up realistic images, feel what I felt. Others might well be marked "return to sender" for all they would convey. The couple on the ferry were staying at the hotel. We spoke of travel, of politics, agreed on all sorts of issues back home. But roads that meant their rental car got dirty had been a problem. Of more concern to me were the odds on those same roads destroying my tyres before reaching Reykjavik. I left them taking afternoon tea and made my way back round the bay to catch the bus, at last, for Ísafjörður.

Stykkishólmur.

Ísafjörður ..... contrasting with the harsh landscape left behind, a breathtaking combination of mountain and water.

We jolted and slithered at an alarming pace through spectacular, high level rocky barren regions on roads that had clearly been frozen and snow covered until recently. The glistening mud surface would have made difficult riding. Vistas from endless summits bore down on long fjords, then after descending we motored alongside them for mile after mile, twisting and turning at every whim of the landscape. A first taste of mechanical travel in ages felt odd, like cheating perhaps, but the 80 miles we covered in just three hours would have taken a full day, possibly more, looking at the terrain. The driver had frowned when he first saw my bike. The twelve seater bus had just a small space behind the seats for luggage. But after unloading panniers and removing the front wheel, it packed down easily enough amongst my four companions' trappings. Everyone on board was a tourist ..... traveller, I think they're called on this sort of venture. Who else would pay 3,000k (£21) for the evening trip? We stopped a couple of times to do the thing properly, be amazed by waterfalls and the like, be photographed next to one. Owing to the remoteness and distances involved, our driver had a second home which he uses when he takes the trip north to Ísafjörður. Not so much a luxury holiday pad, more a necessity as he simply cannot get back to base each evening. As for a wife in every bus depot: this, he denied.

The tunnel was awesome. Opened in 1994 to replace a difficult route over the mountain, time machine-like it whisks users from rock to coast. I have no idea how long this dark craggy hole was, though it is clearly several miles. Somewhere near the middle there is even an underground junction for Suðureyri, a small settlement to the North West. I've cycled through many tunnels, but this one would have been desperate. If you've been caving, know the hollow clank of equipment on rock, the patch of light deep underground, the sense of excitement, anticipation, potential danger, then you have the tunnel. Beamed through the mountain, wreathed in stagnant fumes, only headlights lay between us and oblivion. Leaving the tunnel, Starship Enterprise-like we might have landed on another planet. Contrasting with the harsh landscape left behind, a breathtaking combination of mountain and water was the reward on our final approach to Ísafjörður. The town looked like it had been planted, grown there from seed. Nurtured, yet natural, like the classic country garden. For deciduous trees rustling gently beneath the evening sun, read snow dusted mountains. For tall herbaceous plants, read tastefully presented offices, hotels. Well proportioned and juxtaposed timber housing with multi-coloured roofs took on the role of annuals. Shipping, tied up in the harbour – ferry boats that connect with the outer fjords, brightly coloured fishing boats and a multitude of smaller craft combined to make up the borders. The calm waters of Ísafjarðardjúp took on the role of well groomed lawns, setting the whole thing off beautifully, thus completing the analogy for arrival, and throughout the short time I was to spend there.

Martin and I set up our tents in the grounds of a smart hotel. It was all perfectly legitimate, as advised by our bus driver, who had set us down close by. Luxury toilet and shower facilities: but no one to pay, reception closed. And somewhere in there, the feeling that someone, an angry hotel manager, perhaps, would be along shortly to tell us that he had customers paying good money, and to get the hell out of there before he called the police.

It had been only hours since meeting on the ferry. Now we prepared meals in respective tents and talked through canvas like old friends ..... of travel, aspirations, our homes. And next day, he would take the bus south, too. The rest of the bus passengers arrived later. Having failed to find budget accommodation they, too, had been directed to the hotel campground. If we had co-ordinated our erections better we would have set up our camp like they do in the Westerns. It would have been a fairly small circle, but we could have repelled a whole squadron of angry managers. It had been a long day. Too late for that, I thought, dozing off and listening to the new arrivals trying to set up camp quietly, knowing how conscious they would be of every rustle, every clink in the perpetual daylight.

16

My low-slung ridge tent is as old as the hills. Stuck on after our cat used it as climbing frame on one of the occasions my son camped in the garden as a youngster, brightly coloured patches are a reminder of just how much service it has given. Bought second hand, it was far from new then. My son is grown up now. Close encounters with streamlined, modern tents make mine look distinctly past its sell by date. But there I was, cosy, brewing up coffee in the large storage area. The others were doing the same, but outside, sheltering from the rain under the roof overhang of a nearby building. Fat aluminium poles support the fly sheet. This pegged out, I climb out of the weather with all my gear to hang the inner tent from the ridge. Thus set up, it is hard to believe that my son and I used it together. We had to take it in turns to sit up even when he was a youngster. How we managed on the three week trip over the Pyrenees from Spain, then through France when he was a student ..... unbelievable, looking at the equipment I had with me. It has been all over the world with me, even been posted to Australia along with my bike, to avoid carrying all my gear on the domestic leg of the journey. Now on its second sewn in ground sheet, it has never let me down. Even the slightly run-down image it presents, I regard as a bonus, for what potential malefactor would notice it when shiny new equipment, with go-faster stripes shouting just that, cries out for attention. The same goes for my bike. Technically, mechanically, in use, it's the biz ..... but casual viewers see a time-worn image represented by the fact that it has covered a lot of ground and in reality desperately needs a re-spray. Each time I return from a trip, I vow to do something about it. Each time I leave it chained to a lamp post I am pleased to have resisted the temptation.

The rain had stopped by the time I was packed up ready to leave, but not before finding someone to pay for camping. My straightforwardness in seeking to pay for the facility was accepted without comment. Basic honesty is the norm here, expected and reciprocated. It's a concept close to my heart. The bus would leave at eleven thirty, giving me just a couple of hours to explore this lovely town.

I had changed cash at banks until that point on the journey. The fact that I can put a card into a machine almost anywhere in the (developed) world, punch in a few numbers, and out trots local currency still surprises me. I still find myself saying thank you to the machine. No fuss, no waiting for banks to open, or queuing with traveller's cheque and passport. No different to popping into town for cash at home. Until it eats your card. Still awed by the concept, oblivious to its shortcomings, I will never forget that time. Late at night, small town on the West coast of the USA. The machine wouldn't give me any cash, spat out all kinds of incomprehensible questions. Meanwhile, my wife was sitting in the restaurant anxiously wondering what had become of me. I had simply nipped out after ordering food to find myself locked in mortal combat with a machine that clearly didn't understand me, my card, bank, or account. Pressing buttons in increasing desperation, visions of a fund milked dry flashed through my mind. Although the machine finally gave up the struggle, gave back my card, albeit without money, I now try to make a point of only using machines next to banks that are open. This way, language difficulties apart, I stand a good chance – as yet un-tried – of going in there and convincing someone that they ought to retrieve my vital bit of plastic. Now, with a clear view of staff working in the refined air beyond, I cautiously approached the machine in the lobby. It offered no resistance. Icelandic kronor without a fight. Like so much of this ordered society, it had worked first time. The rest of the town, with a population of 3,000 reflected this aura. By dockyard standards, even the port area was clean, tidy, ordered. Everywhere, a feeling of trust. And utter security. Now well into my second week in the country I was happy to leave my bike unsecured, in the full knowledge that it would be there for my return. In truth, cyclists are few and far between in Iceland. A fact confirmed when quizzed by locals, who regarded me as some kind of madman. I guess demand for stolen bicycles would not be high.

Keeping the public areas spick and span, here, once again, were students. Hard at work close to the camp ground, those I spoke to were happy with their lot in life. No wall-to-wall flattened chewing gum here, no graffiti, no litter, no uprooted young trees. No angst. Quite what odious young malcontents do here, I never found out. Whatever they do, where ever they lurk, if they exist at all, it is kept under wraps. On the face of it, this uncluttered society, without the pressure of a high population, offers a lesson that many would do to learn. While purchasing the largest sticky bun I have ever seen, the young girl who served me, who had left school only the previous year, told more about the community spirit engendered by work schemes for students. Paid little enough (under £3.00 per hour) in this expensive country, there is no shortage of labour. It might just be that there are few alternatives for this group, though I would like to believe it is a reflection of a straightforward society that is prepared to put something back, rather than the take and more take philosophy so prevalent in many parts of the world.

Seated on a tall stool in the window of the bakery-cum-café was an excellent position to observe the world go about its business. Endless coffee, a delicious, if time-consuming, pink iced bun. And talkative company. Confirmation that it would be a lengthy procedure. Fridrik plainly appreciated someone to practice his English on and share his coffee with. Typical of deep and meaningful transitory friendships that are the hallmark of travel, we covered a lot of ground in a short space of time. A former fishing skipper who has travelled extensively, as well as advising on fish stocks and quotas, he explained that sixty percent of modern Iceland's economy is based on fish. Against this background I learned of the 1976 Cod War from an Icelandic fisherman's point of view. Remember the kerfuffle when Iceland declared a 200 mile exclusion zone? So, you're too young to remember. Fact remains, though, that it did stir up a lot of feeling on both sides and impacted on the UK fishing industry in a big way. On lowered fish stocks, he offered the theory that it is not the size of the holes that is to blame, but the nets themselves and their associated gear, destroying habitats as they scrape along the sea bed. Having seen the amount of ironmongery associated with trawl nets it was easy to believe the theory. After brushing on tourism, still a relatively small but growing part of the economy, we moved on to aluminium. Bauxite, imported from Australia, is smelted in Iceland because of cheap and plentiful electricity generated from natural sources. Next, the Icelandic currency, then quite recently floated and responsible in a small way for making my journey simply expensive as opposed to prohibitive. Right wing politics and capitalism, he went on, were prevalent in modern Iceland but thankfully, as yet, little of the crime that so often accompanies it had surfaced. Quizzed as to why people appear so cool to outsiders, his theory was that the country was so poor for so long that it grew to be self-sufficient, independent, having little contact with, and no need for outsiders. And old habits die hard, despite the modern view that a nation of 270,000 can no longer afford to be isolationist. Today, most speak at least some foreign language, English being at the top of the list and learned by all school children. I can vouch for the success of its teaching. With few exceptions, almost everyone I had cause to speak to had good English.

Climate change is taking place here too. Ísafjörður now has snow for only two months in the year. The fjord no longer freezes, as it did when Fridrik skated there as a youngster. Approaching seventy years of age, he was in the process of setting up a new venture. Neither party, we agreed, rated age. You are what you feel, and no less. You take opportunities when they present themselves. You do what you can, when you can. We parted after a warm handshake. A lot of ground had been covered, sadly none of it in real depth, but nevertheless an introduction to all sorts of issues. And between all of this he had learned a little of life in the UK. An hour had rushed by. Thanks, in part, to that heavy duty sticky bun.

After that there was just time to gently pedal through the streets to gain some kind of a feel for the place before moving on. Much of the town and the harbour beyond is built on a narrow peninsula, with vistas of mountain, sea, or both opening up beyond almost every street. Shops, offices, and houses try to out do each other in style and colour – with mown grass and a sculpture or two for added value. A place to savour, I considered, hastily pointing my camera in all directions before making my way to the bus. It had been a wonderful couple of hours.

The wings almost clipped the valley side. Low enough for me to see every detail, it hurtled inland, straight for the head of the valley, before making a startling one hundred and eighty degree turn for the landing strip on the opposite shore of the fjord. I ought to have got my camera out again: capture the near surreal image of modern technology in close encounter with nature. Too late: I was transfixed. For the pilot it would have been just one more landing, a workaday event that locals don't even notice. They must do scary take offs and landings each and every day in this unforgiving, if spectacular landscape, though our bus driver did add that the wind is often too ferocious for either. Beyond the airport, where the plane was now parked serenely on a narrow runway next to the water, with surfaced roads a recent memory, our bus was slowly destroying itself as we lurched over the rocks that passed for a road. Occasional surfaced stretches brought relief, made conversation possible, only for us to rush all too quickly on to the next rough stretch. Road gangs plainly work throughout the short summer season on maintenance programmes. Long stretches were subject to the whims of these gangs and often we would shoot past giant equipment hard at work with just a hair's breadth to spare. Tourists could be forgiven for not wishing to travel on these roads. In an effort to encourage this relatively new industry I guess that the ultimate aim is to surface the entire route to Bru, where it picks up the route to Reykjavik. By the time you read this, that task may well have been completed. This, despite the fact that harsh weather will give it a hard time. To this end, difficult stretches were being by-passed, bends cut out, bridges widened, or replaced. This will be a much easier journey one day, but the sense of achievement, having made it against the odds ..... that will be lost, I feel sure, as developments take place on the heels of improved transport links.

It was interesting to see a road from the motorist's perspective for change. I could see vehicles coming towards us from miles away. That is, I could see the cloud of dust that surrounded it, to pass in a hail of flailing gravel and stones clattering wildly against our bus. On a bike it is worse. Even wearing safety helmet and glasses, and lowering my head for the inevitable deluge of stone and dust. Drivers here see few cyclists and plainly have no concept of the mayhem they cause. Or perhaps they don't care, for they will doubtless be foreigners!

Distances, as the crow flies, were small. But before reaching Hólmavík, on the eastern side of the long peninsula, we had followed the shores of six major fjords on a twisting journey that, in the words of Tina Turner, was "simply the best." Here, snow capped mountains, swooped dramatically downwards from peaks that brushed the clouds. Scree runs and scrubby grass completed a dazzling picture wrapped up by seemingly endless fjords. A vista round every corner that repeatedly drew breath from us passengers. Away from the fjord now, snow melt rushed off the hills and mountains, through scrub, moorland and rocky outcrop alike. Sheep grazed at low level but little stock was to be seen as we climbed steeply away from the sea, always a stream for company, and always safe to drink in my experience, after making sure there were no buildings in sight upstream. A stop for lunch, another to take in a view or two, eyes closed from time to time, to be jolted wide awake by particularly rough stretches. Real tourist stuff, it all felt close to cheating ..... but the fare at 6000k (£42) sharply reminded me that I was not. Indeed, the ploy risked making unreasonable demands on my wallet. In open moorland, a young river tumbled beside us. On past waterfall after waterfall, tumbling over black rock, each one fit to be a tourist attraction in it own right. Bouncing along the winding mountain track above the snowline, alarmingly our driver was talking on his hand-held radio. On past another emergency shelter hut ..... this, a traditional stone construction. Others were made from wood, even plastic moulded ones. But without exception each was roped to the ground. With lakes and ponds in every direction I cared to look, a new stream grew visibly beside us as we descended. Giant road scrapers and the like were left, I guess, where they were last used with little or no security evident. In many parts of the world they would be interfered with, or worse. Not here. Our stream had grown rapidly, was pounding now between rocky banks it had carved through before widening, pebble and gravel strewn in a valley that opened out to Steingrímsfjörður, and Hólmavík where we would change for the Reykjavik-bound bus. Our descent from the summit was amazing: amazing, that is, for the fact that the bus reached new speeds, the noise a new crescendo as we tore downwards on the rubble road. In a matter of minutes the upland stream had metamorphosed, to become meandering gravelled estuary. From bleak upland where even sheep fear to tread, to holiday shacks set in rural charm. Truly a land of contrasts. Our young river ran obediently under the bridge, to be easily absorbed at head of fjord. Parts of this would have been grand riding if I had the time to spare. But still I'd been there, seen it. I had no regrets. Hólmavík and its fishing port looked as though someone had forgotten about it. Lurking in there, the feeling that it all needed a coat of paint. And one of sunshine. But it saved on films. Most of the buildings looked relatively new and I got to wondering where folks used to live before. This, in fairness, from the perspective of someone familiar with stone and brick buildings that go on for ever. It brought to mind a discussion I'd had with someone in Australia years back. It concerned the relative difficulties of altering timber and stone built structures. Putting a new window in the former: "you simply take a chain saw to the wall", he said. None of the propping up, chiselling out, inserting hefty lintels and jambs. I guess that here, replacing or re building a complete timber structure is less of a deal as well. Having said that, much of the newer building stock is in concrete, a material that needs to be used with caution if aesthetic appeal of the final product is part of the brief. Here in Hólmavík, I suspect that it wasn't.

A train-spotter in my youth, it was a fine thing to find myself at the nerve centre of transport services for the entire region. Smartly uniformed porters carry our luggage, passengers check the monitors for connections. Everywhere, a bustle of people on the move. In the excitement I forgot to write down the number of our bus. Back in the real world, on Tuesdays, Fridays and Sundays, one bus service links Reykjavik to Ísafjörður, with a change in Hólmavík. Half a dozen of us triumphant travellers arrived: shaken, somewhat stirred and, not entirely unexpectedly, a little early. Our connection south was waiting. And in charge was the same driver ..... the fellow who had unhinged my plans on a grand scale just a couple of days earlier. But unmoved by my revelation, his main concern appeared to be catching up with our racing driver in the nearby café that doubled as waiting room.

Almost at the end of mechanised tourism I needed to get my head round riding again, together with all its uncertainties. Our new driver was a good deal steadier, and despite the fact that he had cobbled up my plans I felt confident enough to sit in the front seat of the smart twelve seater. Sea, cloud and mountain merged in the early evening haze ..... our road often the only hint of human activity. Back to the junction for Búðardalur, and I had been in a spoon. From walks with my parents, this childhood expression described the journey well. After a circular tour of the North West by bike boat and bus, here I was back on the handle. Stopping to pick up someone waiting at the roadside, probably cold and disgruntled with waiting in a cold wind, the look on his face said he might have been there for several days. But unlike me, at least he caught the bus. You'd think he'd be grateful, pleased even. But this mournful fellow gave nothing away. The driver might have been a ticket machine for the expression on his new customer's face. It was an expression that said "I've just stepped in some dog shit!"

With tents set up behind the café and free use of the facilities I didn't have the gall to complain. But stir fry and toast is not an Oriental combination that springs readily to mind. They had run out rice, the waitress explained. The beer went down well though. Martin would take the bus for Akureyri tomorrow. Something of a novelty, companionship for the meal made a pleasing change. As it had on the journey that brought us there. The South African had gathered that we were foreigners too. Now settled in Ísafjörður, together we touched on all sorts of topics in the short space of time allowed to travellers. He told tales of the fishing industry and the opportunity it presents for young people; of seasonal permanent darkness followed by everlasting daylight. And the mood swings it generates. It was here that I finally discovered the answer to a question that had occupied my mind for some time ..... concerning the whereabouts of livestock in the winter when much of the upland is snow covered and many roads closed. Answer: kept indoors in gigantic barns, sheep included.

Iceland has to be one of the safest countries in the world. Straightforward respect for person and property is the norm, we learned. And a breath of fresh air for someone with roots in modern South Africa. Like Fridrik only that morning, now fluent in Icelandic, Paul was plainly appreciating speaking English. He told more of the community work scheme ..... many students apparently taking part to offset some of the peripheral costs of their education. For me, the spirit of life in the far flung communities was summed up when we learned of letters arriving with simply a first name, and the town for an address. Mindful of this, we were surprised to hear of an unfulfilled bid for North Western independence on the back of a fishing industry that, at one point, he said, was generating a vast proportion of the national income. It is a fact, though, that the area has been in decline for some years now. The idea of independence, if it ever got beyond bar room banter, seems incredulous in this sparsely populated region. Tourism is the new kid on the block. But infrastructure issues need addressing before any but those prepared for a degree of hardship will put this spectacular region on the must see list. As for me. I was rapt by the whirlwind tour of this stunning region.

A hitchhiker's ride to .....

"He had probably woken up, full of the joys of life: and wound up with a squeaky voice, his manhood in a bucket. And that bucket was travelling right beside me" .....

17

My first diary entry for the 20th of June, a Wednesday, reads "What a bloody morning!" Sheltered though it was, behind the café, my tent was flapping fit to bust in a huge wind and torrent of rain. It had been a poor night. Trucks would pull up, leave their refrigeration motors running, their drivers shout above the wind, then slam doors before moving on noisily. It was hard getting out of my sleeping bag. But it was to be Reykjavik, almost a hundred and twenty miles away that day. And nothing was going to stop me. I had to get on the road. Fast. Put this weather business back where it belonged. In my head. A real test of resolve, a question of putting my money where my mouth was, so to speak. A hot shower would be just the ticket. Only it was too early. The café would not open for hours. Privacy beneath the bridge found me tramping some distance and slithering down ridiculously steep slopes beside the raging torrent of a river. Then, flapping clothes, a cold backside, and toilet paper near impossible to light in the breeze. The delights of rough camping were brought into sharp focus in those early hours.

High on caffeine, I was on the road before six o'clock. But not before saying goodbye to Martin, my travelling companion for two days. He would spend a leisurely morning, before taking the bus north. It had crossed my mind earlier that if I stayed inside my tent there was a strong likelihood that, together, we would be picked up and blown all the way to Reykjavik. It wasn't anything like so bad once on the move. Wild wind hurried me along to such an extent that near-horizontal rain had little effect. Only when slowed down on steep hills was I conscious of its full force. And this, on my back. Stopping at a rest hut after an enormous ascent, I had difficulty standing up against the wind and rain. Inside ..... peace, tranquillity, a Mars bar and banana for energy. Outside ..... nature in the raw, uncontrolled. It was a wrench getting back on the road again. But still, you have it to do! The front tyre finally gave in amongst all of this. The wobble had been getting worse for miles. It had become a question of when rather than if, so the hissing death throes of tube blowing out through bulging tyre walls as rim met road came as no surprise. Back on the road in minutes, manna from heaven like, who should pull up with offers of fresh coffee and biscuits, but my Israeli minders. On the home straight to Reykjavik for their flight home, Itzhak and Reuven had covered four thousand kilometres in little over two weeks in their rented four-wheel-drive. This was the fourth time our paths had crossed. And still they were insisting I visit them one day.

The Coke salesman translated the menu for me. The truck driver commented that "I maht as vell go to zi moon", on hearing of my journey. Like so many others, the concept of cycling in Iceland was beyond him, despite admiration for my spirit and determination. Lunch in that transport café was a relaxing affair after coping with the morning's weather. But it was thanks, in part, to that weather that I was well over half way to Reykjavik and still feeling strong. South, through Borgarnes, over yet another enormous bridge cum causeway across the fjord. Then storm along the Southern shore with a tail wind and, better still, it was no longer raining.

In my experience, when things go this well there has to be a snag. And close to the tunnel under Hvalfjörður that would save a thirty five mile ride round the head, it shouted "Gotcha!" I'd stopped for a short rest. And waking, something about it had caught my engineer's eye. Spinning the back wheel revealed a buckled rim and broken spoke. On the drive side. The difficult one where the gears are. So much for earlier good fortune. To ride on would plainly be madness. With the load I was carrying, more damage might well occur if I didn't do something about it. After a heart sinking assessment of the situation, the practical fellow in me took over. After taking off the tyre for the umpteenth time I removed and stripped the block, carefully placing tiny parts of the freewheel mechanism on plastic bags laid on the grass, desperately hoping that they didn't get blown away. With the block out of the way I fitted the new spoke, trued up the wheel and, unlike all the king's horses and all the king's men, did put the whole thing back together again. Ever lateral thinker, but carrying no grease, the margarine I used to cook with came on as an admirable substitute. That I could do the work at the roadside without a bunch of specialist tools was down to the good fortune that I had fitted the high quality, if rather expensive, hub before leaving home. A full hour later, having once again showed my bike who was the boss, I made for the tunnel. Seventy-seven kilometres to Reykjavik, the sign said. Under fifty miles. But bikes were banned. Earlier, in the day it had been the tyre. Now it was my turn to be deflated. The prospect of riding right round the fjord, with my goal so firmly in sight was too much. Weather, puncture, breakdown. And now this. There used to be a ferry that ran from nearby Akranes all the way to Reykjavik. It had been discontinued since the tunnel opened. I considered riding on ..... would claim that I didn't understand the sign. But there might be toll staff and police to contend with before getting through. Against the odds I had made it this far. Banned from the tunnel. Detour unthinkable. There had to be a third way. And fresh from a castration, here it was.

Like me, Martin, my travelling companion in the North West fjords had cycled in Norway. We had got to talking of tunnels, for it is impossible to go far in those parts without encountering them. My son and I rode through countless numbers of them there too, and had no problems. But Martin had come across a particularly long one. With a ban on bicycles. Maps give no indication of these restrictions. It had happened to me in France. Where I had to tackle a huge (and unexpected) mountain pass late in the evening. At a stroke, plans are turned on their head. The joys of cycling. But with no alternative route available Martin had told of standing at the tunnel entrance and hitching a ride through, courtesy of someone with a camper van. Thus emboldened, willing to try anything rather than have my journey plans upset, I stood by the offending sign, deflated, but not yet defeated. As a motorist I do give occasional lifts to hitchhikers. It seems the right things to do sometimes. And here I was, calling in a favour ..... naively, perhaps, testing my belief in consequences. Plainly it would have been pointless thumbing those in small cars, no matter how sympathetic or willing their occupants might be. I had been standing there no more than five minutes. It was the first vehicle of any size. But the driver of the Land Cruiser had caught the eye of a balding, middle aged fellow with a problem bicycle. And in moments I was on my way again. I could scarcely believe the turn round in fortunes. One moment stranded at the roadside ..... the next, with wheels removed and kit stacked inside a mighty Tonka truck, my plan to reach Reykjavik that day realistic once more. Indeed, the world was a wonderful place, I reflected, as we motored under the fjord.

It was the horse I felt sorry for. My day had started badly. There'd been a problem or two but still, the clouds finished up with that ubiquitous silver lining. He had probably woken up, full of the joys of life. And wound up with a squeaky voice, his manhood in a bucket. And that bucket was travelling right beside me, I conjectured, as the tale unfolded. Hinrik and his companion were vets, returning to base having just castrated the lad. So much for getting back on my bike once through the tunnel. Interested in their new passenger, they were keen to hear my necessarily summarised story. Why I wanted to see Iceland? Why I chose to cycle when there are cars for hire? How could a young chap like me take six weeks out to travel? For fifty miles I responded to all these questions and more. We talked of farming in Iceland, of sheep indoors in winter, of horsemeat, of the fact that in a country with a population of 270,000 people there are no less than 100,000 horses. Imagine Britain with twenty million horses? Hinrik had spent time in Germany as a student. He had found the language easy to learn, having developed from the same base as Icelandic, we concluded. This conclusion went a long way towards explaining why I was having extreme difficulty getting a handle on the language. I found it near impossible to equate to the language, and failed miserably to hazard a guess as to what even the simplest words might mean. I speak only holiday French, yet can often work out the meaning of words when travelling in other countries with Latin-based languages. Hinrik explained that he found the same with Germanic based languages. We talked of farming, of the differences between the UK and Icelandic conditions. He was interested to hear that my wife's family are crop farmers in the flat lands of Lincolnshire, and of their operation. On hearing of my home close to the Yorkshire Dales, James Heriot, the vet about whom countless books have been written, was brought into the frame. He told of a colleague, faced with a prolapse in one of his patients out in the field, so to speak. I'm no medic, but did gather that this is something to do with the uterus that has pushed out and will not return easily. With no specialist equipment to deal with it, and a real emergency on his hands, having seen the film "All Creatures Great and Small" he was able to locate and use sugar, an anhydrous substance that absorbed the excess liquid, shrank the offending organ, and hey presto! But, away from work, just what do Icelanders get up to? About to take time out himself, he would hitch up his caravan, leave home in Reykjavik and find a quiet spot to spend time with his family.

Getting back on the road straight after the tunnel had been out of the question, with so much to talk about. In less than an hour we had covered a whole lot. Necessarily, none of this was in great depth. More the sort of elementary level one achieves as a dinner guest. But my hitchhiking with a bike tale is good for many a meal yet. Travel offers much to anyone that takes the trouble to seek.

Approaching larger places by bike, it is easy to get into the scene. My normal practice is to stop well before built up areas, take a good look at my map and work out some general directions. Now, having exchanged addresses and said goodbye to my knight in shining armour, suddenly I was standing alone beside a dismantled bicycle and heap of luggage at a filling station in suburban Reykjavik ..... Iceland's capital city, with a population of 175,000. Convivial company one minute. Out on my own in concrete suburbia, the next. It was as though I had been beamed there from the tunnel entrance. Leaving me with the odd feeling that I needed somewhere to sort myself out. The burger bar was everything that I dislike about fast food. But I needed that coffee. And having got a fix on my map, set off beside the busy dual carriageway amongst factories, supermarkets, housing, and open parkland. On, through increasing traffic and, with a stop or two for directions, heading for the sea. There were two reasons for this. As ever, I was drawn there simply to absorb the scene, but secondly, my city map wasn't a lot of help until I got right into the centre proper. Reykjavik is built on a narrow spit that faces west into Faxaflói, a large bay bounded in the North by Snaefellsnes peninsula, and the South by Reykjanes. Riding west, into the evening sun, I would eventually get close to the city centre and the grid system that my map indicated there. Thus far, it worked. Then, simply by following my nose I found the coast and headed ever closer to the tall buildings and port area. Pausing for a moment or two, I did feel just a little emotional. Downright privileged, if I'm being honest. The capital city of Iceland. Somewhere I had imagined for years. And here I was, arrived by bike ..... a simple way to travel. Like walking. Only more so. Back where I had come from, the now standard issue backdrop of water and snow capped mountains. Turn 180 degrees, and a thoroughly modern cityscape, complete with all the trappings. The contrast, quite simply enormous. Here, I would forget the tent and use the Youth Hostel. Only it didn't feature on my map, and the tourist information office had closed for the evening.

The women spoke no English, but their map was a good deal clearer than mine. And sorted out in French, before long I was booked in to a room of my own for two nights, for a total of just 3,600k (£24). The sense of space unimaginable, I sat at the table, mesmerised by it all. Slowly, the fact that I was staying here, albeit for a short time, began to sink in. I desperately needed to get myself together. To chill out. Be a proper tourist for a while. But short term, what I needed was food. After so much emptiness in the wilder regions, the whole experience left me with the feeling that I was merely an observer. That all of this was happening to someone else. From bustling city streets and suburban supermarket, to the communal dining kitchen where I prepared a feast. But pork chops, fresh vegetables with potatoes and an interesting sauce. That was real enough. So, too, a full range of beautifully presented facilities for the hardened traveller. Here were singles, couples, and families from all over the world. Each and every one, it seemed, wrestling with maps, guide books, and cards for the relatives. Wall to wall information told of attractions unlimited. Coach trips, white water rafting, glacier tours, to name but a few. Space to stand up, room to walk around. And all of it a million miles from wild solo camping. Flapping canvas, thrashing rain: that might have been another life.

But what to do while here in Iceland's capital? Guide books are fine, but a little local knowledge spreads a long way. And with this in mind I sought a list of 'must sees' from hostel staff. The Golden Circle, the blue lagoon ..... they would have to be included on the hit list next day. And my bike could have a rest because, one way or another, I would be a proper tourist. But content with seventy miles by bike and another fifty in the back of the Tonka truck, what I really needed was sleep. Basking in the glory of a plan that worked, if not quite how it had been planned, I was confident of a decision by morning.

Tourist

"People photographed their daughters next to this orgasm to beat all orgasms. In a whirl of mutual imagery, those without daughters had to take pictures of each other."

18

Having woken up with a decision, I would have to be really brave, for there would be no minder beside me. No one to tell me I was on the wrong side of the road, that I'd driven clockwise on the last roundabout. And to make sure I've seen the chap that wants to pull in from the right. My own car, rented left hand drive cars ..... I've done a deal of driving in foreign parts. With my wife, also an experienced driver, beside me ..... the extra pair of eyes that turn the phenomenon of opposite side driving into a team event. The possibilities are endless, taking into account map reading and direction finding as well. But the alternative was an air conditioned coach ride that keeps reality firmly beyond sealed windows. Thirty minutes here, stop at the trinket shop there, time for a look at the view somewhere else. And back. To work out that you've spent far more than you anticipated, because you didn't want wait to on the bus with your sandwiches while everyone else ate at the over-priced restaurant where the driver gets his cut. I had made all the decisions so far and rather liked it. Today would be no exception.

Feeling the need to do the route under my own steam, I drove back through that tunnel, the one that had been such a problem the day before. With a name like that, it sounded like it ought to be an interesting kind of place. Before the tunnel was opened, Akranes, situated at the end of a peninsula separating Hvalfjörður from Borgafjörður had been the ferry port for the fifteen mile crossing to Reykjavik, saving a sixty five mile drive round the fjord. Now, complete with its population of five and a half thousand, the town gave the impression of having been closed down along with the ferry. OK, it was cold, windy, unfriendly. And I stretched a point. But when the guide book says that cement-minded visitors might arrange a visit to the local works. Need I say more? On then, to follow the route I would have had to take If the lift hadn't come along, round the head of Hvalfjörður, to find it not unlike motoring round

Reykjavik ..... a thoroughly modern cityscape, complete with all the trappings.

Reykjavik ..... What charmed me was the near-universal vista of sea and mountain as a backdrop.

some Scottish Loch, dark water reflecting rolling moorland before giving way to snow covered peaks.

The local tourist industry can't decide what shape it is. But they are quite certain what it is made of. Be it the Golden Triangle or Circle, one thing is for certain. The fact is that tourists with a tight schedule are swept up from the streets of Reykjavik. And before they know what is happening, are traipsed at breakneck speed around a well trodden circuit in South Central Iceland, to find themselves deposited in Eden. Seductive as glasshouses with a name like that might sound, just down the road from Reykjavik, the naturally heated attraction at Hveragerði, where almost anything grows, has a reputation for inducing overheated wallet syndrome. Fine, if you like mass exposure to all that glistens. It is so easy to sit there and have the guide's waffle drift right over your head as she tells you the in depth story, and how long you're allowed to look at it before being rushed to the next one where you can stay a little longer and spend all you like.

Time was when Youth Hostels were pretty basic. The rather fine place where I had found myself resident was more akin to a smart hotel than just one rung up from camping. With a room to myself, lounge and dining facilities complemented an up-to-the-minute kitchen where I could prepare my own meals. In addition to this, tourist information was available on tap, plus booking facilities for all types of activity. Not knowing much about the region, I had sought information on how to get the most from my brief stay in the region. Learning of that triangle, or maybe circle, I had decided against wallet-sapping whirlwind tours. Tick sheet tourism was not for me. The hired Nissan Micra cost less than the tour. And it was ready, right there at the hostel. So, my triangle ended up with four attractions: Þingvellir, Geysir, Gullfoss, and The Blue Lagoon. Apple biting would not feature on my agenda: Eden would have to cope without me. On this occasion.

Leaving the comfort of a surfaced road, I headed for Þingvellir on roads that would have been hard riding. Thoroughly appreciating the contrast, driving was fun. Sure, it was less than easy starting out in Reykjavik's traffic. And changing gear with the window winder never works well. But settling down quickly, I found the new challenge of solo driving in foreign parts a refreshing change. New found freedom reminded me of the first time I had taken my father's car out alone, the day I passed my driving test. Setting off a little too enthusiastically from a junction, the back end of the car had lurched round as the wheels spun on a wet surface. Traffic was much lighter in those days and I got away with nothing more than a fright. That was almost forty years ago. And there I was, reminded of that day. The power of travel. The car handled appallingly on gravel, or was it was me that had forgotten? ..... having previously only driven rear wheel drive cars on that kind of surface. The front wheel drive Micra really wasn't up to roads like that, and it went a long way towards explaining the number of four-wheel-drives about.

The island was six days north of Britain, one day before the end of the world. So found Pytheus, a Greek explorer who, in the year 330, sailed north from Marseilles, in France, to learn, amongst other discoveries, of an island he called Thule, or Ultima. Frozen seas one day's sailing still further north confirmed proximity to the end of the world. Iceland, then thought to be uninhabited, is believed to have been the island he referred to in his travel journal. Towards the end of the 8th century, some in Ireland knew of Iceland, though the earliest recorded settlements there are referred to by the Irish monk, Dicuil, in the early 9th century. I first came across King Harald of Norway in Lerwick, capital of the Shetland Isles. Confined, now, to the street named after him there, he was a force to be reckoned with back in the late 8th century. Having driven his enemies out of their homeland to those Scottish islands, Harald followed, and further harried them. My journey across the North Atlantic on the 12,000 ton Norrona had been uneventful. Though the bar room tables simply wouldn't stay still as we ploughed through the force seven gale, and showering had been a problem as we tumbled over the waves. That same crossing in an open longboat, heading for somewhere close to the end of the world, ousted, pursued, perhaps, by Harald's men must have been less entertaining. Some, at least, made it, to become the Scandinavian ancestors of modern Iceland. One in the eye for Harald, these exiles, plus others direct from Norway settled in Iceland, possibly driving out or enslaving the Irish monks, for little is known of them in the years that followed.

Alþing, Iceland's present parliament, was set up at Þingvellir (Parliament Plains) in the year 930. Founded by descendents of those early settlers, it is the world's oldest national assembly. I had parked a couple of miles back to look at Þingvallavatn, Iceland's second largest lake, centrepiece for the oldest National Park in the country, set up in 1928. The rift between the European and North American plates is an obvious 'must see', and responsible for a whole lot of spectacular sights that include canyons, caves and water features. Walking in such surroundings was a humbling experience, as I tried to imagine the forces responsible for such a landscape. Here were trees, not struggling horizontally as they clung to life, but sensibly sized silver birch and pines that had made it to maturity, sheltered, to an extent, by the nature of the terrain. Here was a softer Iceland than any I had seen to date, where a casual glance in the right direction might have transported me to parts of the Lake District in Northern England.

Metamorphosed. Yesterday, a cyclist ..... and wherever I went people would take notice, wave, ask about my journey. Today, a motorist. And already melting into the background, yet revelling in the novelty of being indoors. Before further exploring the site, I ate a picnic lunch parked next to crystal clear water that filled a volcanic ravine. Deep beyond imagination, lined with shining coins it had plainly seen service as a wishing well. Or so I thought. For in reality it turned out to be more versatile. Jeeves-like, the water has a reputation for answering all sorts of questions at the drop of a coin ..... provided a simple yes or no will suffice for an answer. See the coin hit the bottom and the answer is "yes": "no" if it is lost to sight!

It might sound naive, but I really didn't know what to expect. If I'd done the job properly, I would have gone on a bus, listened to a tour guide potted history. Or read all the guide book had to say on the subject. I know someone who, before travelling, reads about destinations like it might be going out of fashion, only to find that on arrival a surfeit of information serves only to muddy the waters. It is a fact that, as tourists, we can only hope to scratch the surface, get a general picture of an area. I prefer to take an overview, let the whole scene wash over me, then settle down to reading the story later. That way the places, the innuendos ..... they are points of reference, a trigger for the memory, and it all makes sense. In your face, rapid transit from one tourist hotspot to the next leaves me quite cold, and no wiser for the experience. I knew that the seat of Icelandic government is in Reykjavik, and has been since the end of the eighteenth century. So, what would there be here? Fine buildings? Their remains? Foundations? Perhaps just post-holes of ancient structures, with artists' impressions of what had been there in times past? Not a bit of it. Þingvellir was chosen all those years back for its natural amphitheatre and acoustic effect

Hvalfjörður ..... its dark water reflecting rolling moorland.

Deep beyond imagination, crystal clear water filled a volcanic ravine.

provided by the great rock fissure. Writings from the time describe booths owned by chieftains, used as shelters and meeting places. Here, in addition to other activities, petitions might be heard. Seeking remains that I was assured are still evident, fleeting analogies with modern UK politics were brought to mind ..... of the surgeries that MPs conduct as a way of keeping in touch with constituents. Important proclamations were made from the Lögberg (Law Rock), a natural soapbox close to the Oxara River, later falling into disuse when a site further east was used. Real life open air theatre, held annually over a period of a week or two, might come close to describing what went on at this place. A modern day rock concert, with its stages, trade stands and temporary accommodation in the form of tents springs to mind as the closest we might come to understanding the ethos of this site. At these meetings, the supreme authority made decisions concerning the entire country. It was here that Christianity was adopted around the year 1000. A large proportion of the population would make the effort to attend, to have legal and business issues settled, marriages arranged, to hear laws made, and witness punishment of those who transgressed.

King Harald must have had the last laugh, for after more than three hundred years of independence, in 1262 Iceland surrendered, to find itself under Norwegian, later Danish rule. Although the Alþing lost its power, it still convened at Þingvellir as a legislative assembly and judicial court. Festivals, it is believed, were held there at the same time as assemblies, confirming that the site remained at the heart of national life right up to the move to Reykjavik in 1798. Since that time there have been several more gatherings at Þingvellir. In 1874 the King of Denmark attended a large assembly in recognition of 1000 years since the first settlement of the country. In 1930 a huge crowd celebrated 1000 years of Alþing: another witnessed independence just a few years later. Changes in legislation took place over a seventy year period, culminating in an end to Danish dominance. The Republic of Iceland was born in 1944, and 30,000 people are reputed to have gathered there to recognise the fact. Even more celebrated the 1100th anniversary of settlement in 1974. Figures like that were quite beyond me as I walked round the near empty natural arena, a powerful place, where history could be felt, as much as observed. Today, there's a hotel, a delightful church, and an enlarged farmhouse used by the park warden. They all blend in beautifully with their dramatic surroundings, look like they've grown there from seed. Protected since 1928, Þingvellir is regarded as the sacred site of all Icelanders.

Earlier in my journey, finding myself in a world of sulphur smelling steam and hot, plopping mud, I offered the notion that four letter words have an aura, a life form of their own. My visit to Þingvellir added fuel to this hypothesis, for it is not possible to avoid another all embracing four letter word for long, when lifting the lid on Iceland's past. To sag is to sink, slump, or subside under pressure. A fairly ordinary, run of the mill, three letter word, no matter which way you look at it. But add just one vowel and it metamorphoses, sheds its old meaning, chrysalis like, to emerge quite different. At a stroke it has got provocative, raunchy, perhaps. It has become one of those powerful four letter words with real clout.

The word saga is an inconspicuous noun that describes long and involved stories, often rooted in history. Who over the age of fifty, and many a good deal younger, can forget that time of an evening? The dishes had been cleared away. It was seven o'clock, and for the next fifteen minutes, talking was a risky business. Set in the fictitious farming community of Ambridge, Dan and Doris Archer, Walter Gabriel, even his shady son, Nelson have all passed on, been replaced by up-to-the minute-characters. It was in 1951 that "The Archers" hit the wireless waves. And still going strong, it has become Britain's longest-running soap. Like good design the world over, it has stood the test of time, for it's much the same in millions of households the length and breadth of the country fifty years on, while Americans have their much younger "Friends" and Australians make do with "Neighbours." With story lines that fall somewhere between fact and fiction, there is no doubt in my mind that the above – others will spring to the reader's mind – can be regarded as modern sagas.

Also lying somewhere between history and fiction, written in the 13th century in Old Norse, the common Scandinavian language, the Icelandic Sagas are the ultimate in long and involved stories. What better place to picture these tales being acted out for real, than the natural amphitheatre of Þingvellir. Like so many places, the world over, that have witnessed a deal of human emotion, these were impressions conjured up from feelings generated deep inside as much as what there was to be seen. To be there was an open invitation for my mind to create images of families sitting together on long, dark evenings, listening to tales of love, hatred, friendship, loyalty, feud, vengeance, and tragic destiny. These are the framework on which the stories, based round people said to have lived in the 10th and 11th centuries, are hung, though to describe them thus threatens an injustice. Much as today's soaps tangle real life events with fictional stories and their characters, their precursors, the grand-daddies of them all are a window on medieval Icelandic life. Artistic licence has probably allowed certain embellishments. But emphasis on action and consequence for individuals in all ranks of society point to democratic ways of resolving disputes, with latent threat and violent outcome never far away. Heroism, courage, generosity, strength, and wisdom feature routinely. These characteristics, and many more besides, are the raw material for wide ranging plots. Honour was the human trait most revered in pagan Icelandic society. Post-Christianity, this might well have evolved to embrace courage, humility, resignation in the face of suffering, even death. There for the reading, these stories demonstrate that virtue is a prized human attribute and backbone, still, to a modern consumer society beyond the wildest dreams of their authors.

Njal's Saga features honour, murder, arson, intrigue and much more, to end with the heroic death of its two main players: friends, Gunnar and Njal. The Laxdæla Saga, a little shorter with only seventy-eight chapters, starts in Norway in the late 9th century, before moving to Iceland where a love triangle involves the country's most beautiful woman. The tale completes its voyage early in the 11th century after several generations. And a death or two. It is beyond the scope of this book to go into the details of individual sagas, but if you fancy a ripping (and sometimes long) yarn, a tale that takes the wraps off early Icelandic life ..... history with knobs on ..... then a good bookshop will point you in the right direction if you want to buy. If you don't, then log on to the Internet. But be warned: there is so much available on-line that it might be difficult knowing where to start. Your local library might be a simpler option, with staff to offer guidance on what's available to match your needs.

Moving on after being moved by Þingvellir was a wrench. Not a big wrench, you understand, for travellers learn to cope with this leaving thing. I guess it's all about the glass being half full, always looking forward, the need to get back on the road, for the next bit of the journey might be more provocative still. That said, I didn't realise I had arrived at Geysir. Until stopping to examine a steaming hot stream running through extraordinarily bright green grass at the roadside. It had been an uneventful journey, the gravel road winding through undulating, surprisingly green countryside. All very relaxed, and still revelling in the contrast with cycling, where every nuance in the terrain or road surface impacts on progress. I had just left the mother of all parliaments, to find myself within a whisker of the mother of all geysers. With just a solitary vowel change, the word has been let loose, to be found, likely enough, dispensing hot water into a sink near you. That this small settlement has unsparingly given its name to hot water spouts the world over is a fact not widely known. The tourist industry in Iceland is making a big effort to put that right. The Geysir Centre, with a car park the size of an aircaft carrier was hard to miss. This Mecca for hot water enthusiasts comes complete with restaurant, information centre, multi-media experience and shop. Where anxious tourists can salve their environmental consciences and spend, spend, spend on memorabilia. Here, bored kids can be bought off. And one can purchase knick-knacks, exclusive proof for the relatives, that you've really been there, and no, you didn't go to that caravan site in Rhyl. Something else to put with the pile of dead tapes and old CDs at the back of a cupboard, to bring out when auntie wants to know what you did on holiday. Ignore my rantings. It's just the cynic in me and I ought to know better. For besides the tourist facilities and razzmatazz, there is an educational aspect that takes visitors through time from Iceland's spectacular creation, to the present. And I did take the trouble to learn a little of Iceland's geology and comprehensive list of natural phenomena. But not for long ..... never comfortable in close proximity to spending sensations, however well disguised.

Outside were a couple of cyclists. It seemed so natural to approach them, but dressed in civvies, I had to explain the disguise before exchanging experiences. Reassuringly, the two men were not young either. Flown in from homes in Spain only days previously, they were loaded up for several days riding in the interior. Like me, they were camping, and carried a good deal of food for their journey. Geysir was the last settlement before the pair took off for wilder regions, and they had assumed that final supplies could be purchased there. This was plainly not the case. Any amount of memorabilia. But food. Sorry. They had considered hitching a lift back to the nearest town, some distance back, but in the event were able play the sympathy card, tell their tale to staff at the restaurant who sold them some basic supplies. As though on cue, like it had been arranged by some travel club, who should

Þingvellir ..... Parliament Plains.

Strokkur ..... a foaming jet of near-boiling water that spouts to a height of 20 metres.

happen along, but Niels, the young Danish motor-cyclist I had spent some time talking to half way up a mountain pass on the second day of my journey. Like old friends, we exchanged experiences, compared notes, did the seen this, been there, what did you think of that thing. He had plainly covered more ground than me, had seen more. But we'd done similar things. And before leaving, we agreed that Iceland offers many interesting challenges for the independent traveller, and that all would be the richer for them. Did you hear the one about a couple of Spaniards, a Dane, and a Brit? Sounds like there ought to be a joke in there somewhere. The entire conversation conducted in English; perhaps the joke was on me.

So wrapped up in talking to fellow travellers, the real reason for my visit was almost forgotten. It's easily done, for the Geysir centre does rather dominate the area. Away from it all at last, to wander in a landscape quite unlike any other I have seen. Apparently, it is often crowded with coach trippers, but they had mostly been taken away by the time I got there. With space to fully appreciate this geothermal area that sits over a vast tub of boiling water I walked amongst this steaming surreal scene. Rocky, terrace-like terrain is punctuated by mud pools, hissing steam, hot and cold springs and streams. All of which support an array of unusually coloured plants and algae. Signs warned of increased activity, and to keep behind the ropes.

The star attraction, the *raison d'être*, the name that has swept around the world takes the form of an 18 metre hole with 20 metre deep chamber beneath. Unsurprisingly, it has been a tourist attraction for an awful long time. In the past, visitors have been known to throw rocks and soap flakes into the chamber in an effort to break down the surface tension of the hot water and induce an eruption. Until quite recently, this was the practice to celebrate Independence Day on 17th June. The practice is now banned on environmental grounds. The Great Geysir was erupting twice each day at the time of my visit, and I had just missed it. Moving on to the next best thing, close by, at a mere 3 metres across, is Strokkur. But it's much more reliable. And that's what you need to keep the punters rolling in. Amazingly clear blue boiling hot water filled its crater. Initially rippling gently like a sea side rock pool, as though driven by subterranean wave machine, its movements grow to a strong swell. The swell increases in magnitude until a final wave of pressure manifests itself in a mass of white bubbles that push up through the pool, to emerge as a foaming jet of near boiling water that spouts to a height of 20m, perhaps more ..... the whole scenario repeating itself every ten minutes. So, you do multiple orgasms. But every ten minutes, round the clock. That's got to be beyond even the wildest bar room banter. That was the closest I got to an analogy, but to be there, to feel the spray as it falls gently back to earth is to see nature in the raw, nature untamed. Those special moments that wrap up a successful union. Perhaps?

People photographed their daughters next to this orgasm to beat all orgasms. In a whirl of mutual imagery, those without daughters had to take pictures of each other. The Japanese were best at this, patiently taking it in turns in front of each eruption. When that game was over, they took pictures of each other taking pictures. Not wishing to be left out, I took a photograph of them photographing each other, then found a fellow Brit who took a picture of me surrounded by hot water and steam. I did the same for him. All jolly stuff. Then we went our separate ways.

Having missed Dettifoss, Iceland's (and Europe's) greatest volume waterfall, early in my journey, I determined not to miss Gullfoss, with a reputation for being one of Iceland's star attractions. Having left one centre just half a dozen miles down the road, another, Sigridarstofa, proclaimed arrival there. One of them, I guessed, must be off-centre, just a teeny bit. That would explain it. Or would it, for this has got to be one of the modern English-speaking world's most overworked nouns. From Antiques to Zen, with Health and Tyres somewhere in between, it is not difficult to find one for practically every letter of the alphabet. Dispensing something vital to life as we know it, there'll be a Centre near you.

Sigridour Tomasson would have been pleased with her Centre, situated on land formerly owned by her father. But for her campaign early in the 20th century, Gullfoss might well have been annihilated under a hydro-electric scheme. Today, along with its appropriately named facilities, it is included on those triangular, or maybe circular tours. Here, the river Hvita, which translates to "white river", tumbles a total of 32 metres in two spectacular falls situated within a 2.5 kilometre chasm that is 70 metres deep in places. I guessed that tourists are normally discharged from their buses straight into the Centre before realising that it is a simple matter to take the wooden stairs and walkway to reach

114

viewing points for all aspects of the spectacle. Pleased not to have been sucked in, vortex like, by another spending sensation; pleased also that, like all the other tourist magnets, access was actually free, I positioned myself for taking the obligatory photographs. Near empty, now late in the afternoon, most of the punters had left. To an extent, this loss was offset by the arrival of a mini-bus load of Japanese tourists who, in a photographic extravaganza, steadfastly took it in turn, ever closer to the edge, to be framed with the falls as a backdrop. Families would also take it in turn to do the same, outdoor types relaxed and at one with their surroundings: the heels, handbag and suits like fish out of water. Nevertheless, all would return to base with tales of intense bravery in the face of gravity untamed. And all would have photographs to prove it, should any challenge their stories of attendance. I, too, was impressed, the more so, leaving manicured walkways behind, ever closer to the mountain of cascading, foaming water that is Gullfoss. Yet another example of nature in the raw, complete with unlimited rainbow-inducing spray that might have been a torrent of rain. The whole scene left me humble in the face of so much power.

My day of 'must sees' was to be rounded off by a visit to the Blue Lagoon. A spa where visitors can bathe in geothermally heated sea water, it is situated near Grindavik, close to the end of the Reykjanes Peninsula. And it was at least a hundred miles away. An uneventful drive via suburban Reykjavik took me well into a cold, blustery evening. It is a surprising place even if you've seen it on the Holiday Programme. Set right next to a Geo Thermal power station, the outflow is what people swim in. A reflection of its industrial heritage, the building is constructed of cut volcanic rock, steel and glass. Surrounded by stark, rough lava with the texture of a natural sponge, it is clearly the place to be seen.

In addition to people who had plainly come for a relaxing evening with friends, smartly dressed pre-dinner guests milled about. Part of the restaurant had evidently been booked by Nokia, the phone company. Congratulatory speeches told of increased sales, targets met, who had won this, that, or the other. How do I know this? The fact is that almost everything for this meeting of minds – including banners, directions for guests, and the speeches – was in English. Eating in the restaurant amongst smartly dressed sales folk and tourists who use hotels, I was conscious of just how little clothing it is possible to carry on a bike.

But the pool is simply amazing. After a compulsory naked shower, bathers (no longer naked) step into the pool then pass through a (partially under-water) glass door, to find themselves outside. A cold wind means that everyone stays near totally immersed in the 70 degree C hot water. On then, through the lava cave grotto, where bathers sat, sheltered from the wind in a sauna-like hot, pungent, sulphurous atmosphere of amplified voices. Strong American accents competed with loud German tones, and those of the English woman so rapt by the whole experience that she'd missed her tourist bus once, but hoped to be on the next one. Not normally the sort of person to spend time drooped in and around pools or beaches, two hours rushed by without trying.

The water, and in particular the mud at the bottom, is supposed to cure all sorts of skin ailments. But would it cure baldness, I wondered? ..... scooping handfuls of the stuff and rubbing it discreetly on my head. It would need magic properties for that one, I conjectured, the putty coloured slime squelching between my toes as I walked. In chest deep bright blue water the temperature of a hot bath I swam a little, floated a lot. And drifted both bodily and mentally in the breeze. If smell and salty mineral taste were a measure of its properties, it simply had to be healthy. At the very least it would knock ten years off my age. And women would find me more attractive. They would have to have a thing about salmon pink though. If they could see me at all. For, from time to time steam obscured the scene, until dispersed by the strong wind. All of these images combined, to produce a package that might best be recorded in some kind of surreal painting. To cool down I sat on rough black lava that surrounded the scene, only legs immersed in the amazingly hot water. It was at times like this when a partner would have come in handy ..... couples, families and groups being the order of the day.

The group of US Servicemen were on some sort of exercise at a base close by. We engaged in small talk concerning quite different life styles, comparing 23 years in one school that was a large chunk of my professional career, to their transient life styles. And coping strategies for each. But what we did have in common were wives or partners at home. At which point I fast forwarded to the bit where I leap on my hobby horse, proclaiming that I wish to be considered as an individual in my own right, not half of a couple. Solo travel, I guess, is a manifestation of this ethos. Thankfully one both my wife and I feel strongly about, while still appreciating the companionship that long term partnership

Gullfoss ..... where the river Hvita (white river) tumbles 32 metres in two spectacular falls.

Reykjavik ..... suburbs built on volcanic lava.

offers. Brought together from many of the States, these men knew a thing or two about travel, yet expressed interest in my journey, and were unfazed by my need for challenges. All in a day's work for them, I guess.

It was late by the time I drove back through Reykjavik. This travel thing is all about contrasts. My journey had been punctuated by hard times and moments of doubt. That it should include high points too seemed only reasonable. The car had been a complete success. 250 miles that day, and experienced more than I could have dreamed of. Driving, for a change, had been fun. Having watched coach loads of people being discharged into the various attractions I was pleased to have been independent. It was equally refreshing to be back amongst people. And rooms. That's travel for you.

Capital

"Funny thing, this travel business, I thought, as the three of us promenaded through the streets amongst fellow late night revellers."

19

Ingolfur Arnarson, Iceland's first settler in the year 874, allowed the Gods to make the decision for him. Approaching the south coast, he threw the pillars of his high seat (the rightful seat, the seat of the master of the house) overboard. Brought over from Norway, he would set up home where they washed ashore. So the story goes. Thus, named after steaming hot springs, Smoky Bay (Reykjavik to you and me) got its first inhabitants. Only in the mid 18th century did the small farming community begin to develop, when wool dyeing, weaving and rope making industries were established as a way of breaking down Danish trade barriers. Reykjavik's population was still less than 200 when granted market town status by the Danish government in 1786. Over many years that followed, all the administrative, educational, church, and legislative bodies, not least of which was the Alþing, were moved to, or established in, what was becoming an urban centre. At the beginning of the 20th century the population was 5,000. By independence in 1944 it had risen to 45,000. Since then it has grown at a faster rate than the national population as people move in from the rural areas. Greater Reykjavik is currently home to more than 170,000 people, around 60% of Iceland's population. Anonymous concrete suburbs house much of that growing population. Those same suburbs had been my introduction to the capital when I had arrived at the filling station with a heap of dismantled bicycle and luggage after hitching a lift through the tunnel. Trade, services, fishing, and light industry keep the economy afloat in a city large enough to have that certain confidence, yet small enough for visitors to get a handle on the place. Having said that, I hadn't travelled to Iceland for its cities. Far from it. But I was there. And needed to chill out. The contrast with nature in the raw gave it just that hint of an edge. And just what I needed.

Two more days. That should fix it. Done the Golden Triangle, maybe

Circle and Blue Lagoon thing. Now all I had to do was see the city itself. OK, I hadn't spent on memorabilia. But it's impossible to carry that sort of stuff on a bike. Either way I had done my bit. But before that, however, I had to move on as my room had only been available for two nights. The campground right next door was a luxury site if ever I saw one. With shelters for cooking and eating, shower and laundry facilities plus twenty-four-hour staffing, it would have passed for a young hotel. Having established camp, literally, I drove into the city to fill the car with petrol before handing back the keys. Driving in foreign parts is always different, and I was pleased to return the car without incident. So, once more, it was bike and tent. A familiar combination.

On foot for a change, following the coastal path into the city, it was well over half an hour before taking to the streets proper. There's an awful lot of concrete ..... much of it, typically, featureless and bland. In contrast, other buildings sport bright paint and coloured roofs. Elsewhere, glass is tastefully melded in up to the minute designs, and tall structures break the skyline. Charming old timber buildings are still to be found, overshadowed, to an extent, by more modern structures. But the whole centre area felt intimate ..... shops, offices, bars, restaurants all within walking distance. The city appears to cope with its traffic reasonably well. On pure population it's not that large, but the suburbs spread over a wide area making for more relaxed attitudes, I guess. It was never my intention to get into the cultural scene. Museum, theatre, cinema, and more: they are all there. But my schedules only allowed for a window on city life. Like most times I visit a city, I did what I needed to do quickly. A new tyre and tube, the zip on my backpack repaired for a pound. But later, after beer and pizza in a trendy lunch bar I strolled around the streets, soaking in the atmosphere of this place, appreciative of the contrasts it offered. Trendy shops, trinket shops, tourist traps: they're all there, but my wallet stayed firmly shut. What charmed me was the near universal vista of sea and mountain as a backdrop to so much of the city: natural and man made environments that contrasted, yet complemented one another beautifully.

My bike had taken a beating on the journey. It was sorely in need of a thorough going over. I couldn't do with bits dropping off on the road, and tightened everything in sight. Once again it was all-change on the tyre scene, winding up with the spangly new one on the back, where all the load was concentrated, my lightweight folding spare returned to being just that. The German woman had worked as a motor cycle courier in London. Now pedal powered, she was at the start of an open ended journey that would take in much of Iceland. Complete strangers, it seemed the most natural thing in the world that we should sit down together outside her tent. The first solo female I had encountered, I was able to tell of ferries, routes, 'must sees', and those to avoid. And the sheer difficulty of maintaining schedules in the face of extreme weather. I wouldn't consider approaching a young female motorist to talk of travel: it's all too easy to be misconstrued. But a bicycle can be a social animal that breaks down so many taboos.

Reykjavik has a reputation for night life. Naturally, almost all of it is aimed at young people. I am young. On the inside. So common sense demanded guidance on suitable venues for music and a beer or two. So, after describing requirements to camp-ground staff, I wound up at a trendy bar called the Dubliner. Here was warm beer, cold Guinness, live music. And a fellow alone amongst a sea of friends and couples. But sitting at a table I quickly found myself deep in conversation with two travellers. Amelia, visiting from the UK, and Lucien, a Belgian, were at the end of a journey round Iceland by bus. They had met at the start of that journey and travelled together ever since. Young enough to be my daughters, with travel the common denominator, and intense competition from loud music we went through the "did you see" routine effortlessly, had both British and Belgian education sorted and made a start on international banking. The Norwegian plainly appreciated my attractive companions too, and in heavily accented drunken English that might have been Rab C. Nesbit, TV character, late of urban Glasgow, told them so. Many times. Thrown out for unacceptable behaviour, he plainly had the scent and like Jack-in-the-Box, bounced back repeatedly. Just one dance. That was all he wanted. Unimpressed, they invited me along to another bar and we left together. Funny thing, this travel business, I thought, as the three of us promenaded through the streets amongst fellow late night revellers. We had a rough idea where the Fógetinn, Reykjavik's oldest building, now restaurant and bar, was but, by the time we ordered another round of rather expensive drinks there, we had seen a considerable proportion of the old town. All in a day's work, though they were plainly planning to make a night of it, and I did begin to think that I was cramping their style. Their company was much appreciated. It's good to talk. But it is equally good to be alone at times. At which point I left them to it, to find my bike exactly where I left it. Would I do this at home? Too damn right I wouldn't ..... leave my bike in a major city centre while I went drinking for the evening! Riding through city streets in the calm of early morning perpetual daylight, clambering into my tent, conscious of every zip and rustle ..... memories are made of this.

Before going to sleep my mind was made up. The idea had not gone away since the ride to Stykkishólmur. The wind dropped away as I got further into the night then. And riding back the night before, the calm had been uncanny. Not only that, weekend traffic on my route east, I had been advised, would make for scary cycling. So ..... I would spend the day checking out more of the city, rest up for a while, then ride through the night. That way, I would avoid both traffic and wind. That was the theory anyway.

20

A lazy morning catching up with my notes then lunch in a rather chic bar was followed by a ride amongst more of the city sights. The Alþingishus (Houses of Parliament), the Supreme Court, the National Theatre, Museums, Galleries. These, and many more imposing buildings, all within a stone's throw of the central area. Presiding over it all is Hallgrímskirkja, the local landmark-cum-viewing tower for the city, and striking modern church that resembles a lava mountain. So many of the nuts and bolts that hold a modern society together were to be found close to that central area, I got the feeling that if it didn't happen here, then it didn't happen at all. Situated in lovely old premises, I will not forget my visit to the Tourist Information Centre. Drawn to the Bureau de Change in there by good exchange rates, it was a done deal before I had read the small print that told of 8.75% commission. Normally unmoved by glitzy bargain offers, it quite spoilt my day. City breaks are fine, but with schedules to maintain, Reykjavik's museums and galleries would have to wait. Picking up the banks of Lake Tjörnin, backdrop to many of the municipal buildings, and much more, my overview of the city continued with a ride along the cycleway that hugs the southern shore. Leafy suburb dwellers share their site with endless bird life. Gardens, open parkland, water, and well proportioned buildings combine to produce a uniquely colourful vista that is my lasting impression of the city proper.

The golden sand beach was something of a surprise. Behind a pair of breakwaters, imported, handy size, and available for the usual activities, it was down only on clients. In fairness, the weather was being typically Icelandic: not encouraging for those wishing to get their kit off. But a handful of fully clothed smaller souls were investigating the potential of this fascinating facility. In a country renowned neither for its sand or its castles, I guess the tourist information folks could be on to a winner with a handy guide to what to do on finding oneself on a beach. The view from the geothermal water storage tanks situated on a slight rise was of lupins, volcanic rock, pine trees, suburbs, sea. What struck me forcibly was the space, the contrasts, the houses of all shapes and forms, a good deal of brightly coloured corrugated metal both as roofs and cladding. Even the odd stone built one. Naturally heated from the communal scheme, spread out over miles, the suburbs have their own services and, to an extent, are separate communities within the city. In ethos it felt not unlike Canberra, Australia's capital city, thoroughly modern, with quite autonomous regions spread out over a vast area.

I wound up taking tea at the Botanical Gardens. With tables set between plants and trees it was awash with students and their lecturers attending end of year celebrations. Dressed in formal wear, they added to the Palm Court atmosphere, once again drawing attention to my restricted wardrobe. The British couple's visit to Iceland couldn't have been more different. Restricted by gardening interests to short breaks, unsurprisingly they had made a bee line to the botanical gardens. Necessarily, we went through the "did you see" routine pretty rapidly before settling on to gardens. Now, don't get me wrong. I wouldn't be without my garden at home, but my wife is in charge there and, try as I might, this growing business does not come naturally to me. Thus, I found myself taking part in a somewhat one-sided conversation on the subject.

Back in my tent by late afternoon I tried to pretend it was late, caught up with my notes, and bedded down in my sleeping bag in preparation for my night ride out of the city. But try as I might, my brain refused to shut down as it ploughed through recent events. That done, it went into turbo mode and took me through the whole of my life to date. Clearly, sleep was not an option. OK, I'd rested a little and somehow it had got round to half past eight in the evening, at which point I got up and went through the breakfast routine in an further effort to trick my body into

Reykjavik ..... Lake Tjörnin, backdrop to many of the municipal buildings.

Reykjavik ..... Gardens, open parkland, water, and well proportioned buildings.

Reykjavik ..... In a country renowned neither for its sand or its castles, an imported beach.

Reykjavik's suburbs ..... autonomous regions spread out over vast areas.

believing it was the start of a day and get it used it to the idea that there was a whole lot of work to do.

At ten o clock I set off amongst the Saturday evening traffic, on the second stage of my journey, that would take me along the south coast, and back to where it started. Booked on the ferry in eleven days time, the sign told of Egilsstaðir, just a short distance from the ferry port, 683 kilometres away. On the right road after a couple of false starts, and not a breath of wind. Simply amazing. And how riding ought to be. Night came and went, and though visibility was never a problem, I used my rear light as a precaution. Waving and blowing horns noisily as they passed, there were an amazing number of people about. At half past one in the morning I crept past Hveragerði before anyone out there had realised. Here at the Garden of Eden, vortex-like, a million tourists a year are sucked in to the geothermally heated banana and coffee growing extravaganza. Iceland's largest tax free shopping experience ..... by opting out of coach trips ..... I had managed to avoid it earlier, too.

It rained hard on the mountain pass, but I had dried out by the time I reached Selfoss a little after two a.m. The place was awash with people. And many of them were milling around the burger bar. An all night place, it seemed the most natural thing in the world to stop for a bite to eat. Situated in a car park next to the bridge over the river Olfusa, spectacularly flooding with glacial outflow, it was staffed by just three young girls. And it all felt very safe. Quite American movie-like in ethos, local youths and their girls constantly arrived and left in smart cars. I spoke to a young man who told me in text book English that they were just having fun, drinking ..... that sort of thing. Riding into town, bars churned out loud music, and cars roaring from one to another. All this in an out-of-the-way small town ..... though having said that, with a population of four thousand, it's the largest in the area and a centre for local agriculture. I have heard it said that people make the most of opportunities that everlasting daylight presents: that they squeeze more out of life in those summer months as some sort of compensation for life on hold in winter. Civilised rowdiness might be a way to describe what I found in that never never land of permanent daylight.

At three a.m. a dozen horses dashed past in the opposite direction. Some were being ridden, the rest galloped along beside. Nothing seemed odd any more in the surreal quiet of early morning. At four a.m., too weary to carry on, I called it a day (or night, maybe) and set up my tent

Leaving Reykjavik ..... At ten o'clock I set out amongst the Saturday evening traffic.

At 3.00am a dozen horses dashed past in the opposite direction. Nothing seemed odd any more.

by a bridge over another river. In the still of the night I had covered almost fifty miles: something of a success, I considered, swiftly asleep to the sound of rushing water.

21

Unsurprisingly I woke late, and equally unsurprisingly, it was raining again. Caught out in rain is one thing. Setting out in it is quite another. With the bit firmly between my teeth I desperately wanted to get back on the road, but it simply poured. A leisurely meal and a great deal of coffee solved the dilemma. By which time it had eased off. Well into the afternoon I hit the road; what struck most was the traffic coming in the opposite direction. I had been told of the weekend exodus of urbanites bound for wilder regions, and just down the road was Þórsmörk. Guide book descriptions of the valley tell of a birch-wooded nature reserve, partially hidden amongst three glaciers. And amongst all of this, crystal clear brooks and mountain scenery. It was on my hit list too, but thankfully a midweek slot, for, I had been reliably informed, at weekends the area would be wall-to-wall gizmo-touting trippers. Now Sunday afternoon, touting over until next time, they were heading back for Reykjavik. Back came the "lifestyle" vehicles in one long procession. Cruising, Ranging, Roving, Discovering. Big tough toys for big tough boys, as everyone tries to out do the other fellow. Wider or higher ..... it didn't seem to matter. The thing, it appeared, is to have the most bits and pieces stuck to your Tonka Truck, have tyres so wide they almost meet in the middle, and suspension lift that goes a long way towards competing with a double decker bus. I suppose they have to be that big to accommodate all the logos like super, challenging, turbo charged, indoor toilet, show off, macho man. Many have enormous racks ..... substantial enough to carry a spare truck up top, and room for another behind in the trailer. And for that little extra, a row of spotlights on the roof. Just the ticket for a trip to the supermarket at Hvolsvöllur, where in the car park of the attached café / filling station I don't think I've ever seen so many Tonka trucks in one place. Surrounded by their chattering owners I could only imagine the sort of conversation they were having. Though it wasn't too difficult.

In complete contrast, earlier in the day, at another roadside café I had found myself in the company of a coach-load of older people. With not a word in common, and time to reflect over endless coffee refills I was conscious of the gulf between us. I guess that we all feel the need to express our personality in some way or other. My bike, without doubt says something about me. The four-wheel-drives make a statement about their owners, and probably their overdrafts. And coach travel, too, has its followers.

A relaxed thirty-something-mile ride through rolling countryside saw me camped on bright green mown grass. Warm enough for my first meal cooked outside, I was the sole resident. For company, only noisy waterfalls that tumbled down huge rocky cliffs overlooking the site. Seljalandsfoss would be the stepping stone for an out and back trip to Þórsmörk next day. On my list of 'must see' for some time, I would either hitch-hike there or cycle light, leaving all my gear in the tent. The forty mile round trip would be a relatively easy day, and with a return to base camp it would make an interesting change. Or so I thought.

Day tripper

"Was it sensible? I guess not. It's certainly not the sort of thing you would let your children do," .....

22

In the event, I couldn't leave my bike out of the adventure. Together, carrying nothing but tools, extra clothing and lunch, we set off. With a known destination and route, a relatively short ride would allow time to look, without the frenetic need to plough on, regardless. Odd to think that only a week before I had been heading for the ferry port, bus ride and Western Fjords. I had done so much since then, it seemed almost unreal. More relaxed about the whole package, my state of mind had improved. A relatively wind-free day, and the night ride before that, had somehow made it all seem possible again. The need to maintain schedules creates its own kind of pressure. But, for now, it was all in the bag. Open ended trips must be less demanding, I conjectured. All of this, and more, whirled through my mind as we skipped along the semi-surfaced road. Time to address the sheep, stop for a closer look at a flower here, a view there. Twenty miles. Two hours at most. Relaxed lunch. Return to base. That was before the Þórsmörk road proper. The original south coast road, since bypassed, used to cross the river on a now-seriously dilapidated concrete bridge over the wide glacial outflow, before running beside it. I had assumed that this was the Þórsmörk road, and how easy it was going to be. Just how wrong a fellow can be came to me immediately I left the old route, bound for the secluded valley. It would have been near impossible to ride fully laden. As it was, I delighted in the challenge of pure mountain bike riding, for that is what the boulder strewn road threw at me. But more was to come. The bright yellow sign warned of river crossings for the next 20 kilometres and depicted a 4x4 in deep water. In Icelandic it said "Vadid krefst varudar." The English version read "Crossing requires caution."

The following instructions were set out:-
Where is the crossing? - Rivers change.
Tyre tracks do not tell the entire story.

Has your engine been waterproofed?
Is somebody watching while you cross?
Probe the crossing yourself.
Use a safety line.
Wear warm clothing in bright colours.

Not a word about what to do if you're a bike rider. But back in Akureyri, repairing my seat post at the bike shop there, I had learned that many repairs resulted from riders taking their machines through deep water, causing wheel and bottom bracket bearing damage. Close to home it wouldn't have mattered, but with hundreds of heavily laden miles to go the last thing I needed was bearing trouble. But more of that later. I had heard of them from other riders. Seen the warning sign. But here, right in front of me was the reality. Not that wide. And using my bike as a sort of crutch, with a hop, skip and a jump from bank to boulder I got across without even getting my feet wet. And the water wasn't deep enough to cause any damage. So what's all the fuss about, I thought, riding beyond. As it happened, that was just the introduction, a starter before the main course. For it got more interesting as I rode deeper into the valley. Green on the lower slopes, rocky then snow capped as they rose beyond, on either side the mountains began to close in. I had read of glaciers in this region and now, for sure, something shone in the distance. This was the edge of Mýrdalsjökull, one of Iceland's permanent ice caps. And from that first doubtful sighting, to actually arriving at its base, I made regular use of my spy glass to examine the river of ice. I had seen glaciers once before on a helicopter trip in New Zealand. I remember flying low enough to see the angular blocks, the crevasses between them ..... then lower down, the plain filth of moraines, scraped from the mountain on the way down. And fuel for wide, fast moving, sediment laden rivers heading for the sea. To see it from the air was truly remarkable. To cycle in a deserted valley and examine the scene from afar ..... then witness the spectacle, this tongue of moving ice, getting closer as I worked at the pedals, is quite another. But in between was a whole lot of water. And it was clear that there was no way I was going to keep my feet dry. With bike lifted over my head, that day I waded carefully through a dozen or more rivers. From simple stream, to deep, fast flowing multi-choice affairs with channel and sub-channel alike spread out between islands of gravel. Unsurprisingly, given the source of the water, it was mightily cold, but the schoolboy in me took over and I wasn't turning back. All of them a tad risky, worst were those so sediment-laden that I couldn't see the bottom. Here, with bike balanced overhead, before advancing I would gingerly put each foot forward to test for a firm river bed. Only a little fellow, sometimes it would be thigh-deep and I would be forced to brace against the current, then stabilise myself before taking the next step. Was it sensible? I guess not. It's certainly not the sort of thing you would let your children do. And I was just pleased that I didn't have my wife with me. For she would have pointed out all the dangers and I would have had to catch the bus instead. That's right, a regular bus service from Reykjavik follows this route. But I'm still here to tell the tale.

Route 249 and I continued our merry way, climbing steadily, crossing and re-crossing a myriad of rivers that dashed down from the mountain snow melt, to form a criss cross pattern of water and gravel that is the outpouring of permanent ice above. Gigjökull had been no more than a speck in my spy glass. Then, cresting a particularly rocky approach I was upon it. Close up it was awe inspiring: a mass of white, broken into every shape imaginable, and blue tipped where the light refracted. Brought with it were masses of ground rock scraped from the valley sides, to be deposited at the bottom in heaps that could have been spoils from a mine. Disappearing into the sediment laden lagoon at the bottom it sourced yet another of the rivers scurrying through the valley. For a few delightful moments it was all mine. Then a couple of coach-loads of cameras and their German minders arrived. For their drivers I guess that this trip is just another day, another dollar. But the sight of four wheel drive buses crossing the river where it left the lagoon, water half way up their radiator grilles, grubby glacier as backdrop, was something else. This one would have been a real problem for me, but fortunately there was a footbridge. The plus side of other tourists, I guess, is that you can get them to take photographs with you on them: useful stuff if ever proof of attendance is required, provided that you can get them to understand what you want. Surprisingly, for a German party, there wasn't an English word between them.

Here would live Trolls, leaving only to wreak havoc and mischief upon unsuspecting passers by. Narrow, with towering cliffs of volcanic rock either side, grass clung precariously to life on slender stratifications. At their base the stream tumbled over boulder and gravel. I would have

Seljalandsfoss ..... For company, only noisy waterfalls that tumbled down huge rocky cliffs.

Here would live Trolls. A magical ravine where shafts of sunlight cut through the shadows.

133

missed it but for the buses. One of them had stopped back at Gigjökull (glacier), and now it was parked up beside another at the side of the road. Chatting in the calm sunlight, their drivers told of the chasm. My reward for just a few minutes walking? A magical ravine where shafts of sunlight cut through the shadows, picking out rock, bright green grass and tumbling water. All of this, a beguiling frame for snow capped mountains beyond. With footwear that said much about their holiday expectations, many of the bus passengers had not made it beyond a step or two. All the more for me, I thought. But what a treat they missed.

Þórsmörk is set in a bowl created in the mountains and consists of a couple of small huts plus a substantial building available for renting. Those daring enough to drive there need some substantial vehicle. The final approach was through a river too dangerous to wade. A tour bus stopped beside me on the approaches. Its courier, concerned for my safety, advised using the footbridge downstream. But reaching that involved scrambling over an obstacle course of boulders and wading through asset-shrinking fast moving water. From the river-side footpath beyond, the view of glaciers still at work carving out the scene was amazing. The more so as now I viewed them through a wooded grove, carpeted with violets, buttercups, dandelions even. What a contrast with the icy scene beyond, while right next to me flowed its summer melt, loaded with sediment and far from clear. Experience on earlier rivers had taught me that these were the difficult ones, where it was not possible to see how deep, and what's in the way. This, with a bike balanced overhead, too. The bus courier had been right: there was no way I would have waded across the Krossa. For that, ironically, is its name. But I made it to the hut, sat on the balcony, shared my lunch break with the Germans' tourist guide, and drank her coffee. Again, there wasn't a word of English in her party. From Berlin, they turned out to be the same group I had caught up with earlier at Gigjökull. I assumed, wrongly perhaps, that they must be from former East Germany, isolated from Western influence for so long. That would explain it. Only afterwards did I begin to think that I should have asked her. Too bad. But what I do have is a photograph of me, looking rather pleased with myself, in Þórsmörk's modern ice age mountain setting.

Leaving was hard. I regretted having no time to ride still further into the valley to look at other glaciers some distance beyond. But I would have needed to camp, or use a hut, perhaps. Besides, my gear

With bike lifted over my head, that day I waded through a dozen or more rivers.

Seljalandsfoss ..... landing in the most delightful ice cold pool.

was a hard ride away, and with schedules to meet it was never an option anyway. Still, a privilege to be there at all, and with nothing but pedal power. The footbridge was new. So new that the courier who advised me to take the one downstream hadn't seen it before. With bike balanced overhead, I picked my way across its narrow plank, all that was between me and deep, racing water close beneath. The tour bus crossed at this point too: no way could I have waded through. The detour had seen me in the deepest water of the day, though comforted by the courier's concern for my welfare. And it was something to laugh about over lunch!

On the return trip I stopped again at Gigjökull, and walked right to its base. Quite alone now, and treading carefully where others had plainly been, the moraines were squishy. Small cracks appeared all around and, somewhat uneasily I took each step ever more carefully. Water dripped from the ice into narrow channels of muddy water. The toilet end of a glacier is seriously unromantic. Surrounded by cliffs of ice topped with crushed rock, I walked on a whole lot more of it. Where streams had carved their way through I could see and touch the dirty dripping banks, and with ground rock clearly visible on top, felt justified in watching every step. Warm by the standards of the trip, gusts of icy wind blew across the scene, kicking off a sand- (or moraine) storm as I took in this somewhat unreal scene. On the point of leaving, I was joined by a couple of Swedes I'd spoken to back at the hostel in Reykjavik. Their story was that they had intended to cycle tour, but found nowhere to leave their car at the ferry port in Denmark, to wind up motoring round Iceland with their bikes remaining firmly attached to the rack. But the river crossings had got the better of their smart BMW, and the bikes had an airing. Iceland's tourist circuit is sufficiently small and well trodden, I concluded, for the same faces to show up time after time. The ride back was tremendous, downhill. And fast. With the wind behind for a change I flew over the rocks that passed for a road, waded back across countless rivers, saw them combine to form just one huge, gravely, sediment laden glacial outflow that rushed along beside me. Checking this out as I walked across all of this on the now-disused long, low bridge was a little scary. Cracked concrete, rusted steel, and gaping holes with icy water clearly visible rushing below. All of this, compounded by a chilly wind and rain that had just blown in. Back home, there would be rules about this sort of thing ..... a big notice at least. And security fencing. Here, common sense rules OK. I was, however, pleased to be back on firm ground.

A complete contrast, back in my tiny tent, out of the pouring rain, cooking inside again, a little music on the radio. Thoroughly cosy after an exciting and challenging day, it was like arriving home. Time to record my thoughts and feelings on the day. One of the best.

On tenterhooks and tyres

"I felt so privileged to be there. Beyond a little sand gently whistling, slithering across the surface in the breeze, few sounds interrupted my thoughts" ---

23

For a change I had managed to get my act together early next morning, and made time before leaving for a closer look at Seljalandsfoss. Where a fluffy stream delicately cascaded over an enormous cliff ..... landing in the most delightful ice cold pool, so clear it was impossible to guess the depth. So undercut is the cliff that viewing the tumbling water from behind was perfectly safe. Clouds of spray constantly wet the carpet of bright green grass and wild flowers surrounding the pool and stream that gurgled away from it. Contrary to expectations it was bright, fine ..... and, more importantly, still. Skógafoss was next. Another spectacular waterfall, another photograph. Another bunch of tourist buses gathered for the kill. Iceland is not too hot on palaces, galleries ..... that kind of thing. On the other hand, I came to regard the country as one enormous natural sculpture park. And, between the hardships of cycling, a source of constant delight.

Dyrhólaey, the 120 metre high lump of rock sticking out of the sea, and connected to the mainland by a narrow spit, just asked to be included on my tick list. Picking my way along the rough track that left the coast road, recognising a kindred spirit it seemed so natural to stop and, once again, exchange travel stories the world over. Although he was walking at the time, Simon and his partner had flown into Reykjavik from their home in Australia and were at the start of a five week ride round the country on their tandem. This, he explained, was better than two separate bikes as it harmonised differing riding strengths. But I did wonder how they would cope with the rough stretches I had covered earlier. Synchronised falling off might just take the edge off all that harmony, I conjectured. Then, underwhelmed, I quickly left Dyrhólaey and headed for Vik ...... Iceland's most southerly village, and the country's rainiest spot. Here were cliffs, headlands, a huge surf bearing down on sandy beaches, bright green grass, delightful coloured buildings, and a dinky church perched high above to keep an eye on things. All this beneath a cloud of mist that cut off the mountain tops and ice cap above. I ought to have spent more time there, but with schedules to meet there was time for little but shopping for food, a coffee or two, the postcard thing, a photograph. And memories.

It was early evening by the time I got back on the road again. About the same time that the bubble on my front tyre got big enough to hit the brakes as it revolved. But only hours later, while eating the meal I had cooked at a table in a car park next to a river, incredulous, I noticed that the sidewalls of my almost new rear tyre were in a desperate state too. It could only be a matter of time before that one failed as well. A disappointing discovery ..... with my spare tyre now in use, and nothing better than hope as a solution, I pressed on through desperately dull, scrubby countryside. It was the sort you wouldn't notice at all in a car. Loud music would be a better option here. But with the wind behind and the road near-level I rode like a machine, making rapid progress and covering the last thirty miles to Kirkjubæjarklaustur in a little over two hours. Arriving late, after a journey of almost ninety miles, I slept to the music of yet another spectacular waterfall.

24

I hadn't dared to take another look at the (second) ailing tyre for fear of spoiling my night's sleep. But the reality of it next morning was the fact that its sidewalls were broken in places, and between strands of remaining reinforcement the inner tube showed. My exuberant ride to Þórsmörk had left its mark. The coffee and sticky bun thing, great comfort though it was, simply avoiding the issue a little longer. Here, over endless refills I realised that a whole lot hung on the fact that, one way or another, I had to get hold of yet another tyre. Cycle repair facilities, according to the guide book, were to be found only in Akureyri and Reykjavik, both left miles behind. With this information whirling through my mind, my first port of call, as recommended by the filling station attendant in seriously broken English "where the man has a house" turned out to be a garage. Where any number of tyres for trucks or cars could be had, but all he could offer for my predicament was the schedule for the once-daily bus that would get me and my bike the 275 miles to Egilsstaðir ..... and within a stone's throw of the ferry port. If the worst came to the worst then I'd have to do that, I decided. But the thought of it made me feel ill. Then I pressed on. The bus would pass me in any case.

"Gremlins rule OK" seemed to be motto of my trip at that point. I hadn't gone far that morning before they struck again. It had happened once before. Years ago, when my son and I rode from Bergen to Narvik, beyond the Arctic Circle in Norway. That time, it had been the one and only breakdown. Now, as the cranks of my pedals began to crunch and seize, my reaction was "here we go again". Before leaving home, just about everything that moved had been stripped, cleaned and thoroughly greased, but Iceland was taking its toll like no riding before. Despite the fact that I had carried my bike through all the rivers, just like the repair man way back in Akureyri had said, there was no option but to fit the new bearings I had taken the precaution of bringing with me. Once again I set up as roadside mechanic and, with no regular grease to hand, once again used margarine to ensure things would keep on turning.

The unremarkable countryside of the previous evening had nothing on this. With the exception of the dead straight road, for miles around, nothing but black sand. Skeiðarárjökull, Iceland's largest valley glacier together with its myriad of shifting rivers has created Skeiðarársandur, a broad expanse of sand desert. Here, spaghetti like, the map shows a mass of rivers crossing the region. So many I lost count of the enormous timber decked concrete and steel structures that carried me high above silt laden, fast moving water hungrily seeking the sea. Building and maintaining structures against waterways that continue to bring glacial sand and silt with them on ever changing courses is a nightmare for road engineers faced with the task.

Laid on the ground, my bike was something to lean on. It was sunny, only a little breezy for a change, and warm enough to ride wearing just tee shirt and leggings. Miles away to the east, just visible beyond the sand and glinting in the sun, no less than three glaciers ground their way down from the Vatnajökull icecap. Deserts, it seemed, are not confined to hot countries. Surrounded by black volcanic sand, I'd heard of travellers being caught in sandstorms here, and could well imagine it. For there was a good deal of sand on the road, blown into ripples not unlike those the receding tide makes on a beach, and squeaking under the tyres as I rode. Feeling so privileged to be there, I'd had an overwhelming desire to stop and record my thoughts. Beyond a

Vik ..... Iceland's most southerly village.

Eating the meal I had cooked at a table in a car park close to a river.

little sand gently whistling, slithering across the surface in the breeze, few sounds interrupted my thoughts ..... the oneness I felt with my surroundings. Time to contemplate, time to reflect on the journey to date, to anticipate what was to come. And remember reading in the guide book about cycle hire facilities in Höfn, almost a hundred miles beyond.

At that, my mind went into overdrive. My rear tyre couldn't possibly make it that far. The most casual glance confirmed that simple fact. But Skaftafell National Park, complete with lavish information centre and camp site, where I planned to spend a couple of days was, perhaps, only twenty miles away. And where there are bikes for hire, there would be tyres. The once-daily bus service that called there completed a solution to my problem. With my mind instantly at rest, and confident now of completing the journey, I could get on with appreciating my surroundings.

The sky looked like great rolls of cotton wool threatening to fall in on the whole scene if we didn't behave ourselves. Distant mountains disappeared into cloud. For the second time in as many days I was within a whisker of permanent ice. To the north, Vatnajökull, Iceland's largest icecap, steadily supplied the raw material for dozens of glaciers that are still at work shaping the landscape. Spreading out in all directions like tentacles, desperately dirty in their nether regions, they discharged their loads into any one of the dozens of rivers I had crossed on bridges that went on for ever. I'd felt slightly threatened, such was the force of sediment laden water rushing seaward as I passed overhead, with nothing but a low guard rail between it and me. And wind is always stronger at these points. For days to come, Vatnajökull and its outpourings would never be far away. With new found confidence concerning the tyre, I reflected on the problems I'd had with my bike. The same rig took me a thousand miles round Tasmania and then to Northern New Zealand and back with almost no problem. Still, it had given me something to think about. If I had a piece of advice to anyone contemplating this trip, it would be "don't." Unless you're the practical type, or willing to take tuition first ..... because there are not so many folks around to help when things go belly up.

Tourists went by in their coaches and cars. But I felt sure that I was getting the better deal. The physical act of making the journey possible makes it a very "hands on" experience, more meaningful, a feeling of communing with the real world. With no glass and air conditioning to filter out the difficult bits.

By then I'd been living outside for three weeks. Home seemed like something over there: an awful long way from current experiences. Much of what it's possible for a body to do is in the mind. The older I get, of that fact I become ever more certain. Having the bike with me is the link with previous journeys. It is like having a friend alongside all the time. Sometimes I spoke out loud, apologised for giving it such a hard time, thanked it for being so strong and making the journey possible. Sometimes I would systematically touch all its vital parts ..... mentally picture us working together, and completing the journey. For me it creates that oneness, that working relationship between man and machine. And before setting off from my desert sojourn, I made a point of doing just that with my rear tyre. Daft, or not: it's the way I like it. We made it to Skaftafell.

On the final approach was a sharp reminder of just who is in charge here. Dumped at the roadside, crumpled, twisted like so much waste paper were steel girders ..... the remains of substantial bridges tossed aside during floods caused by volcanic eruptions beneath the ice cap in 1996. This, despite the efforts of engineers to divert excess water, a process that, it appears, is ongoing. At several sites, diggers were at work shifting gravel and creating dykes to ensure that glacial melt flowed safely beneath the many bridges rather than push through the causeways between.

Rather than phone, myself, and risk language problems getting it wrong, I explained my predicament to the woman on duty at the information centre. Within moments she had the telephone number of the cycle rental people in Höfn, and following a brief conversation with them said that, as requested, a tyre would be delivered to the Centre next day. And would I put cash to pay for it in the envelope they provided? Staff on duty when the bus arrived would hand it to the driver. I could go off walking for the day. What a turn round in fortunes, I mused, setting up my tent on the large, well tended site.

After setting up camp I phoned home for the once-weekly reality and "I'm still safe and well" check. Apparently we'd had to have a new washing machine. And the car had passed its MOT. For those few minutes I had a foot in both camps: pictured images of our summer garden ..... together with distant views of walled pasture and moorland

Just one of the enormous timber decked concrete and steel bridges that went on for ever.

Morsárjökull ..... glacier & lagoon.

144

beyond: the domestic scene inside. But it might have been on another planet, such was the distance I felt at that moment. Like news flashes interrupting a TV programme, tranquil domesticity clashed with reality. Reality at that point, sitting in my tent with Skaftafellsjökull (glacier to you and me) clearly visible beyond a hillside covered in a young forest of silver birch. Reality also concerned cooking at floor level. Curry and rice from a packet never tasted so good. A sense of relief. Of having made it against the odds. Of gratitude towards helpful people. Delight with the natural grandeur surrounding me. And the rest of the trip could happen. It had been up in the air for most of the day. I'd even been forced to consider finishing my journey on a bus. But it was meant to happen. I'm a great believer in that sort of thing.

That evening became a watershed. My head got the idea that with only 250 miles to go it was almost over. And downhill all the way home. The relative scale of my venture was brought sharply into focus as I recalled stopping at the roadside only that day to chat with a couple of young Australians. Each wore a large rucksack. And between them they carried a huge plastic tidy box of equipment. With an unexpected time slot to spare they were hitch-hiking to Skaftafell for a few days climbing. They had sailed to Iceland from Plymouth UK, and on the journey their 35 ft yacht had been battered by force 9 gales. At times the venture had approached stupidity, they admitted. Part of a group setting out to tackle unclimbed peaks in Greenland, having safely arrived in Reykjavik they had intended to sail on, but late pack ice made that impossible. Now they were to fly there instead ..... the result being time on their hands. And the surprise trip to Skaftafell. From Canberra and Townsville respectively, we exchanged travel experiences the world over. Once more, my theory that there is always someone doing that bit more proved to be the case. It put my venture sharply into perspective. Closer to home, so to speak, on a cycling holiday from Germany and camped right next to me, Robert had tales like my own. Of tyres, of spokes, of river crossings. Honour satisfied, I slept easily. Tomorrow, I would check out glacier activity.

'Caps and 'bergs and contemplation

"This surely had to be a place to contemplate one's soul: the sense of space, of nature in the raw, nature in charge, crept in on me, the more I looked at the scene."

25

Sitting quietly in emotive settings was becoming a habit. On discovering that glacier skiing or snowmobiling would cost an arm and a leg, plan B, the walk, and free, was just the ticket. Quite alone at the edge of the glacial outflow lake at the bottom of Morsárjökull, once again I was moved to record my thoughts. Floating in the lake were great lumps of ice, many extremely "dirty" because they'd scraped a whole lot of mountain away on the way down, I guess. The shapes were simply amazing: it took little imagination for them to become animals, vehicles, houses, towers, almost anything. Like watching the flames in a fire, look long enough and there it was. The schoolboy in me wanted to throw rocks at them, but it would have been sacrilege, so I didn't. The water, unsurprisingly, was icy cold. Isn't it one of those laws of physics that tells us water remains at 0° C until all ice is melted? Well, I guess that's the temperature there because great chunks of it regularly creak and crash into the lagoon as they break away from the glacier. In turn pieces break off these enormous chunks, float away and melt, to join the silt laden outflow. Pooh-stick-like, some make it to the river intact, nudging their way downstream, catching between rocks, scraping on the gravel before disappearing for good. Like last time in Þórsmörk, the bottom of the glacier was covered in moraines, and looked like a small mountain range, the ice being underneath. I was in a sort of bowl, a corrie, if my Geography teacher is to be believed, only here glaciation isn't confined to pages in a text book. Here it is still happening, complete with U shaped valley, arrêtes, hanging valleys: the lot. Above, and all around, were pointy mountains, themselves formed by the scraping action of ice which, not unlike my hair, continues to recede as the years go by. Back by the lake, the sediment laden river flowing from it was seriously unromantic, but attractive for its own sake. On the ground, woven into the moonscape of rock was scrubby grass and a delightful array of what I can only describe as Alpines plus a good deal of moss, which it seemed unfair to walk on. I'd walked for something like three hours, through scrubby willow and small birch "forest" then along the banks of the gravel-strewn outflow river to reach the base of the glacier. To counteract the effects of erosion, walkways had been constructed over difficult stretches. Nothing surprising about that. Some were made from old railway sleepers. So what, one might ask. Until the reader learns that, with the exception of a short stretch used only during the construction of Reykjavik's harbour, Iceland has had no railways.

The party was led by a guide. Tagging on to the end, I was pleased to learn of a couple of bridges that crossed the fast flowing river, enabling us to get right amongst the moraines. Here, the raw power of ice and gravity had combined to produce an effect that might have been a quarry. Black sand, gravel and boulders, some the size of a bus, had plainly been scraped effortlessly down, to be deposited in heaps, as though giant earth moving machinery had been at work. Philip knew my home town well. Retired now, at one point he had worked there. We even had a common friend, a former colleague of mine. His wife being French, it was unexceptional that they should join a French speaking party to tour Iceland. For us to meet at the foot of Morsárjökull ..... it's an odd thing. Coincidence, perhaps. Or is there more to it?

Back down through the mist, in full view, waiting for me to collect it was the tyre. The receptionist at the Information Centre, the bus driver, the cycle rental shop in Höfn. Between them, they'd got everything right. And me out of a serious fix. To celebrate I started off with a beer. In Iceland this is not a decision to be taken lightly. But having parted with the cash it went on from there. And wound up with a full scale meal in the company of a couple of women. Half my age, Canadians living in California, they were cycle camping too. And like the pair in Reykjavik, we had a whole lot to talk about concerning travel experiences the world over. It was well into the evening before I left. Then, after fitting my (third) new tyre, confident that all my bicycle troubles were behind me, I rode out to a swimming pool where the hot tub made a perfect way to end the day. Despite the fact that by now it was a thoroughly miserable evening, nothing could dampen my spirits. And tomorrow, I would go to Jökulsárlón to check out the iceberg lagoon.

Reflecting later on recent events, I couldn't begin to imagine how the tyre I had bought back in Reykjavik had made it so far. My exuberant ride to Þórsmörk had plainly wrecked it. But just how little held it together had only became clear when I'd removed it. Parts of the sidewall were near-disintegrated, leaving only odd strands of reinforcement. And enormous gaps. Despite this, against the odds I had made it, and, once again, found myself fixed up without a whole lot of drama. Somewhere hanging in there, again the odd feeling that I was being looked after. I offered thanks to whoever was in charge. And meant it. For was it not privilege indeed to have the opportunity to make these wonderful, sometimes challenging experiences possible.

26

Travelling is so many hello and goodbyes. And somewhere in between, deep and (at the time) meaningful conversations with near-complete strangers. Thus, I made my way over to their tent and bade my evening meal companions, Mel and Jane, farewell. I thanked them for putting me on to the swimming pool, and was further reminded not to miss Jökulsárlón. I have said it before: a bicycle is a great conversation opener, a tremendous leveller. It bestows membership of an exclusive travel club, where the more difficult the terrain, the more its members band together. And in this instance, turning up sound tourist information as well.

Thirty five miles to Jökulsárlón would be like a jolly afternoon out with no pressure to perform. Even the weather took a relaxed view of the proceedings. Riding away from Skaftafell, at times it was difficult to keep my eyes on the road. To the left, one glacier after another ground down from the icecap above. Close enough to be clearly visible, detail through my spy glass revealed more of what I had come to associate with the business of creating the jagged landscape that is Iceland. Identifying everything from terminal moraine to hanging valley in a somewhat belated revision exercise, this was the visual aid for O level geography that I ought to have seen forty years before. More enormous bridges crossed the outpourings from all of this as they fed unremarkable countryside with an unvarying diet of sand and gravel. But as I had come to expect, the joy of riding with the wind behind was short lived, and came to an abrupt halt on reaching the coast. From here, following a startling ninety degree change in direction, I would roughly follow the coast for the next 200 miles, heading north east and back to where I started, seemingly months before. Now head on, for the remainder of the ride, the wind would rarely leave me alone.

Jökulsárlón..... camped within a stone's throw of so much beauty.

Cliffs of ice, shimmering, near luminescent under the surface sank from view.

Sheltered from the wind, to an extent, by enormous banks of gravel that interrupted my view of the ice cap, it caught me unawares. Like the main film just started following endless mind-numbing commercials. Through a break in the ocean of gravel, almost unreal, yet there they were. The translation gives little away. Jökulsárlón simply means glacial river lagoon. This was what I had come to see, and after dropping my bike on its side I dashed up the gravel bank to come upon a sight that took my breath away. Before me was the lake. And floating on water so deep in colour it defied belief, there they were. Great lumps of ice, some perhaps 20, 30, 50 ft and more in length, with height to match. That was above the water, just a fraction of the total volume. Cliffs of ice, shimmering, near luminescent under the surface, sank from view in turquoise water, reputed to be 100m deep. Some clean, white, with blue light shining at the edges. Others with a deal of volcanic debris evident. All this, for standing on a flat grassed area above the scree bank that ran to the shore. I knew that boat trips amongst the 'bergs were a popular attraction, but vowed to return and spend the night right there with that captivating view.

Not half a mile down the road, it might have been another planet. A far cry from the splendid isolation just moments before, here were coach parties. The bunch of continentals treated the queue at the self service café more like that for an Italian ski lift. It had been some time since coming across this kind of demeanour and, familiar with more genteel, thoroughly British queuing it went down like a lead balloon. Nevertheless, eventually I found myself seated outside, in the company of yet another sticky bun and gallons of coffee. Beside me was the lake, together with its exotic contents. And I was about to take a boat trip amongst them all. Most of the trippers took to the water en masse, landau-like, in large amphibious craft. A jolly experience that had the look of a grand day out in an Edwardian charabanc. Just three of us, with the near personal service of a guide took to the water in a rescue-type rubber dinghy, so small we could dip our hands to test the temperature. The shapes, the colours, the cold raw impact of ice towering above, most pure white, some moraine covered, others streaked with ice-melt deposited moraines. We ghosted past shapes, only 10% of which were visible, to see not white, but thousand-year-old pure ice beneath turquoise water. The closest I can get to describing it is icing that one might find in the bowl after it has been mixed: random shapes, no order, pure white,

Jökulsárlón ..... the shapes, the colours, the cold raw impact of ice towering above.

From cliffs to cartoon characters. All these and more.

delicate bits, huge chunks, textures that one couldn't hope to design. Some looked like the prow of a ship, others, as though someone tried to drill enormous holes in them; many where the wood carver had been busy. Imagination constructed the rest, turning up with animals, shells, and mushrooms where the water had undercut. From cliffs, to cartoon characters. All these and more, along with little floaters like those in the iced water jug: only these babies were a thousand years old. Beyond that spectacle was the glacier that spawned them all. Full of crevasses, a river of ice pushing, creaking ever downward from the icecap at a rate of up to a metre a day only to have great chunks, some as big as houses float away in the lake, finally melt and join the incredibly short river and sea beyond.

Earlier on my journey I had speculated on the power of stones. But ice? Great lumps of it, some the size of a young tower block. Relentless creator of landscapes, old as the hills, seen a thing or two. As for powers. Who knows? But I got to spend the night there. Camped within a stone's throw of so much beauty. To prepare food there. To eat it there. To sit outside in the gathering cold there was to enter heaven. The very thought of it brings tears to my eyes as I write. Picked out in the evening sun, stratified cloud settled over the icecap and snow capped mountains beyond. The quiet, for even the wind had died off, broken randomly by great splashes as lumps of ice melted and fell off. Just part of the inexorable journey to the sea. This surely had to be a place to contemplate one's soul. The sense of space, of nature in the raw, nature in charge crept in on me the more I looked at the scene. Every shade of turquoise was reflected in the fading light. Cobalt blues and near greens melded ..... these gently rippling colours in turn reflected on to the white above. All of this for simply lifting my head. A shark fin, caterpillar, human skull. My imagination was still hard at work as I crept into bed.

I had a disturbed yet relaxing night. For sheer excitement it was hard to beat. Only a steamy night in the arms of some exotic new lover could have come near. But truly, that is the stuff of dreams. Back down to earth, quite alone in the calm of that half lit northern night, drifting between sleep and what passed for being awake I dreamt of shapes. Of gruyere cheese, tail of a plane, pulled teeth ..... yet sharply conscious of ice noisily crashing into the water beside me. Memories of that evening will be with me for all time.

Thank you

"Like so many, he questioned my sanity: the "why on earth do you want to do all of this" thing. But nevertheless I was pleased to shake my saviour's hand.

27

I could barely wait to unzip my tent. The 'bergs right outside had changed shape dramatically in the night. Huge chunks were missing and many had changed position as well. Continued ice falls demanded attention. The spreading ripples they spawned lapped gently against ice as I ate breakfast, grateful in the cool of early morning for the womb like security of my sleeping bag.

Later, in no hurry to leave, sitting on a large rock I breathed in the scene, lit now by early morning sun that offered yet more exciting perspectives. A microcosm of the Arctic, or its rival a good deal further south. So realistic it's been used as a film set, yet just for a time it had been all mine. Or had it? For there, up on the hillside perhaps half a mile away, was an intruder. I'd noticed someone up there while setting up camp the previous evening but made nothing of it. And earlier, scrambling over rock strewn gravel shore I'd wondered. Now, still in the exact same spot, that someone was sitting quite motionless and, like me, plainly appreciating those same extraordinary (even for Iceland) surroundings. Sufficiently far away for me to feel quite alone, I guess that we were both intruders on nature at work.

Quite what the flotilla of ducks found to eat down there in the icy water I cannot imagine. Repeatedly diving, as though part of some synchronised swimming team, normally I would have been content with the notion that they were ducks. But so finely honed were my senses, before I knew what was happening, I'd made a note of their markings. OK ..... brown all over with white neck bands. Or all black, apart from a wide band of white above the water line. What were they? Cold, I guess.

Not wanting to leave my perch by the icebergs, I delayed leaving that ethereal spot for as long as seemed decent. And a little beyond. Then I scrambled down to the water's edge again for the dipping of fingers goodbye thing. Several last looks later, I finally hauled my bike over the grassed bank and back on to the road, only to abandon it and dash all the way back to the top for another.

Beyond doubt it was an excuse. I could have got water from anywhere. But the visitor centre afforded yet another in that series of last looks. Besides ..... there was coffee. Seeming like the most natural thing in the world, it was here that we finally met. Walking along the short road that led off to the Centre, complete with large pack she was plainly a traveller. It turned out that we had been neighbours. And she, the mystery hillside guest. With several days to spare before starting a research project, the American woman had spent three days up there with nothing but a bivvy bag for accommodation. Before parting, by bus and bike respectively, we agreed that it is an awesome spot. And for me, an all time best camp site. Truly a privilege.

Draining mountain ranges in one country before powering though another, they disregard international borders in their quest for the sea. From racing stream to navigable artery and wide estuary, they have been the lifeblood of nations, the world over. Enabling everyone from explorer, to trader and invasion force to journey inland. Britain's longest, the Severn, starts her journey in Mid Wales, to wind up in the Bristol Channel 220 miles later. But from sources in Burundi and Ethiopia to its delta in Mediterranean Egypt, the world's longest is in excess of 4000 miles. The Nile. A source of life, almost from the beginning of time, passes through no less than ten countries, its basin occupying roughly a tenth of the African continent. I have clear memories of cruising past scenes straight from biblical times, complete with fishing nets being cast from small boats. That luxury Egyptian time warp had been so realistic, I remember half expecting to see a young bearded fellow feeding several thousand from just a single catch. And the rest.

With all of that in mind, following the course of an entire river that races, ice-laden, from source to sea seemed like an exciting prospect. Yet Superman-like, in a matter of moments I did just that. Lumps of ice jostled for position to leave the lagoon. Water danced, swirled menacingly, to race noisily through a narrow channel in the gravel bank and threatening supports for the girder bridge that carries the southern ring road. Like the no-frills airlines, extras are dispensed with. No messing about with playful young streams, no puddle-prone Gloucester at the crossing point, no antiquity-strewn Cairo awash with the trappings of a major city. This movie channel cuts straight to the main film ..... a short, fast moving thriller. But at least there'd be the soppy bit where the plot slows down and everyone makes up before we can all go home. Not a bit of it. For after cutting a fine pace through the shingle beach, this young stud dashes, fully clothed, into the North Atlantic surf where, momentarily, what remains of the ice is thrown about mercilessly, to drown and disappear for ever. Indecent, unseemly after a journey that had taken a thousand years. Alive and kicking one minute. Despatched, crumpled and lifeless the next.

Like all the king's horses and all the king's men, who failed to put Humpty back together again, they could only watch helplessly as the ice disappeared, taking their frustration out on me. A fleet of arctic terns had taken it upon themselves to do something about the situation and plainly considered that I was interfering with their task as they swooped and screeched, in their efforts to drive me off their patch. Superman would have known just what to do. He'd save that ice with a single whoosh. Nevertheless, hazardous as it was, I crouched on the beach with both hands in the sea and thought of England. Before cycling into the rain. Superman would not have appreciated my black leggings and waterproofs.

In my head it was roughly 35 miles to Höfn, pronounced Hupn, because the o has two dots over it. Hunger had settled in on that basis. The realisation that it would be closer to 50 was all I needed that morning. Spectacular glacial river crossings came and went. And by early afternoon I was almost there. When an estuary, the first of many I would encounter on that south east coast, got in the way. On my left had been the icecap, its several tongues heading seaward. To my right I'd had the sea for company much of the way. But the wind, the rain, the mist had all crept inside my head. I was in poor form and needed good food.

The fellow caught my eye the minute I walked into the place. He addressed me in English as though we were long lost friends. Windswept and more than a little disorientated, I was concerned that I was losing my grip. Nevertheless, maintaining the presence of mind to draw myself up to a full five feet six inches, I found myself telling Erik that I did not think we had met before.

My companion for the much needed full scale meal turned out to be a young German Air Force Tornado pilot. We belonged to different worlds. He, a racy, split-second-decision, life-threatening, supersonic existence that included recent service in some of the world's troubled hotspots. Me, a semi-retired teacher, twenty years and the rest older, ... who does a little joinering and building to make ends meet. I had ridden round the streets, looked at menus and finally selected the Italian restaurant for its interesting pasta selection. He, too, was cycle camping and it meant instant camaraderie. The connection established, over starter, main course, dessert, coffee, and a beer or two, we exchanged experiences.

We were both taking six weeks out to pedal through some of the most difficult climate and terrain that Europe can offer. The practicalities involved meant a good deal in common to start with, but the similarity of emotions conjured up on the trip was uncanny. Rapidly going through the "did you see" thing, our agendas might have been worked out from the same hymn sheet. Our responses to difficult situations had been similar. The way I psyche myself up, will myself on to ensure I get through, it seemed, was not mine alone. Both parties admitted that some of the challenges demanded a degree of madness, maybe more. But something inside drives us on. Each, it seemed, had enough material for a chapter on roadside repairs. And another exclusively concerned with tyres. The feeling of being in harmony with the world when travelling under one's own power, of living at floor level under canvas, aware of each and every nuance in climate and terrain. And respective partners who prefer warmer climes. All of this and more, together with our responses to them, meant that two hours swept by before we left. In opposite directions.

Haraldur took some finding. I eventually found him working in the shop at the local garage. Now, why hadn't I thought of that? It's such an obvious place to look for a fellow who hires out bikes. Responsible for organising my tyre back at Skaftafell, I just had to thank him, personally, for getting my trip back on the road. Like so many before he, too, was concerned for my sanity. And once again I was trailed through the "why on earth do you want to do all of this" routine. But nevertheless I was pleased to shake my saviour's hand.

Höfn (which means harbour) had little more to offer as I rode round the place looking for something memorable to photograph. The welcome sign below the water tower said it with flowers. And was as good as it gets on the interesting-ness scale. I have a photograph of my bike laid in front of it.

When travelling by bike, ever present is the need to "buy" time. Just in case. In case of breakdown. In case the weather is simply too desperate to carry on. In case the road ahead is steep. Or the wind is in the wrong direction. The list of possibilities is endless. And a constant source of (mild) concern when schedules are important. And they were. For with 200 miles to go, I was booked on the once-weekly ferry bound for The Faroe Islands. In five days time. Just one fold of the map. Then it really would be the home straight. No problem. If there were no problems. Seriously relaxed after food and beer, but nevertheless mindful of this fact, it was a reluctant cyclist who took to the road late on that cool and windy afternoon.

What Erik hadn't told me about was the hill. Back at Skaftafell the two Canadian women had "mentioned" it. Maybe they were simply being kind. Perhaps they didn't like to tell the old bugger he'd probably have a heart attack half way up. I could scarcely believe it. It must be a four-wheel-drive track. The main route would be just out of sight. For, like the proverbial house end, it tackled the slope head on. From this distance they were mere specks. But, focusing my spy glass, they turned into cars, buses, trucks. And the surfaced road into rough gravel. It was the steepest road I'd ever seen. And it was in my way.

Mental preparation. That's the thing. And, as so many times before, beyond the initial intake of breath, welling up out of nowhere came the resolve to ride it all. Down to tee shirt and leggings in the cool evening light. A pause, a long hard look at the hill before me. A Mars bar, banana, a long drink of water. OK, I might well need to rest. But pushing. Never. So steep, the front wheel momentarily unweighted, with each thrust of the pedals. So enormous, the unguarded steep fall away to my right that I rode in the centre for fear of wobbling too much and tumbling over the edge. So soft, the surface, that the front wheel was in constant danger of whipping out from under me. Impossible to get my feet back in the toe clips, starting after my rests. But I pedalled all the way. And the view off the top. You'll have to take my word for it. An unbelievable perspective of steep cliffs, watery sunlight ..... and the North Atlantic. The ride down the other side back down to sea level was pretty good too.

Ask for directions in the UK, and it isn't long before we're told to turn right at the "King's Head" then left at "The Fox." Down a tad on pubs, progress in Iceland is charted in bridges. Unsuspecting motorists crossing these most remarkable structures of timber, steel and concrete see little of the torrents raging below. Cyclists cannot fail to notice the fact that, caught off guard by a particularly strong blast of wind, it would be all too easy to be swept over low guard rails into oblivion.   Five. Or maybe six glacial river bridges further on I set up camp. Although Stafafell appeared on the map, far from hamlet or village, it was just a single farm. With basic site facilities and price to match. The only other residents were a young French couple from Paris. A well known fact amongst foreigners is that the all Brits drink tea like it was going out of fashion. And that is what the young woman brought over to my tent as I prepared my evening meal. A delightful gesture ..... my first cup of tea in months ..... that had me wishing I'd packed those snails. Later, cosy inside with the stove lit, despite the fact that it was cold and draughty outside, I caught up with my notes. Hard to beat. If you like that sort of thing.

Proceeding in an easterly direction

"To spend a night in close company with a gently breaking surf: what better antidote for an invasive weariness that had settled in as I'd battled with increasingly aggressive road surface and weather."

28

It was still early. I hadn't been riding for long. But the distant dot had turned into a bike rider. We had both expected to stop. Jon, Iceland's only touring cyclist, he speculated, a telephone engineer by trade, was cycling to his sister's home near Þórsmörk. The 600 kilometre journey from home in Reyðarfjörður, using overnight hotels, had been an ambition of his for years. His wife had steadfastly refused to accompany him and it turned out to be a solo event. Well into the trip, having covered over a third of the distance, he was thoroughly pleased with himself. We exchanged traveller's tales and swapped e-mails before moving on.

With the ice cap left behind I was amongst quite different terrain. Now, tongues of sea crept deep into steep sided mountains that nudged the coast. The East Fjords meant that for two days my route would cling to ridiculously steep slopes as it wound interminably round a jigsaw of submerged valleys. By lunch time it had turned cold and unfriendly again. A couple of hot drinks sheltering from the wind provided the perfect antidote as I reflected on my experiences. There is something special about a boiling kettle out in the open. But there again ..... you might be thinking ..... plugging in that shining electric one in your luxury kitchen sounds a whole lot better.

The route round the East Fjords had a number of gravel stretches. And it was clear that my suspension seat post wasn't functioning properly. Its softening action was plainly important, for already my backside had the beginnings of bruises. Without it, the remainder of the ride might well be torture. It had happened before: to the extent that I had to rest up for several days on that trip. Having sorted it out weeks back in Akureyri I knew how the thing was put together. This time it wasn't coming apart. Now it was seized up and in need of grease. Deep inside the works. Once again turned roadside mechanic, accessing the fittings

159

required a little lateral thinking. And with two Allen keys bolted and taped together to provide the required length, I dismantled that vital component and, margarine to the rescue, was soon back on the road.

Spectacular vistas of mountain and water were constant reward for doing battle with increasingly unfriendly weather, but the café in Djúpivogur was just too tempting. Spectacularly ordinary, even for the sort that is bolted on to almost every filling station in Iceland, it came equipped with tired looking Formica topped tables and metal framed chairs that might have seen service in some 'fifties milk bar. But at least it wasn't windy in there. And the beer went down a treat. I did feel the need for treats at that stage in the game, and when a young woman bought the ice cream I simply couldn't resist one. No ordinary ice cream, the woman placed the truncated cone under the dispenser and pressed go. With deft swirls of the wrist, the helter skelter built up. She just didn't know when to stop, the result being an extraordinary structure that resembled another of Dusty's hair dos. And "would I like it dipped in hot chocolate" as well? The local toughs and their girls sat the wrong way round on their chairs. They leaned them back on two legs. And furtively fingered videos from the rental display. Discretely situated in a corner of the café, titles included "Blair Witch 2." What it's about, I could not begin to imagine. But headline writers for Britain's fun-packed vitriolic right wing tabloid press would have been proud. Were there more? Was this simply one of a series? Were other Prime Ministers so honoured? This burning issue occupied my thoughts for all of half a second. Maybe less. Just the same I smiled a sickly smile, thought of England: and further punchy titles that Jo Public and his Icelandic neighbour could barely wait to get their hands on.

Here was a fishing harbour. Just the second I'd come across on the south coast. And quite delightful. Unlike Höfn, pronounced Hupn. The café overlooking all of this was not closed after all. If I'd seen it first I'd have gone in there, given the milk bar tables a wide berth. But did I want to get back on the road? A firm "no," I replied, sitting down for a second time and ordering chips with yet more coffee. What tipped the scales in their favour was the view of a tiny yet vibrant harbour. With what looked like on-shore processing facilities it plainly featured strongly in the local economy. If I'd spent time gathering everything together I'd have missed the shot. Leaving all my possessions, palm top computer included, on the table I rushed outside to photograph a fishing boat that was manoeuvring out there. Faith in human decency. Or sheer stupidity? Where else in the world would I think of doing that? Nothing had been touched when I got back to my chips.

Battling with weather, roads and hills needed all the concentration I could muster just to keep riding. Spectacular scenery round every corner required similar attention to detail. But sitting quietly on the right side of a coffee or two, watching the world go by, it is easy to drift on to issues that rarely get an airing. My head was beginning to get the idea that it was all over ..... the "done that now" sort of feeling. Firmly on the home straight and getting to the point when it would be good to move on, I found myself contemplating three stopovers on the way home. May be it was the weather. It wasn't particularly anything. Simply unfriendly. The sort when it is best indoors.

It was a wrench. I'd ridden just 45 miles and was fresh out of excuses for not resuming my journey. I would carry on, "buy" time to chill out and, more practically, wash clothes before the next phase of the trip. Djúpivogur is situated at the mouth of Berufjörður, which stretches inland for roughly fifteen miles. I could clearly see the road on the northern shore, but it would be hours before it saw me. The southern shore was easy. With spirits raised and a following wind, I whistled along the surfaced road. Then, back to rough gravel on the undulating northern shore, with rain threatening I pedalled straight into a biting wind for ten miles.

My intention had been to carry on, camp at the site a little further on. But the sheltered bay was irresistible. Establishing camp in poor weather can be a wonderful experience. A casual glance from the road said that it was a distinct possibility. Lots of water: no problem there. So leaving my bike at the roadside, I walked the few steps on to the black sand and shingle beach. The grassed platform that I'd observed was a little above high tide marks. To spend a night in close company with a gently breaking surf ..... what better antidote for an invasive weariness that had settled in as I'd battled with increasingly aggressive road surface and weather. There are many who would not have appreciated it. But wheeling my bike off the road and establishing camp in that cold drizzle had the potential for a perfect end to a hard day. With a suitable area of flat grass selected, the next vital decision was wind direction and the view I would like to wake up to. So often one requirement contradicts the other, but on that occasion, like someone knew just what I needed, it all fell into place. One moment it was a tightly rolled package held on to my rack with bungee cords. Next, flapping, inert, on the grass. Then three dimensional as poles begin the Frankenstein like task of injecting life. Finally resuscitated as pegs are pushed home and tension applied to the guy ropes (thin cords really, but rope sounds more boy scout-like), it is time to open the front door. A little over five minutes after arriving, with sharp end into the wind, I flung my panniers under the fly sheet and climbed in to set up the inner tent. Wet outer clothing discarded in the luggage area; sleeping mat and bag laid out; the smell of food cooking. What a contrast with just minutes before. Glancing away from that domestic scene, out through the open flap, I was reminded that the sea gently breaking on black sand, just a stone's throw away, would be my companion for the night.

Later, after washing up in a tiny stream that trickled through the shingle using a little sand to scrub the pans, I settled down to catch up with my notes. By then it was bucketing down. But there's something special about camping in the rain, cocooned, cosy, warm ..... two fingers to the weather. Like the previous evening my stove featured as the added ingredient that completed a satisfied feeling of comfort and security. Another cross on the map reminded me that I had been on the road for twenty five days. And experienced so much that it was difficult to know what to think about first. Continuing rain amplified the feeling of security within as I contemplated the fact that the same time next week, Iceland would be but memories. It would be my last night on the Faroe Islands and I would be pondering life back home. With that, I retrieved the map of that country. Dormant, in the bottom of my rucksack for weeks, now it actively compounded the feeling that I was almost ready to move on. Already I was anticipating the next stage of my journey. This, with over a hundred miles to go before joining my ferry back in Seyðisfjörður. Much of the route I had planned clung to a coastline that might have been a child's drawing of someone's hand ..... its fingers pointing to the promise of vistas to equal those that so thrilled in the North West. I'd ridden a long way to be amongst the East Fjords. I could have just popped down the road from Seyðisfjörður if I'd known. Missed out the difficult bits. These thoughts, and a whole lot more flashed through my mind, but my head was still ahead of the facts as I tried in vain to address the present, in the full knowledge that in two days time a journey that had festered in my mind for years would be over. With that the stove went out. "Time for bed", said Zebedee. And with that I slept to the sound of rain and gentle surf.

Housing estate ..... Icelandic style.

Djúpivogur ..... just the second fishing harbour I had come across on the south coast.

On fjords

"With fingers deep amongst the tangle of mountains, shining in the morning sun, a demure North Atlantic Ocean completed the postcard."

29

Awake in the night listening to the waves, momentarily concerned that I might have got the high tide marks wrong, plans for swift evacuation did battle with a sleepy haze. That Monday morning feeling had taken a powerful hold. So near the end, my head considered the event complete. So what was this fuss about getting the show back on the road? With just 120 miles to go, my legs could be forgiven for feeling that they had been overlooked in a dash to complete the journey. But today it would be work. As usual.

A day amongst the fjords promised spectacular sights. But my feet were dragging when, with packing complete, it was time to dismantle my tent. No complaints about the weather, no excuses there. But the (temporary) home that had offered so much inner warmth was about to lose its status. With panniers pitched on the grass outside and inner tent rolled up, a last look at my home for the night in that tranquil setting. The first peg or two made no apparent difference, then, with crucial support removed, the tent collapsed, to lie bedraggled, helpless on the ground. That moment, that point of no return is always one for quiet contemplation but, on high emotional alert, near journey's end, rolling up the lifeless form took on special meaning.

In the absence of tree, lamp post, or willing assistant, holding a bicycle while loading up a tricky business. It is a process which near guarantees angry rebuke and oily extremities as securing straps pass within a whisker of gears and chain. It is at this point that the front wheel, seemingly with a mind of its own, flips at right angles and the whole lot threatens to tumble over. Having pulled all these tricks, and more, it was plain that my bicycle did not wish to get back on the road either.

But several meaningful last looks later I was breezing along beside the sea under a bright, if cool, sun. Errant wheels and oily fingers forgotten ..... that start of a new day feeling. All was well with the world. Early July and still-snow-covered mountain peaks nudged the clouds, their lower slopes awash with scree runs that, in their sprint for the sea, plainly keep the road gangs busy. Sheltered in gullies were the first signs of a visible growth line. Here, scrubby grass reluctantly gave way to more vigorous growth on the lower slopes, surrounding me at road level with a riot of green, brilliantly complemented by slashes of vibrant yellow dandelions and buttercups. Closer examination revealed yet more colour in the form of what, to my untrained eye, can only be described as Alpines and lichens clinging to life amongst the rocks. And breaking up the scene, a mass of tumbling streams and waterfalls, too numerous to count, made a dash for the sea, their contents clear and icy cold. With fingers deep amongst the tangle of mountains, shining in the morning sun, a demure North Atlantic Ocean completed the postcard. Fjords 10 miles long, and the rest, knock large holes in schedules. Time to work up quite an appetite as I steadily made my way along a route that hugged the shore.

Clearly visible across the water, with wanton disregard for the welfare of my wallet, Breiðdalsvík tantalised and titillated with the prospect of another fine restaurant meal. The morning's riding dragged in anticipation of good food, but all too soon the three course meal had gone. However, endless refills of coffee took some time, affording ample opportunity for watching the world go by. Clad in full leathers, their gait that of saddle-sore horse riders, the macho pair mounted enormous motor cycles and swept away. People gathered for a bus that was plainly imminent. Not so much a bus stop in the traditional sense of the word, it was more a staging post between different parts of everyone's journeys. Buses arrived and departed; passengers getting off one to wait for another. Tonka trucks, awash with all the trappings of an outdoor life, came and went, their drivers sporting obligatory base ball cap and dealer boots. "Lifestyle" transport in realistic surroundings ..... all of it a dream for those on the school and supermarket run back in the UK. Who get to spend the weekends washing off all that mud with some kind of religious zeal. But only after the lawn's been cut.

For no good reason Sundays as a child flashed across my mind. It was probably something I'd eaten. Or maybe it was the religious zeal thing. But there I was, back in the 'fifties, simply for observing Tonka trucks and their drivers. I wasn't allowed to play out. Stream blocking was off. And no den building. Had to stay clean that day. And we only used that room on Sundays. Church in the morning. After my mother put the meat in the oven. Always, it was roast beef with all the trimmings. And always the cabbage. Followed by rice pudding with a thick brown skin on top, because the oven was on and it would be a shame to waste the heat. After I got back from Sunday School we sat in the front room, then had sandwiches for tea sitting round the gas fire. Then we played games. "Brains Trust" was one of my favourites. Players picking up an alphabet card, followed by one from the question card heap. Which would ask the name a breed of dog, a capital city, something found on the Christmas tree, even ..... and beginning with the randomly selected letter. Easiest of all, my favourite as I was an avid train-spotter, the card that said "seen from a train window". A player couldn't fail with this one. Almost anything would do, be it beach, boat, bus, bauble, even. For couldn't we see brightly lit Christmas trees in people's homes as we trundled past. Fifty years later the trains flash past so quickly we'd miss the tree. Or the railway has been dismantled. Unless you've taken the kids to a preserved line in December for the steam-driven Christmas experience. Pure nostalgia, a trip back in time for many of the older visitors as steam hangs around in damp air. Perhaps nothing more than the "Thomas" experience for younger clients. A train zoo, where locomotives that used to roam the length and breadth of the nation can be seen frustrated, caged, slowly pacing back and forth on memory line. Back from a somewhat convoluted trip down Memory Lane, the answers for "Seen from a café window" might not be far removed, I mused, carefully noting buildings, buses, boats ..... baubles, even. At the right time of year.

Day dreaming done with, back outside it was time to check out the village. Breiðdalsvík is stunningly situated on the northern shore of a large cove bearing the same name. There did not appear to be a great deal on offer, but as ever I was drawn to the harbour on the tip of a short spit of land. Important enough to have been upgraded in the mid 20th century, the centrepiece for a population of around 200, it was awash with all the paraphernalia of a vibrant fishing industry. Vessels moored in water so clear that I could see their hulls below the water line as well. Engines thudding gently, men aboard, busy. And ashore, maintenance facilities in a huddle of purposeful, if somewhat ramshackle buildings. Observing the way others live is one of the joys of travel. It helps to get one's own existence into firmer perspective. On jetties that provide a safe haven for the boats were people whose way of life is far removed from the one I have led. No registration, assemblies, lesson notes, writing on the board, demonstrations, homework setting, marking. And endless corridors. No noisy break duty, eating in the hall with hundreds of youngsters. I could write pages, but ask you, the reader to remember school days. Compare them to a life style that, each and every day brings those involved in contact with the North Atlantic Ocean. Before returning the catch to a tiny village port on the south east coast of Iceland where, in summer it rarely goes dark, and in winter it rarely gets light. All of this occupied my thoughts as I walked around the harbour before gently pedalling back past coloured timber buildings set amongst scrubby grass and shingle beaches. Just one more of those places it was becoming increasingly hard to leave, I climbed a rocky headland for a final overview of the cove and village it had spawned.

I hadn't been out of Breiðdalsvík long before coming upon another building site currently in use as a road. For three miles, the ring road might have been a river bed. Fortunately, on this occasion, I guess the workmen hadn't got round to directing water along it yet. In fact, the workmen were doing nothing at all. And notable, like most of the major road improvement schemes I'd come across, by their absence. Fact was that early Monday afternoon, there wasn't a hint of activity: not a workman on site. I guess the unions have it all stitched up. "Don't work at weekends, you understand, then, following negotiations, it's like this: Mondays, help the wife with the washing: Tuesdays, need time to get used to the idea: Wednesdays, that's our day off: Thursdays, planning the weekend: Fridays, start weekends early here: and in any case, roads need time to settle, you know." There might be something in that. For many of the roads round the Eastern Fjords perch perilously close to massive drops straight into the sea. With not a guard rail in sight. Maintaining a sensible gap between me and the edge seemed like a good idea ..... for crawling up steep hills at a snail's pace, the slightest wobble could so easily have caused a major problem.

Just round the corner, in reality a whole fjords worth of riding, was Fáskrúðsfjörður. Established in the late 19th century, it was once home for up to 5000 people. Surprisingly, French people. Fishermen. Who knew the town by another name. Budir. One of their main bases for fishing off the Eastern Fjords. Although they had left the town behind by the beginning of the First World War, much evidence of their presence remains to this day. By now it was early evening and the museum of life in the tiny French outpost had closed. It's at times like this that I have pangs of doubt concerning cycle touring. I really ought to have spent the night there, made time to visit all the town had to offer, for everywhere evidence of times past could be seen. Sadly, I had to keep riding long into the evening, and settled for simply soaking in the atmosphere of the place. In fairness, just being places with a lot of history behind them often puts me in the picture. So much in evidence, the tricolour flag helped. So did the municipal hall that used to be home to the French consul, the French cemetery and, moved to its current site in the late 'twenties, the (derelict at the time of writing) former French hospital. Shown in French as well as Icelandic, for once I could get my head round the street names, and with these as catalyst, added to the mountain setting, it might have been the French Alps. A little imagination is required but it is almost as though something of times past has soaked into the streets and buildings, and is still there for those who seek it out. All of this made me think of my childhood, and the three years I had spent at secondary school studying a subject that would be the only foreign language I ever got a handle on. Here, at a time when I sorely needed a reason to be doing what I was doing, it gave me a lift.

If only I could have delayed the next part of my ride. For six years. I could have avoided the gravelled, exposed and often steep route clinging to rocky hillsides that threatened to cascade down on me. Camping there while they built the tunnel would have been tricky. And my family would have missed me. The views were spectacular as I made my way round the long spit of land that separates Fáskrúðsfjörður from Reyðarfjörður. Motorists will miss this treat when the tunnel between the two fjords opens, saving 34km of driving. But will cyclists be allowed to use it? Perhaps it is just as well that I decided to press on, for waiting six years, only to be turned away, would be disappointment indeed.

I had intended to camp in Reyðarfjörður, the small town on the northern shore, but flat grass within a whisker of the water was too attractive. It was just a phase. I knew it would pass. For to go through life being attracted to soft, flat grass might well be regarded as a serious condition in polite circles. I guess it's OK if you happen to be a sheep, but it's not the sort of thing you'd tell just anyone. And what would people say?

Concerns over what people might say were overtaken, once again, by the pressing issue of the view I would like to wake up to. Looking east, a narrow, curving, mountain-flanked stretch of water almost as far as the open sea. In the opposite direction, shallow water gently washed a shingle beach, before my eyes were drawn upwards to follow the river valley and mountains that soared on either side. And somewhere in there, my route north. Almost certainly there would be a hard climb. Tomorrow. This would be as close as I got to Reyðarfjörður. But peeping a little in each direction, I got the best of all worlds. And on the opposite shore, through my spy glass, a clear view of the harbour, together with numerous smaller fishing craft and a couple of large ships moored there. Right next to the water, I could see the camp site I had originally intended to stay at. Behind all of this, a small, straggling town of brightly coloured buildings huddled, as though wary of tumbling into the water. I'd missed the War Museum: Reyðarfjörður was an Allied base in WWII. But it would have meant a short diversion off my route. Through the spy glass was easier. And at that stage in the game it had become an important issue. Thus, I spent my last night on the (Icelandic) road. And to celebrate, following a swim and a little relaxing in the hot tub, tomorrow I would buy the most amazing meal. Even a cursory look at the map confirmed the fact that I would probably have earned it by the time I had covered the 20 mile ride to Egilsstaðir. All that would remain after that was the further 16 mile hike back over the mountain to Seyðisfjörður. Where I would chill out at the Youth Hostel. For that is where I vowed to spend the last two nights before leaving the country. A chance to sort out practical issues like clean clothes for the next part of my journey. And more emotive ones, too. Like the need to draw a line under what had been a most amazing, and truly privileged experience. Time, also, to get my head round the remainder of the journey and work out how to make the most of it. It would be easy to let things slip. But there was the voyage, The Faroes, Shetland, and Orkney. And the train ride home. I would enjoy it. I would make the effort. I would not become demob happy.

All of this and more, much much more, washed over me as I tended to the practicals of life at floor level. Sea water is fine for washing in. Together with a little sand and a few pebbles it's fine for pans too. But riding is thirsty work and cooking a meal soaks up drinking water, no matter how frugal. Mixed with dried milk, my regular breakfast of muesli needed more. Then there'd be coffee. The extra water, that third bottle slung under the down tube on this trip had made those instant decisions concerning camp sites feasible. Rough camping had been pure delight.

A night in close company with gently breaking surf.

Fáskrúðsfjörður ..... once home to 5000 French people, with street names to match.

Recognised sites with all the facilities have their practical advantages, but to happen upon a glorious spot, to sleep right there, and wake to the sound of gentle waves. To see icebergs simply for opening a zip. To eat there with nothing but nature for company, I found truly wonderful. In bad weather, once inside, a sense of well being, cocooned, alone against weather that could do its worst. To hear rain thrashing down, to know it is blowing a gale out there. A meal, the stove and a down feather sleeping bag, together make a good antidote. It is at times like this that I am pleased to be using that same sturdy tent, so small that those in charge of the weather barely notice it. To lie there, warm and comfortable while all of that is taking place outside is inspiration indeed. At times like that, my palm computer top gets quite a bashing. That evening was no exception as thoughts were consigned to chip.

Was I safe? To be honest, Iceland is a particularly safe country, but I've camped in all sorts of places over the years, both in the UK and abroad. And the only strife I ever had was quite recently on the Lleyn peninsula, in North Wales. Where, for reasons that never became clear, a bunch of local twelve-year-olds lobbed a few stones at my bike and tent. It might have been their idea of fun. It might have been because I was English. But having failed to engage them in conversation, with some sadness I moved on. I will not visit Aberdaron again. Iceland, with its permanent summer daylight is exceptional, for normally after a day on the road I try to set up camp at dusk, and leave early for another. That way, few are aware that I have been there.

Back, then, from a short reflection on my journey to date, and brief consideration of what was to come. Nothing wrong with a bit of reflection. It provides opportunity for a perspective on where life is at. And time to plan for the future. Call it day dreaming, call it what you will. But it is a fine way to draw things to a close. And for me it's as exciting as planning new ventures. With whirlwind trip over, it was back to my tiny tent by the fjord, a view to die for in every direction. And one last look at them before sleeping.

Decompression

"Accordions, bass guitar and percussion: a super enthusiastic conductor, the rest of the cast apparently less relaxed, and one fellow with an expression that most would reserve, for example, when a finger's gone through the toilet paper."

30

Waking for that last ride I was aware of a certain end of term feeling. It would be no distance at all. Just 35 miles that included a couple of steep climbs. But with a shower, swim, hot tub, and cracking meal at half time in the frame, who cares? And for afters I would sleep in a bed. Still, it was hard to leave yet another stunningly beautiful spot by the sea and, as so often before, it took several last looks before finally tearing myself away. Having only just set off I had to stop again. Not another last look. This time a whole squadron of geese waddling down the hillside, to cross the road in front of me. As though on parade they crossed the beach to swim off in the fjord beside me, the entire performance acted out in strict vee formation common to flight. I was back in Tasmania. Camped within a stone's throw of the beach at Bicheno, on the East coast, woken at five o'clock on that late August morning to the sound of penguins squawking in their sand dune nests, close by. Quickly dressed, creeping through the red, half light of sunrise to watch them cross the beach, and paddle through the Pacific surf, before swimming off to feed at sea.   There, they would stay, until dusk found them clambering ashore with food to regurgitate for their young.   Their truly graceful demeanour at sea, I recalled, contrasted with an amusing, somewhat laboured gait on land. The geese were much the same. Time warp over, I pedalled gently away from the fjord, heading East beside the river. The mountains began to close in and I got to guessing where the road would get through. Just when it looked impossible, we swept sharply northward through a steep mountain pass that took me from sea to snow and back again. The river kept company all the way to the top ..... hard to believe that the torrent tumbling beside as I worked in low gear was the same one that gurgled serenely into the fjord at the end of its journey. Equally spectacular, the myriad of glistening snow melt streams. For them, it was "make your mind up time" regarding which team to join, for the summit was plainly a head for river systems draining both north and south. I never knew its name, but I'd seen its birth, development through tearaway adolescence to maturity, and tranquil demise: albeit in the wrong order! My mind firmly fixed on the delights to come, I pedalled like a machine, before an exhilarating descent that went on for miles, beside waters heading north.

It had been almost four weeks since I'd left to head north, but back in Egilsstaðir it all felt very familiar. Like meeting up with old friends. With urgent business to attend to, I set about it with a will. Losing one lot ..... that's carelessness. To lose two is verging on stupidity, yet Iceland being Iceland, they'll almost certainly still be there, waiting for me to go back if only I knew where to look. It left the third and only remaining pair under a lot of pressure, to the extent that if I'd left them unattended, they might well have walked away on their own. Such was the plight that had befallen me. Soaked by rain and river crossings, dried out as I rode, the whole performance repeated time and time again, my last remaining pair could well have qualified for a long service medal. With all of this in mind I furtively entered the department store. Cycling for weeks in all weathers, the last two nights of rough camping, me and my still-damp feet. People might have been forgiven for giving a wide berth. To wander amongst clothes, furniture, TV and hi fi ..... the stuff of household life ..... was to land on another planet. To select new socks from the racks on display was from another life ..... one temporarily suspended in my nomadic existence. To walk the streets of that small town, to peer through shop windows, to see at close quarters the homes and gardens of those who live there was to feel invisible. I guess that I was being ultra-sensitive to my surroundings in a way that those who travel by car or bus, and stay in hotels, could be forgiven for not appreciating. To travel by bicycle, to camp in solitude. Unimaginable for some. An eye on another world. If you like that sort of thing.

Taking a shower, naked, before going in the pool was one of the rules of engagement and, in the circumstances, probably the least I could do. The outdoor pool was wonderful, the hot tub better. To lie in hot, sulphurous smelling water, a powerful stream of bubbles to sooth my spine, was to truly relax. Steep hills, high winds, stinging rain, bone jarring roads. They were then. This was now, as I bathed in the glory of it all. But everything has a price, and this was it. Men in various states

Mablik Endar ..... where surfaced roads run into the gravel. And more!

Just when it looked impossible, we swept sharply northwards through a steep mountain pass.

of undress. Loose, unfettered flesh in every direction. Stale body and aerosol in mortal conflict. Changing rooms are not pleasant places, but the worst was yet to come. It had served me well, no complaints on that score. Better for cycling with, but furtively looking around, there was no getting away from the fact. Mine was the smallest. It crossed my mind to smile a weak smile but, decided against it. The shame of it. These Icelandic men had bigger ones. Much bigger ones. It's probably what your average coracle owning Anglo-Saxon had on his mind when those pesky Vikings called in for drinks. To have nothing more than a skin-covered bird's nest parked outside when the fellow next door was sporting a four-wheel-drive longboat must have been disappointment indeed. At twentyfour inches by eight it took up no space at all in my panniers, served its purpose well. But dabbing dry with my micro towel, an all embracing, bath sheet would have completed the luxury, I conjectured. Refreshed, clean clothes, a bounce back in my stride. But it was the socks that did it. To pull on fresh socks before stepping into almost dry trainers was to enter heaven.

Re-entry to the real world took another step forward. In perfect English, following my request for the "do the best you can" style to which I am reduced, we went through an Icelandic version of the "did you have a good weekend?" routine that is the stuff of hairdressers. For £10 I was metamorphosed, to emerge with a go-faster streamlined look, and four weeks of beard reduced to designer stubble. To say that I felt like a new man is to risk being misconstrued. Nevertheless, the effect was dramatic.

Starters included things I hadn't tasted in weeks ..... prawns, a whole variety of salads, fish soup, and real crusty bread. For main courses, fish in delicious sauce, or a spicy bean thing, with potatoes, noodles, pasta, or rice as appropriate. Tempting desserts, a couple of beers and finally coffee completed the feast. A whole squadron of cutlery at my disposal, outside on the terrace at the café Nielson, an "eat as much as you want" Icelandic buffet lunch, an umbrella above my table, trees rustling gently, the sun on my back. Civilisation indeed. Incontrovertibly, the world was a wonderful place.

Civilised, and ready for anything. With just 17 miles to go to Seyðisfjörður, and journey's end. Egilsstaðir had taken on the role of decompression chamber, prepared me for the outside world. I had ridden into town, an unwashed traveller. Somewhere in there I became a tourist. And that's who left ..... one who travelled by bicycle, but a tourist nonetheless.

The climb away from Egilsstaðir twisted and turned for 9 miles. Near journey's end and my enthusiasm was evaporating. To an extent, the feeling compounded my theory that so much of what it is possible for a body to do is in the head, for part of me knew that it was all over. I'd been there, done that, seen the movie. Certainly, I did want to get there, no doubt about that. But grinding up that last hill for over two hours, I felt up against it. And I was. The switchback route had me alternately battling against ever more powerful wind. One moment, it was pushing me upward, the next, it almost stopped me in my tracks. A last look back at the summit reminded me of four weeks earlier, the splendid vista that presented itself then, like pulling back the curtains on a glorious morning. Now they were closing again, a chapter, a small, but significant part of my life consigned to memory.

I'd been in a spoon again. And this was the handle. There I was back for a moment or two on childhood walks with my parents. The circular route, with an out and back stretch at the start and finish. Back amongst snow the plateau seemed to go on for ever, then the hill like a house end and speedy descent back to Seyðisfjörður. And the hostel. An awful looking building ..... pink vertical timber clad and a single pitch roof added to the impression that it was a large garage. But inside I could make a drink, sit in a chair, eat at a table. Outside was over. For a time. I realised as evening went by that I was pretty tired. Exhausted, in fact. My head had kept me going for past few days and now it could let go a little.

Secure in the knowledge that I'd been there, done that, taken on the challenge and come through, for once it was good to watch the gentle lapping of the fjord, comfortably seated behind glass. Difficult, near impossible at times, but intact, relaxed. And already impatient to be getting on with the next phase. After so much isolation the company of others was most welcome. Cooking in communal kitchens is a social event, besides being an exercise in co-ordination as cutlery, crockery, utensils and cookers are collectively optimised. Later, aimlessly relaxing with a magazine, the thought occurred to me that I ought to go for a walk. Fact remained though that I'd had enough of the physical thing for a while and, for the duration, would thoroughly appreciate apathy. No pressure to be somewhere else, make an early start, find somewhere to use for toilet purposes. Civilisation after the nomadic lifestyle. The luxury was complete. Revelling, still, in my spacious surroundings, the realisation that I had not a single item of clean clothing to my name was dull: indeed, dullness redefined. Pre-requisite to life as we know it, domestic chores are, at best, dull. Fact was that the last time I had been this close to a washing machine I had been in Reykjavik almost two weeks past. Swilling clothes under a cold tap or in a stream then dangling them from my rack on bungee cords to dry as I rode had been the norm. Thus, the very necessary and long overdue task of washing all the clothes I had with me, save those I wore.

31

I could scarcely believe it, having slept till almost 10 o'clock. The feeling that I could stay there was simply wonderful. As was breakfast at a table, again with the fjord right outside. Then I picked books off the shelves, read a little. But so finely tuned to images, "Landscapes - Images of Iceland" leapt out, and asked to be opened, its preface entitled "Landscape of Dreams" written by none other than The President of Iceland, Vigdís Finnbogadóttir. In it, she asks "what makes a group of individuals, large or small, into a nation?" Snorri Hjartarson, the poet provided the answer: "land, nation, language, a trinity, sole and true." Amazing images provoked an instant recall and a powerful rush of emotions. It's how Alice must have felt. I, too, was in Wonderland and, delving further into memories of experiences on my journey, risked a flood of tears. Looking back over the trip, feelings about it had changed almost by the minute, an emotional roller coaster at the mercy of challenging landscape and weather alike, yet rewarding beyond imagination for all of that. To say that I was on high emotional alert is to understate my feelings.

The woman on holiday, with her young family, from Reykjavik had several favourite holiday spots in Iceland. Sometimes she camped. Sometimes she used hostels. But by way of a contrast she might take a cheap flight to London, soak up its frenzied atmosphere. And a bargain or two. To an extent, we had similar demands for travel. Contrasts, we agreed, is what it's all about. Being honest, I was ready for a change and already wondering what The Faroes would bring. I do wonder if it's the journey that's more important than actually arriving, for having got back to Seyðisfjörður it would have been so easy for the time there to turn into something of an anti-climax. Already I was anticipating the voyage, and getting on the move again. With someone else in the driving seat for a change. Now, it was time for practicalities. Like cleaning my bike, checking it over. And reading up on formalities concerning entry into The Faroes.

In the lounge, large windows on two sides overlooked the fjord and small town with its obvious marine associations. Sunlit reflections of snow covered peaks danced on the surface of the fjord, no more than a stone's throw away. And clustered round the water, brightly painted buildings, their coloured roofs so much a part of that Scandinavian scene. Newer constructions in corrugated iron blended easily with older timber structures from the 19th century. To me with a feel for buildings and their construction techniques they had a presence, made a statement about the region. Beautifully juxtaposed between mountain slope and water, many looked like they, too, were part of the landscape. So powerful is their presence that even the 21st century utilitarian demands of modern commerce and industry fail to dent the charm of Seyðisfjörður. Heavily dependent, still, on the fishing industry, tourism is becoming increasingly important in summer. But curious about winter and how people get about I quizzed my host. Most use four-wheel-drive vehicles but rarely chains now, on roads that are kept open throughout the year. Before the current trend in Tonka trucks, Land Rovers, Willys Jeeps and Snowmobiles were common. And before that, everything came in by sea.

It struck me that I'd not left the hostel since arriving the previous afternoon. Twenty four hours and not a step outside. Sitting at one of a pair of long trestle tables, beyond my immediate surroundings and separated by half wall was a sort of lounge. Complete with a couple of cushion clad settles it also fielded a pair of those inverted Chinese-hat-on-legs chairs, popular in UK in sixties. In the typically-hostel dining kitchen beyond, multilingual signs indicated what to do with your garbage, that sort of thing. Hostels are host to many languages, so often a disparate band with only travel in common, but Iceland does have a common denominator. Thus, Danes, Swedes, Americans, Germans, Icelanders, and myself washed up together. In English. Inside the hostel simple things meant so much. And stayed there when I put them down instead of blowing away. But already I was feeling the need to lick lethargy, to tackle torpor, to get myself out there and make the most of last few hours in Iceland. Fellow guests included a party of musicians who were putting on a concert that evening. I would make the effort, go to that. And I would make a bit of an effort that afternoon.

Half knowing that it would be too late, I set out for a walk. Aimlessly ambling, a little shopping, free coffee at the supermarket, a beer in a thoroughly pleasant bar overlooking the harbour ..... a vista in every direction. Time wasting at its best.   The museum was indeed about to close. Sighted out, part of me pleased with the disappointment, I meandered beyond the buildings to sit on a headland overlooking the town and its magnificent setting at the end of the fjord. With nothing better to occupy my mind I quizzed myself.   Nothing difficult, mind. Just a little preparation for the sort of question the neighbours might ask when I got home. "What will my firmest memories of this trip be?" "Tough, challenging, wind, spectacular, geothermal activity. Luxuries like drinks and meals out of the wind, finding shelter to stop by, and taking good care when pissing in the wind!" "What did I miss most?" "Occasionally my wife, people generally, books, conversation, trains." "Weren't you scared?" "No." "Would you do it again?" "Not the same trip, but in principle, so long as my bits and pieces all work properly, then, yes."

Back at the hostel the atmosphere was electric ..... safe, low voltage. But the convivial ambience of communal cooking is like no other as multilingual evening meals are co-ordinated, prepared, eaten and cleared away.   The closest I can get concerns my year working in Australia, and memories of Australian friends who would phone to ask what we were making for tea. That established, an entire family would descend on us to mix and match ingredients and culinary skills, resulting in an instant soirée.

Dinner jackets, posh frocks ..... and me with my one pair of lightweight trousers, fleece top and trainers that had seen the world. Tourists and locals alike, were entertained by a selection of music that bridged the world. Accordions, bass guitar and percussion: a super enthusiastic conductor, the rest of the cast apparently less relaxed, and one fellow with an expression that most would reserve, for example, when a finger's gone through the toilet paper. A couple of beers with fellow travellers less than half my age and my evening out was over. A fine way to wind up my time in Iceland.

Next

"It was late, very late, by the time I got off to bed: in contemplative mood. After all, I had a whole lot to contemplate."

32

Sitting on a rock within a stone's throw of "Norrona", my ferry to the Faroe Islands, I could scarcely believe it. Comfortable in short sleeves with no wind break. Reluctant to leave the hostel, I had watched the vessel as she had made her way up the narrow fjord, turn and reverse in the small harbour. Only then had I cycled the short distance there, queued with the vehicles, to wait alongside a couple of motor bikes and one other cyclist. Anything less like an international departure would have been difficult to imagine, as I left my fully laden bike unattended to relax by cold, clear water in glorious morning sun. Surrounded, as ever, by pointy mountains, a considerable amount of snow still lay at high level and in the gullies, running off in a myriad of cascading white streams that dashed headlong towards Seyðisfjörður. Clearly visible below the growth line, swathes of lupins, a sea of blue that must be regarded as weed. Though I guess that they must go some way towards preventing erosion on the steeper slopes. Lower down brighter, more cultivated looking grass took over. Then the town itself, its buildings so natural, nestling between mountain and fjord that they, too, might have been planted or grown from seed. Here and there a tree or two ..... rowan, silver birch and the like showed signs of an intention to stay. Many were no more than a metre high. At three times this figure a scant few braved the wind to reach for the sky. All of this has the effect of breaking up the landscape, softening it just a little. For if I'd missed anything, it had been just that. So much of this land is harsh, brutal, raw, untamed. Having said all that, it's the reason I wanted to go there in the first place. And now it would have to be consigned to memory.

On the rear deck until we hit open sea, a little emotional I got someone to take the "been there" photograph of me with slipstream and mountains in the background. A rapid journey round the country ..... a series of flashbacks as Iceland receded. Like some giant lens zoomed in as I made my way round the country. The credits would be next .....

Back to Seyðisfjörður.

Tórshavn ..... capital city, Faroe Islands.

superimposed, for effect, on unforgettable experiences. The crossing went, as crossings do. Claimed my berth, sat in this lounge, sat in that. Read in this chair, caught up with notes in that. Out on deck, meal in self service, affordable beer, a chocolate bar or three from the duty free. To say that I talked to the German woman is to exaggerate. The reality was that she talked at me, the only other cyclist on board, a captive audience. A nod, a mumble of agreement to prove I was still awake, was all I could muster while she spoke almost without interruption of her cycling trips. I ought to have taken more interest, I really ought, yet increasingly it was like being caught off guard at the party, deeply bored by the drunken fellow in the cravat. Until constructing a need to be somewhere else. A body can take so much, then even going for a pee seems exciting. Something of a Scotaholic when it comes to bike riding, the surprise was to find her at sea somewhere between Iceland and the Faroe Islands.

Unlike Jack Spratt and his wife who, between them would lick the platter clean, the German couple on his-and-hers motor cycles had a problem. He won't fly: she hates sailing. So they compromised. And did what he wanted. Only hours into the crossing, desperately seasick, she had taken to her bed. And would remain there for the duration.

The Dutch woman worked for Ministry of Transport as researcher. To hear of reliable, affordable integrated transport that has advanced beyond electoral promises is to be envious. I am saddened by the state of public transport facilities in the UK. Beeching left half the nation without trains. Thirty years later, privatisation of what remained, on the back of political dogma, ensures that a plethora of operators currently scrabble to service their shareholders, with fares that prohibit all but those without alternative, or expense accounts. I have heard it said that extra customers attracted by sensible fares would overwhelm what passes for a national network. No surprises, then, as fares continue to rise, many way beyond inflation. Like Basil Fawlty, we are left with a system that shouts "no riff raff". Meanwhile, travellers without the means to pay the highest fares in the world, or those foolish enough to have cause to visit places off the rail network, clog up our roads big time. Back from that short voyage into public services and politics I learned that my Dutch companion was travelling with her brother, a musician in Reykjavik. Between travellers' tales and a whole lot more, he confirmed that Icelandic folk do infact smile regularly, are wonderfully helpful, and generally good eggs.

Turns on deck, drinks, meals, reading, writing, people ..... a routine like no other. And later, in the quiet of a gently rolling, almost empty lounge bar, I shared intimate moments. With soft music and a whisky or two ..... the most wonderful whisky in the world. Or so it seemed after four weeks of cost-driven prohibition. Just why the Americans didn't think of that all those years back beats me. And, think of all the time it would have saved on gangsters. But Hollywood might have been short of ideas for films ..... and there were probably lots of spare violin cases about ..... what with the radio and gramophone having come along. So I guess it was probably best in the long run. It's odd what goes through one's mind when there's nothing better to occupy it.

It was late, very late, by the time I got off to bed. In contemplative mood. After all, I had a whole lot to contemplate. Only then did it dawn on me that time on the boat was an hour ahead of that in Iceland, and my watch. And I had to be up and viewing, so to speak, soon after five a.m. for a 6 o'clock arrival in Tórshavn.

On small islands

"Compressing a whole nation into a land mass so small has meant some sacrifices. The mountain pass I'd climbed had plainly been scaled back to take this into account."

33

By 5 o'clock land was drifting by. We were already ghosting along for final entry into the harbour by the time I got out on deck. Few were out there to see brightly coloured modern buildings and ancient black tarred ones alike emerge from the morning drizzle. Few watched the crew throw ropes to harbour personnel, huddled against the morning cool, before winches pulled on them to make fast and vehicle ramps dropped noisily into position. Viewed through tired traveller's haze, that early morning might have been happening to someone else. Only when the cars started driving off did brain engage and legs dash to cabin to collect belongings before re-joining my bike.

Arrival was something of a non-event. Even as a non-event it scored dismally. No grand entry, no uniformed officials asking invasive questions. Out through the "nothing to declare" green route. And still nothing. No obvious directions to an arrival lounge where a weary traveller might chill out, find a bite to eat, take a nap. And not a soul to ask. Far from that slight feeling of unease, that bit when passports are scrutinised, faces casually matched to photographs taken years ago, and luggage is given the eye. As though I had just come back from the toilet ..... that much drama. Out on the harbour front in a new country with only a vague plan, early on an indifferent morning. So early that not even the early morning coffee bars had opened up. I had to get a fix on the place. But before that, needed to change out of cruise gear, become a cyclist again. Locating the passenger lounge and, by pure chance the gents, metamorphosis was complete. Riding without fear of flapping trousers and oil in unsuitable places was, once again, possible. Passengers joined a couple of coaches that rolled up out of nowhere. That done they vanished swiftly, almost as though they'd never existed. Then nothing. Like the rest of the passengers and their vehicles had evaporated. Or dropped into a big hole. I guess though that the authorities would get wise to that though, have it filled in before the press got hold of the story. Imagine the furore if such a thing were to happen back in the UK. "Dover Hole", the headline might screech. Then the tabloids would run soul searching investigations into the fishy business of missing millions as those with excess duty free disappeared without trace. Still, an overwhelming need to get an angle on the place. And still no café. But the fellow in the taxi office confirmed times for the ferry that would be the start of a three day route by bike and sea that I had roughly worked out. By now it was almost seven o'clock. I had an hour. Ferries to Toftir were not frequent. Miss it and my programme, rather than I, would be at sea.

After establishing the departure point for "domestic flights" I could relax a little, find breakfast, settle down with lots of coffee, log on to a different country. That was the plan. But with no sign of anything opening, after touring the streets I wound up on the waterfront. Muesli and a brew up sitting on a rocky outcrop overlooking the harbour. Not quite the overture that springs to mind for a damp morning. But a whole lot was going on out there. In most countries, it would have been a bustling railway station with long distance passenger traffic, commuters and freight fighting for territory in a manner that Brunel or Stephenson might recognise, still. But this eighteen island nation in the North Atlantic, even now home to just 46,000 people, would have foxed them. Years on, through mountain pass and tunnel alike, a delayed, hypothetical, well and truly privatised "Islands Express" might make its way from Klaksvík to Tórshavn. Its passengers leafing through a boatload of excuses would be acutely aware of detail like points failure, the wrong sort of snow (now, where have I heard that one before?) fish on the line, a signal failure to respond. Boats rule OK here, however. Humble dinghies, swanky fishing boats bristling with equipment, cargo vessels. And the dazzling tower block of a cruise ship anchored out there, small service vessels like suitors at the ball paying close attention to her every need. All this, and more. A live show that gave a real insight into the way this maritime society worked. Out there passengers would be wading through mountainous breakfasts, others jogging on deck or working out in the gym. Some would be waiting to be taken ashore for wallet stretching exercises. Or the coach tour. Travellers, all of us. But there the similarities ceased. Pedal power, with its inherent hardships, a million miles from the cushioned lifestyle just yards from me and my simple meal. A gulf in more ways than one, I mused. Meanwhile ferries came and went, bringing workers from the islands into the one of the world's smallest capital cities ..... with a population of just 16,000. With map in front of me I followed their route ..... dotted lines between the islands ..... much as I'd done all those years ago as a train-spotter. The Thames Clyde Express, The Yorkshireman, The Lakes Express, The Cambrian Coast Express, The Aberdonian, Atlantic Coast Express, to name but a few. Following the routes of these trains, and many more that ploughed the length and breadth of the UK, I acquired a basic geographical background that has never left me. But setting up a stove, making breakfast on a rocky outcrop at the end of Platform 6 at Kings Cross: that would have been against the rules, I'm sure. Just another travel experience to conjure up emotions from the past. But so realistic that it almost over-ran. To the extent that I had to hurriedly pack up and ride back to the west harbour. Where my ferry, already unloading its cargo of commuters, was making ready for a rapid turn round.

Back on the move again, this time on a small inter-island vehicle ferry, heading for Toftir, situated at the southern tip of Eysturoy. Even the most casual glance at a map of the country reveals a tangle of islands, themselves punctuated by intrusions of water that would meet in the middle given half a chance. Gnarled fingers of water and rock thrust together like no other I have ever seen. Only later would I come up with an analogy that even comes close. Throw up successive volcanic eruptions from the sea bed; precede each course with volcanic ash; allow to settle slowly and unevenly for millions of years; glaciate throughout; inundate with sea water. Thus evolved The Faroes, their characteristic stratified landscape of bright green grass firmly established on softer terrain between layers of unyielding basalt. All of this, I took in as we made our way north through the two-mile-wide channel of Tangafjørður that separates the two main islands of Streymoy and Eysturoy. Toftir, my destination on the latter, lies at the mouth of Skálafjørdur on its western shore. 6 miles in length, this steep sided gash extends almost half the length of the island, effectively cutting that part in two.

There were few passengers on board. Silence lay over us like a cloud, and after taking an initial interest in Tórshavn's maritime suburbs, out at sea it was only natural to exchange pleasantries. Now I've been around a bit, but professional travellers ..... that's as close as I could come to describing the American couple. Near full time travellers, they were well

186

into retirement that included a hundred days skiing each year. But "been there, got the tee shirt" exchanges can be somewhat limiting. Only half way to Toftir, and he'd taken the wraps off all the hotels in the world. Current affairs ..... that would take his mind off them ..... take care of the remainder of the crossing. But he was pretty cross about those. Poor Icarus paid the price for flying too close to the sun. Remarkably similar circumstances had found their plane in the neighbour's garden: like good boys they'd asked nicely, but gotten it back as a flatpack. A storm in a (china) teacup: the most powerful nation on earth. It was all so unfair. OK, you've no idea what all that was about. *In April 2001 a US surveillance plane collided with a Chinese fighter over the South China Sea, resulting in an emergency landing on Chinese soil for the former and the death of the pilot of the latter. The American crew had been returned after 11 days. But the plane had been retained, was dismantled and returned only that day – July 6th.*

The ferry left and my travelling companions took to the bus ..... twelve seats that promised yet another snapshot for the "been there" series. Then nothing bar the gentle lapping of sea on jetty. Not a breath of wind to remind me who was in charge. It all combined to leave me with a feeling of isolation. Three days off the road, and civilisation had begun to creep in. Then, suddenly it was just me, bike and a tent again. But together we would take on The Faroes.

Short on features, even the guide book had failed here. The road north, I concluded, was the best Toftir could offer. Unwittingly I had missed the main attraction, learning only later of the 5000 seat international football stadium located in the hills above. An opportunity afforded to few. And I blew it. Football: that's the one where they kick, or do they throw things, hit them, perhaps? And that's just the spectators. I guess it's a little less dangerous than war, but the rules of engagement for both might have been drawn up at the same meeting. That so-called followers, the world over, should be elated or saddened to the extent that tribal violence all too often follows a result is quite beyond me. Appreciative of personal challenges on a wide front, I cannot get my head round the time and energy expended on the orientation of a ball. Without doubt, great skill is required for its successful handling. But if skill alone was a measure of the esteem in which everyone was held, I cannot help thinking that the world would be a more pleasant place. International kitchen fitting championships; a crowd puller at a stadium near you. First division carpet fitting. Commonwealth cake icing competitions. Police hold back the crowds: the open-top double-decker is just able to make its way along the High Street. Up there is the team: they're holding the cup high. Ecstatic, the crowd is at fever pitch, for they are in the company of champions. No hopers, the press had written. But, all that behind them, the waiters, their waiters, had come good. They had waited longer, faster, more politely. The final had been tough: each team had waited an hour and a half when the final whistle blew. Only extra time had shown just how all the training had paid off. And now, they were to be honoured at a banquet given by the mayor. Laughable: or is it simply a measure of how the skills that keep humanity afloat are relegated to third division while entertainers, for that is all they are, fill the newspapers, and their wallets, on a scale that far exceeds their value to society? Take no notice of my rantings. I don't know what came over me. It's probably something I'd eaten.

Even the most casual glance at the map of this country confirms that a large proportion of the road network hugs fjord shorelines. With few exceptions, the remainder go over mountains. Or through them. Highly engineered, much of it at Danish expense, all this has the power to surprise in a country so sparsely populated. Prepared, then, for surprise, I set out on what promised to be an eye popping experience. Circular routes are best. Spoons, I can handle. Out and back is a definite no no. Bike, boat, but no buses ..... that was my other prerequisite. Thus I headed for Klaksvík, on the island of Borðoy ..... a leisurely 12 mile ride followed by a ferry trip described as one of the loveliest on earth. Like a maintenance platform for the impossibly steep backdrop that swept above, my route clung to the hillside, close to the water's edge. Straggling villages and small towns, their livelihoods clearly dependent on the sea came to life, Brigadoon like, as I approached ..... the combination of water and mountain so perfect that it, too, might have been a creation of the imagination. Or a film set.

Easy riding amongst all of this with comparatively little distance to cover: it might have been a Sunday afternoon out. So what better than a picnic. I had re stocked on food in Runavík, situated amidst what is described as one of the most important developing urban areas in the Faroes. That said, those who wrote the (local) guide might have been describing somewhere else: Milton Keynes, perhaps. For an area looking less urbanised, I concluded, would be difficult to imagine. A

Tórshavn harbour.

Beyond Toftir ..... the combination of mountain and water so perfect.

bustling street, several shops ..... and fishing boats in the harbour. All beautifully juxtaposed twixt (I could be an estate agent with words like that) mountain and sea. The fact that I was in a different country with different systems sank home. "No signature. Just tap in your number". Only I didn't have one. My visa card has seen successful encounters worldwide. But here, with groceries carefully selected for a mixed, if lightweight, diet it was by sheer chance that I was able to pay for them, having just enough Danish (and interchangeable) currency with me. Only later did I learn that language problems had been the real culprit, the swipe and tap machine simply being a more secure alternative to signature. Just another of life's rich experiences. And a look at the future.

I was lucky to make it to the top of the hill. Seven miles into the trip, and almost wiped out. Twice. The fact that I'd seen no other cyclists should have alerted me to government policy. The hole into which ferry passengers must have disappeared earlier was intended for cyclists as well. I'd avoided that but, sighted now, large unmarked trucks had been sent out on seek and destroy missions. To feel the heat of large vehicles as they overtake is not uncommon. Close enough to be pulled into their slipstream is scary. Closer than that is to be grateful to live long enough to curse their drivers, to consider the marital status of their parents and the sexual activity in which they were, without doubt, currently engaged. Also the possibility that they were Merchant Bankers earning that extra crust. Neither of them heard any of this. I doubt if they'd even seen me. In a land bereft of cyclists, I guess they don't feature on the Highway Code list of things for drivers to avoid: sheep, people, fjords, fish, going slowly. But not cyclists. Small boys wanted to be engine drivers when I was young. With large parts of the UK now devoid of railways, the next best thing is to be a white van driver. To hug the tail of the car in front, to overtake in ludicrous places, to deliver the goods whatever the cost to other road users: a fine career; for the mindless. In a country short on other motorists to intimidate, I guess that driving large unmarked trucks at breakneck speeds on winding roads is a viable alternative. Unless you can afford a Fiesta with tinted windows.

It was good to be able to stop without freezing, blowing away. Or both. With stove set up on the table, pot noodles, chocolate, a little fruit and a coffee or two made the perfect break. Compressing a whole nation into a land mass so small has meant some sacrifices. The mountain pass

I'd climbed had plainly been scaled back to take this into account. Having climbed steeply away from the fjord, sea level to summit had taken no more than half an hour. Now, without leaving my seat a vista opened up on the eastern shore, mountains, and islands beyond. In fairness, I guess that a mountain pass of Icelandic proportions would have looked out of place here. Besides being too high, the provision of extra facilities like rocks, mud, and running water might make unreasonable demands on the road gangs.

It rolled in from the open sea, then swept skywards on reaching the end of the fjord. Awesome is the only word that comes close to the change that took place. Like the stage manager had enough of that awful rock band and turned up the dry ice. Like the magician waved his wand and said the magic words. He'd got them right, for if ever there was a case of "now you see it, now you don't", this was it. One moment, bright sun, shirt sleeves, little luxuries like being able to see: the next, grey, invasive, clinging cold had swept up from the sea. Time to leave. Once I'd put on a full suite of weather proofs. The ride down was fast, smooth, beautifully graded, and extremely cold. Down again just in time to watch the mist disappear like someone rolled up the carpet, the village of Sydrugøta appeared, as if from nowhere. The scene asked to be photographed, but I declined on the grounds of bad light. I had begun to get the feeling that there would be more where that came from: just a question of time before I came across another request stop for my camera. It wasn't long before the lights went back up to full. Watery sunshine picked out a vivid green stage set for hamlet and village alike. Mountains had tops once more. Breathtaking slopes resumed their supporting role. Streams tumbled down to scamper beside simple, sometimes traditional turf roofed buildings: a delightful combination that landscape gardeners could only dream of. To pedal beside all of this, to commune with so much beauty is to be a little emotional. Poor Alice fell foul of emotions. It is widely known that on one of her forays, having shed too many tears, the unfortunate girl had to swim in them to escape. Despite the fact that here could be inspiration for the title of Lewis Carroll's book, I had no immediate plans to swim. Wonderland, it might be, but the tears that welled up in its company: they would have to stop. Leirvík was no distance at all. Just three miles and I would join the ferry for Klaksvík. To drop down several notches after the self-imposed pressure to perform in Iceland was remarkable. Aimlessly amble when it pleased, deliberate on demand, stop when it suited, And I did stop. Many times. With no voice shouting how far I'd got to go that day. Like being on holiday after a hard term back at the chalk face.

The local guide subtly describes the climate as quite changeable; the air as fresh and clean whatever the season. With more of a handle on reality, those with no axe to grind tell it like it is ..... of precipitation on a grand scale and high winds. The fact is that, on average, something falls out of the sky on 280 days of each and every year. And it's even stormier than Iceland. Though on the plus side it's marginally warmer. And the harbours don't freeze over. Shirt sleeves, bright sun, not a breath of wind. Precipitation, statistics, could go hang. It had to be day 281 on that great calendar in the sky. Life's a breeze, I considered. But tunnels ..... they are assessed separately.

Lit or unlit, they feature high on my list of things to avoid. Or failing that, get over with as quickly as possible. With high intensity, attention seeking flashing rear light, fork mounted front lamp, and head torch strapped round my helmet, daylight was left behind for two miles. I'd done tunnels years past in Norway and they don't improve with age. A world of echoes, of hollow amplified sounds that are difficult to identify, of cool, damp, pungent air that reeks of traffic fumes, shouts "unclean", of perpetual "wish you weren't here." It starts with a gentle whooshing sound ..... the first sign that a vehicle is approaching ..... and goes on from there. Most tunnels wind their way through the mountain, the result being that from initial whoosh through to angry, deafening roar it is only at the last moment that I know whether I'm to be annihilated from back or front, though headlamps are a good sign. Worst is the approaching certainty of a large truck thundering ever closer, and catching up at an alarming rate. The comfortable armchair where you sit reading bears little resemblance to any of this, but you might wish to try the following. You will need a rickety chair, a run down torch, the services of an accomplice, and the cover of darkness. Turn the dimmer down to a tunnel traveller's romantic glow: with the aerial disconnected have your accomplice very slowly turn up the TV to a full roaring hiss, then snap off the lights altogether. Throughout all of this, grip the book ever more firmly and concentrate on reading it. In the darkness, try to remember exactly which line you were on and fiddle with the torch to resume reading. Before restoring the lights your accomplice will shake your chair violently. Continue reading the book throughout all of this or your accomplice will push your chair over. My hands tighten nervously on the handlebars. I pedal a little harder in order to maintain a straight line. The elephantine roar is upon me. In an instant the overhead lighting is blotted out. The slab front of the cab slams air aside as it passes, pushing me with it. Eyes take time adjusting to the dim pool of light cast by my lamps as I control the wobble. Huge wheels that would squash anything in their path pound alongside, the truck body slides past agonisingly slowly. I hang in there, wait for the back wheels to roll by, hold the bars ever tighter, concentrate on the edge of the road, ready for the tail end and maelstrom that follows. Just as suddenly it is over ..... the noise fades until all that remains is a pair of red lights disappearing into the tube beyond. Normal services are resumed. Until the next one. Apart from the fact that they don't block out the lights, cars are only a little less awful as they compensate for lack of bulk by avoiding going slowly. Fumes add to a scenario that has to rate amongst the top ten worst experiences for a cyclist, rating in my book alongside high winds on exposed bridges for scary. Day to day I don't do scary, but give me a bike or a pair of skis: it's as though the record has been changed. I have ridden in some pretty odd places but if there is anything to be thankful for when it comes to tunnels, it has been a lack of serious traffic in most of them. I've described a worst-case scenario, but hearing that initial noise, I have little idea what I'm up against until it is upon me. The reader might be forgiven for thinking that straight tunnels would be better. In one way, they are: it is possible to see if a vehicle is coming towards me, but the pool of light at the end does strange things to the eyes, which shut down like an automatic camera and in the absence of powerful headlights, makes for poor visibility. Some are lit and lined throughout, with safety markings at the edges. Others, less well equipped are pitch black, provide natural shower facilities, and feature edges that drop away into craggy darkness. Each and every one sends shivers of anticipation down my spine. Drivers miss these delights. 250 watts of halogen headlights, a powerful engine, windows closed, and it might just be a computer game. With me as expendable victim. But I'm still here to tell the tale.

Out beyond that dark tube, that birth canal, a brave new world of seeing things, of being seen. Of something about to start anew. Fresh air, daylight. And another flashback. I will never forget that day in Northern Norway. My son and I had crossed the Arctic Circle the day before, camped at high level not far beyond. It was late by the time we set off next morning but the enormous descent at the start of the journey put us well ahead of the game before taking an early lunch. Then it started raining; real Scandinavian driving rain that looked like it meant business. Wetter than wet, we rode on. Tunnels took on new meaning: up to three miles away from torrential rain that had been our companion for hours. I was never more pleased to be riding underground. Anticipation is a fine thing. Out of the rain we began to get used to the idea. It would be different on the other side. Time and time again, subterranean fantasy remaining just that, we re-joined the real world of rain still bouncing off the road. Many times, I would have booked into a hotel there and then. My son would have none of it, insisting that we carry on long into the evening. Only after announcing that we had covered a hundred miles that day was I allowed to stop for the night. Still bucketing down, we weren't looking forward to the putting the tent up on a sodden site. But moments later we had rented a fully equipped chalet. A shower, a hot meal and a beer or two never went down better. A hundred-plus. It's a good feeling!

Arriving in Leirvík, just yards beyond the tunnel was a close rival. Besides being the ferry port for Klaksvík, where I was heading, it is a delightful little town nestling between mountain and fjord. Brightly coloured craft of all shapes and sizes filled the harbour. Engines idled, their cooling water spluttered out in to impossibly deep, clear water. Timber jetties, stone breakwaters, concrete piers, sheds with brightly coloured roofs. And in those sheds, on boats, everywhere ..... people were busy. Fishing is clearly alive and well here. The contrast with far too many of our small ports at home in the UK is indescribable.

Confined to places that sheep cannot access, this is a country where buildings provide shelter for trees. Few survive beyond the confines of walled gardens, where they share space with simple displays of colour. Still fewer grow higher than their man made minders. White painted buildings, brightly coloured buildings, typical Scandinavian buildings vie with one another for the best view. In fairness, every one is a winner, for which ever direction I cared to look, the view was breathtaking. Behind them, towering green slopes brushed the clouds. And opposite, the northern islands of Kalsoy, Kunoy, Borðoy, Viðoy, together with the waters that surround them. Out on a limb, connected by tunnel only since 1985, Leirvík offers a surprising range of services that include bank and school. School ..... I'm trying to give up, but a bank in a town with a population of 800! That has to be a novelty in a world of rationalisation. But technology triumphed once again, and out popped Faroese kronor. Old enough to be amazed each and every time I use that versatile bit of plastic, I found myself saying thank you. To a machine!

Passing through narrow fjords between sheer mountains rising directly from the sea, the ferry ride did not disappoint. From seaweed to summit sheep grazed vivid green slopes, so steep the joke about being bred to have two long and two short legs might have originated here. Breaking up the green stratified volcanic rock, weathered now it presented a vision that might best be described as Upper Wharfedale on Sea. Those of you who know this, one of Yorkshire's finest dales, might care to picture not a valley floor of river and water meadows, but of deep, sparkling fjord. That is the best I can do. You, the reader, will have to fill in the detail. To the untrained eye, a passage through all of this would have been impossible. Enormous trucks, cars, foot passengers ..... together, we willed our ferry through a confusion of water and rocky shores. Twisting this way, that way, each turn opened up another breathtaking vista. Out on deck for the full thirty minute crossing, I began the task of searching for adjectives that might begin to describe what I saw and felt. Dismissing submissions such as nice, pleasant, pretty, I went on to draw up a shortlist that included amazing, divine, impressive, incredible, indescribable, splendid. None having quite the impact I felt the situation demanded, on the point of re-advertising a late entry caught my attention. A short interview confirmed my gut feeling. Awesome was the only description that came close to meeting my criteria. Yet even this powerful word came only half way to conveying the humbling I felt, surrounded, by so much of nature's finest. Wet-eyed fellow that I am, places that beautiful are fraught with unique danger, as I said earlier. But weep as I might, the ferry was a reassuring place to be. Rising water level would be of no concern. Plainly better equipped for such beauty, the locals took it all in their stride. Unmoved through all of that splendour, it might have been the local bus into town: that much interest. In fairness, it is their local bus, their link with the rest of the country. Ten times each day, everything and everyone travelling in or out of Klaksvík, and the islands beyond, goes that way.

The hamlet I had expected grew as we approached. Like the schoolboy who failed to do his homework, sailing into a town with a population of

4,500 took me by surprise. Forming a flawless U shape round the head of a fjord so narrow that townsfolk on opposite sides might throw stones at one another, Klaksvík clings to the slopes as an infant clings to its mother. With the posture of rock strata, buildings follow the contours ..... reminiscent, in a frivolous fashion, of the grand Regency period crescents that visitors flock to see in Edinburgh or Bath. Grandiose plans, the equal of Victorian Britain's most flamboyant, envisaged both sides joined by a vast, transparent canopy. Flamboyant was fine with boom time money sloshing around freely in the eighties, though I guess that Klaksvík's population might be grateful, still, for fact that credit ran out before the glaziers moved in. Here was the most amazing harbour ..... large and bustling with activity as I had come to expect in a country married to the fishing industry. Shipping traffic on the go, fishing craft of every conceivable shape and size. Awash with the trappings of a vibrant industry. Cargo vessels, inter island ferries, craft no bigger than a poolside inflatable all vied for space in a scene that might have been a dance routine at a musical.

I never got to the campsite. Marked on the map, it was supposed to be somewhere near the swimming pool. The fellow at the Tourist Information office didn't know whether it would be open anyway. I wound up at the Youth Hostel in the company of more vintage youth. No more than a block or two from the harbour, checking in was something of an anti-climax. The sign indicated that I simply choose a room and put my belongings in there. Simple as that. No form filling. Nothing. Open to the world and his next door neighbour, it's good to be trusted, to be amongst people for whom trust is the norm. Leaving all my worldly goods unsecured was no drama. A short walk on the harbour side confirmed that I was exhausted. Just four hours sleep the night before had left me with the distinct feeling that I was just an innocent bystander to what my body was doing. Freely available, the antidote for traveller's haze is simple to apply; my walkabout was abandoned in favour of a rest and a meal. Normal services resumed after a short sleep, the convivial atmosphere of food preparation in a youth hostel kitchen kicked in. The American woman, the New Zealander ..... solo travellers all of us, we were of an age and found easy conversation on a ready made topic. I ought to have made the effort, got on my bike, ridden for miles. Or taken a bus tour, seen more of the region. Fact was that, sighted out, I was quite content to be in one place and couldn't muster the initiative for further foray.

So relaxed about the whole issue, a short evening walk amongst Klaksvík's night life was all I managed. Streets full to bursting, a bar here, a nightclub there. In every basement, a disco. Dreaming on, it was interesting to get a handle on the workings of an isolated community. Banks, schools, shops, health ..... all services and amenities are represented, some plainly diversifying to survive. Welding gear was displayed alongside car parts, stoves, and cookers. Second only to Tórshavn in population, Klaksvík's traders plainly have insufficient trade to justify specialising, but continue to provide the goods by opening up their businesses to a range of goods and services.

The reality of the town's night life is its absence. Youngsters make their own entertainment. In a region short on urban sprawl, the local tearaways have limited options for irritating the locals. Two screamed by on racy mopeds, throttles wide open, at all of 20 mph, and sure to excite the girls. More cruised by in expensive cool hatchbacks with tinted rear lights. But the rising young studs of Klaksvík plainly go for boats. A couple of teenagers whirled round the harbour in some kind of high powered craft, its nose so high out of the water it looked in danger of doing a wheelie. Spectator to these displays of plumage, groups of girls wearing tight jeans huddled together on the harbour front. Others took the task of locating those six packs and that all important triangular physique more seriously. Cruising the streets, regrouping in coffee bar or street corner, these would be the first to review what Moped boy was wearing, or Corsa man's disregard for road safety. Less concerned with being noticed, small groups of boys sat in quiet contemplation at the harbour side. Those too young for any of this had been issued with fishing rods, and plainly knew how to handle them if the shining, slippery, free meals lay beside them were anything to go by. I ought to have gone in for a beer, soaked in the atmosphere of a bar. My yardstick, when travelling is to select the beer most local to wherever I happen to be. In some small way it gives another fix on an area, in the same vein as specialist foods. Klaksvík has the Faroes' only brewery. But I was too tired to appreciate it, settling instead for my bed, but not before lingering just a little longer amongst the shipping and small boats of the town's dynamic harbour ..... a harbour that is the heart and soul of the local economy.

Leirvik ..... Brightly coloured craft of all shapes and sizes filled the harbour.

Towards Klaksvik ..... together, we willed our ferry through a confusion of water.

"Our reward for all of this was to sit in the farm kitchen with the regular hands, the stuff of Enid Blyton, drinking lashings of lemonade, eating crisps like they were going out of fashion."

34

Having been so lacklustre the day before I planned to explore the area before moving on. A notice had asked guests to fill in a card on arrival. What it didn't say was, in the absence of the warden, who or how we were to pay for the stay. Only next morning was I able to catch up with him. Quizzed as to where to leave my luggage while I went off for the morning, he was clearly puzzled by my concern. Right there in the unlocked, unattended foyer. Where it would await my return. It simply wasn't an issue. And I rather liked it. My intention had been to ride south on the shore of Borðoyarvík, the fjord that, together with the one Klaksvík is built around, almost cuts Borðoy in two. Lightly laden, it would have been a terrific ride. The map showed a surfaced road degenerating into a track that hugged the shore right out to the mouth of the fjord. I never got into that ride. Something wasn't working. Still a little tired. Whether it didn't qualify as part of my journey? Whatever the cause, my head wasn't putting pressure on to the right parts of my body and it became clear that what I really wanted to do was to get on with that ride to Gjógv on the most northerly tip of Eysturoy ..... part of a journey round the country as opposed to joy rides within it. The trip back to Leirvík was enchanting. Riding that ferry each and every day for the rest of my life, I could only begin to fully appreciate the majesty and sheer beauty of water and mountain so beautifully juxtaposed. And blessed, unusually, by bright sunshine for a second day. I guess it's not hip to shed a tear on account of all that natural beauty each time they pop into town. So, like the trip out the day before, with not a single ooh or aah the locals took it all in their stride once more. Not a tissue in sight. Like housewives on the bus into town for the week's groceries might chatter. Their men folk. What they did at the weekend. What they plan to do next weekend. And what time your daughter got home last night. Others passed the time in quiet, if malodorous, contemplation, with a cigarette or two. Travellers, each and every one. But the gulf between us immeasurable. Back in Leirvík the café had worked its spell ..... the prospect of coffee overwhelming the need to press on. Too late for breakfast, but they could do something for me as they would soon be starting lunches. All of this, I managed to establish in broken English and mime. The same technique with the menu found me, yet again, on the right side of endless coffee refills and the wrong side of a whole bundle of junk food. Freshly caught lurking around the nether regions of some far flung factory, the burger featured much that is awful about fast food. Apart from the fact that they didn't do fast. And although the chips went down well I regretted taking up the suggestion that they could do me something, and could only hope that it was thus because they hadn't got up to speed, what with it being early, like.

For the first time since arriving in The Faroes I had experienced difficulty communicating. And it was while waiting for my food to arrive that I contemplated the fact that a nation of just 46,000 has a language of its own. No prizes for guessing. It's Faroese ..... a derivative of Old Norse with shades of Gaelic, Icelandic and Norwegian for added value. Some speculate that Faroes is a derived from the word faar oy, or Sheep Island. It fits for, like Iceland, Irish monks and their sheep are thought to have been the islands' first inhabitants in the 7th century. They could have found nothing more remote, for it would be a hundred years and more before the Vikings spread out from Norway to colonise countries that are modern day Scandinavia in ethos. The Faroes found themselves roughly at the centre of this Empire, but like the other individual countries began to develop customs and a language of their own. Norwegian, itself later usurped by Danish power, saw exploitation that is the hallmark of colonisation the world over. Danish then became the official and written language of the islands. In the late 18th century scholars unearthed a language last written in medieval times. But only in 1890 was it finally adopted as standard Faroese. Now it is the official language of the Faroes ..... widely used locally alongside Danish ..... which everyone learns as well. In common with so many countries throughout the world, English is learned and spoken by many ..... a fact for which I was eternally grateful.

Outside, a couple of men were hay-making in a small field. With not a tractor in sight, this was hay-making like I used to do as a boy. Right beside my childhood semi was a steep field. In the good old days of proper winters I sledged there on snow that fell each and every year. I remember tying a torch on the front of my sledge so that I could go out at night. I remember being carried back through the garden gate that led on to the field. I remember the reason why. It was a boy-shaped hole in the asbestos garage at the bottom of that field. And I had just created it ..... concussing myself in the process. But in the summer we would be out there for a quite different reason. Dennis mowed the grass with his tractor, but from then on it would be down to us boys. With pitchforks bigger than ourselves we shook the grass out from the cut rows so that it would dry. Days later we raked it back into loose rows, then small stacks. And waited. Each day, pulling a two-wheel buggy carrying churns, Rose would bring milk to our homes. She would stop outside every house and wait while Dennis scooped milk from the churn and carried it into kitchens, to be poured into a waiting jug. Without command she would move on to the next house where the scene was repeated time and time again. It was Rose who hauled the Hay Cart. It was us boys that loaded her, wielding mighty pitchforks. Rammed into the stacks, twisted to get hold of a bundle, then up to the fellow on top who placed them, trod them down for the journey back to the farm. Just how much we could get on to the fork and carry to the cart for loading was a matter of pride. To be up on top, receiving and trampling it down on the cart was an important task that we all looked forward to as well. Stacked to the height of a young double-decker bus, we all clambered up for the ride back to the farm. Level for most of the way, the last few hundred yards was mightily steep. And between the strips of tarmac were cobbles, just so that horses could grip. Back at the farm it was our job to trample the hay down as it was thrown into the barn. Sitting in that café, almost fifty years on, I could smell the fresh hay, feel it on my legs, the bits that got in my shoes as we threw ourselves into the task of squashing it all down. But the best was still to come. Our reward for all of this was to sit in the farm kitchen with the regular hands, the stuff of Enid Blyton, drinking lashings of lemonade, eating crisps like they were going out of fashion. Small boys have much to regret in an age of high-tech plastic-wrapped hay. But I guess there are rules about small boys and pitchforks now. Once more, the travel had woven its magic. There's so much more to it than looking at things, ticking them off as though stocktaking at the supermarket. The momentary voyage into childhood had been good, a double edged sword though, for it did point to the fact that I was looking forward to getting home soon.

The idea whirled through my mind to incorporate them, make them part of the journey. But almost as quickly the plan fizzled out through lack of interest. Mountain tracks are fine. Fine that is ..... if I can carry my bike over the worst bits, wade through rivers with it held aloft. But carrying a whole bundle of kit turns that option on its head. Still ..... I could just take a peek. Back through the tunnel the sign at the junction pointed up a steep hill. Ahead of the game, 6 kilometres was no distance at all ..... what with Gjógv, my goal for the day, being a mere 20 miles away. My reward was a view that, like so many since arriving on the islands, took my breath away. At this point that I began to take seriously the business of repeatedly having my breath taken away. I was reminded of the catch phrase ..... the one when every parent shakes a wistful head ..... a shake reserved for those special occasions. The one I have drawn on before that warns of the perils of too much of a good thing. That said, those whose breath had been taken away by the sight that met me must have been removed. For only a breathless me sat at the top, overlooking the cluster of buildings that is Fuglafjørdur. As though stones had rolled down the sweeping green mountains behind and turned into buildings where they lay, the town, with its population of 1400, clusters round the head of yet another fjord. Saved the trouble of going there, of losing all that height only to climb back up again ..... through my spy glass I observed yet another settlement that looks to the sea for its livelihood. The colourful buildings and harbour, a large fish factory. And enough shipping to form a fleet. A presentation that is the exclusive preserve of Scandinavia. With no pressure on distance it was some time and a great deal of chocolate before leaving that comfortable hollow in the grass.

Back down the hill a whole lot of vehicles were parked at the roadside. Plainly something was afoot. Delighting in the luxury ..... the fact that I didn't have to ride another 80 miles by the end of the day ..... I stopped to investigate. With bike dropped into grass at the roadside and camera in hand I climbed the rough track that led up the hillside, and hadn't gone far before it became clear that this was a gathering of farming folks. Round the bend it became clearer still. Sheep shearing is a community event in these parts, I learned later. No high tech solutions, here, no g'day and away in moments for their annual haircut with electric shears. Some were crudely built of timber. Others were simpler still ..... plastic fish box with four legs bolted on, a ramp for access and, at the front, a pair of boards with a cut-out to anchor the neck firmly. Held shut by a bucket full of stones on a cord, they had shades of the stocks where petty criminals would have been held and pelted by angry villagers. Or the last an unfortunate French aristocrat might have seen before the guillotine did its work. Rounded up from the mountains in a team event by the local villagers, the sheep are penned. Here, they were discussing the latest styles and whether to go for an Afro, a simple Bob, or Spiked, maybe. Selected and dragged up the ramp by the horns, firmly clamped in position by the neck, most had clearly decided to keep it simple, chosen a crew cut. "Easier to keep clean," they bleated to one another. Two men set to work with hand shears taking, I guess, ten minutes for each. One poor creature had found it all too much and with all four legs bound together lay grumbling on the ground throughout her haircut. The local economy, I felt certain, was the last thing on her mind. That said, others, plainly of a more pragmatic persuasion, understood that luxuries like winter sheds for themselves and food on the table for their owners depended on the woollen industry. And if that meant standing in a fish box with your neck clamped tight, while two men stole your coat, then that's what they would do. If a job's worth doing, it's worth doing well. This, they undoubtedly understood, gravely accepting that humans know best.

Just yards down the road, the most exquisite harbour. Small, but perfectly formed ..... and behind it was a cluster of buildings clearly older than most I had come across. Norðragøta would hold on to me for some time as I ambled amongst beautifully maintained boats, before soaking in the charm of traditional buildings. Stone slates, pan tiles, thatch ..... they point to specific parts of the UK. Turf roofs are the traditional roofing material in the Faroes. With tree bark laid on timber for a base, turf forms the outer shell. Between them they provide a weather proof roof that, to an extent, insulates and, because of its weight, will not blow off. Modern restorations use a base of roofing felt. But those I came across had a little bark tucked in at the edges for effect. They'll never catch on though. Picture Basil Fawlty ducking and diving Sybil's lashing tongue, and proclaiming he was "just off to mow the roof dear." Or the Sunday morning set with that extra chore after the car's been washed. It was while examining the turf-roofed old church that we met. My bike had given it away. I had to be foreign. Plainly well known in the village, the upshot of our exchanges ..... after Jörgen got keys from the curator ..... was a personal guided tour. I signed the visitor's book just a few lines below that of Iceland's Prime Minister, who had been a guest of honour not many days previously. The museum is set in the oldest house in village. Built in the early 19th century, it is constructed of timber on a stone base, turf and bark roofed, timber lined, with a peat burning fire in the corner. In a country notable for an absence of trees, most early Faroese timber is either driftwood or shipwreck material, thus the building was filled with delightful locally made simple furniture that had a history even when it was new! Like many of the buildings in the village, the old church is a simple construction too. Timber built, stained near black, turf roof, and topped by a small white painted wooden spire. Much like others I'd seen, it was the sort of church a fairy princess might choose to marry the handsome woodman. That sort of magic place. But what with there being no trees he'd probably have to re-train if they intended to make a go of it and live happily ever after. Very basic, it possessed a certain ambience ..... but no windows on one wall on account of winter storms. And each pew had an electric heating bar under it. Plainly, the path to righteousness is a warm bottom. Once again, signing the visitor's book amongst the quiet calm of all that old timber, the Icelandic PM had beaten me to it. Little used now, a 24 million kronor (£2.4 million) replacement built a short distance away serves, as far as I could gather, the whole Gøta region, which encompasses two more villages besides. It was in this region, called Gøta, that Viking chieftain Trondur i Gøtu made a last stand against the Norwegian king and Faroese chief Sigmundar Bretison who were urging the population to embrace Christianity. That was a thousand years back but maybe it was on still their minds, for even when roughly divided by an exchange rate of ten, £2.4 million represents religious zeal on a grand scale for the 900 locals who paid for it. Joined by a couple on holiday from Malmo, Sweden, together we did the remainder of the tour, taking in the village hall for that little extra. Despite the fact that the three understood one another's languages they spoke in English for my benefit. In common with many of the newer homes, Jörgen's was three-storey, clad with painted timber and heated by oil. It could have been many places in the world but yet somehow a feel, a scent of the older turf-roofed ones hung in there. I felt honoured to be invited back there to share a beer. A big wheel in the local economy ..... fish, he went on, accounted for 90% of exports from The Faroes, much of it travelling by truck to Tórshavn, to be shipped

Firmly clamped in position by the neck, most had plainly decided to keep it simple.

One poor creature had found it all too much and with all four legs bound together, lay grumbling.

to Hartsholm in Denmark, or Scrabster for UK markets. Friend and neighbour, Ulf, walked in to join us for a beer. A fellow teacher whose home, like most of the population of the village, overlooks the sea, we talked a little of our work, before rapidly moving on to football. Jörgen is a Liverpool supporter. Ulf supports Manchester United. A thousand miles away from Anfield and Old Trafford, their wives listen to results on the radio so that they can anticipate the mood their husbands will be in, returning after watching the matches on satellite TV. Never one to miss out on a chance to discuss my favourite sport, I had to own up! That I cannot get my head round any of it was quite beyond them. But they couldn't understand why I take on huge physical challenges. It was one-all by the time I left and though the result might have been more conclusive if we'd gone into extra time I felt the need to get back on the road.

It was early evening by the time I left Norðragøta, but hadn't far to go. Alongside the Fjord, back up the hill and down to the road I had taken out of Toftir only the previous day ..... and a stop for a vista or two. It must have been longer than that. To have done so much. But no ..... it really had been less than thirty six hours ago. Hard work, losing my grip. Or what. No more than ten miles that day. And knackered. Coasting along beside Skálafjørdur it became clear. Despite resting in Seyðisfjörður ..... despite spending a day on the ferry. Despite riding only short distances for the past couple of days my body was still on high alert for vast energy demands. Equally vast, my metabolic rate. Yet all I'd had since mid-day was a bar of chocolate and a beer. So much had gone on that afternoon that this small factor had been overlooked. Like manna from heaven the restaurant-cum-filling station at the head of Skálafjørdur could not have been better placed.

It might have been a football match. The commentator on the radio was certainly giving it some. Flies past the winger. The centre forward does this. The left back does that. Then it's right back with the other ..... and the goalie didn't stand a chance. Screaming ecstatically into the microphone one moment, near weeping the next, it must have been a meeting of giants. Just what those giants were up to only became clear later. Faroese giants, plainly ..... the faces, the reactions of fellow diners made that clear. I was on the point of asking someone when all our attention was taken by a loud hooting of horns. Outside was a boat ..... best described as not unlike those lifeboats that feature in paintings of famous rescues at sea before the days of steam. And it was slowly making its way past the café. Odd, you might say ..... what with water being some distance away. The young men looked like they would know the score. Explaining the spectacle, they told of rowing contests between village teams. The boat and her crew of six, plus Cox, had just won a contest. Not just any contest, but an elimination round that got them one stage nearer the final. And they were driving round the island to prove it. Behind the horn-blaring Tonka truck containing the crew was a trailer on which the flag-strewn vessel rode. Everyone in the restaurant took a keen interest ..... the team was a local one. And they had a chance of winning the final.   Like a station after the last train has left, with the excitement over, it was with renewed vigour that the diners followed the race commentary again. Gasping on cue, the fact that it was a repeat, and the winners had just driven by appeared of little consequence. All of this with not a drunken supporter in sight. And police presence notable by its absence.

The meal put me on top of my game as well. Mountain passes, coasting alongside Funningsfjørdur for miles, climbing away from it on gradients so steep my front wheel lifted with each stroke of the pedals. The return on so much work? Difficult to quantify, but splendid isolation amongst lush green mountains, stunning vistas of sparkling water and mountain peak. If you like that sort of thing. But to speed down from open moorland, to drop through the deep valley towards Gjógv, my destination. That was the ultimate reward. I would have camped by the sea but there are rules about that sort of thing in The Faroes and, seeking directions for the camp site, wound up at the Youth Hostel. Worth visiting in its own right, it was timber-built in a style that might best be described as Alpine. And turf-roofed, with bark in evidence at its edges ..... where it should be. Inside were sleeping cubbies set into the eaves off a lounge area. Fantastic shower and toilet facilities tucked into similar spaces meant that the roof window opened onto grass. And a fantastic view of the sea filled gorge that is Gjógv. But having set up my tent on one of few flat sites on the area set aside, the brilliant kitchen for us campers demanded full attention. Here, I prepared my third full scale meal of day ..... in addition to breakfast, of course.

It was here that I caught up with the red Volkswagen camper. Not just any red VW, but a British registered one ..... last seen on the road to Búðardalur after missing the bus to the North West Fjords. Three weeks past. In Iceland. Then, I was rushing, insofar as it is possible to rush on a bike, to catch the ferry that would put me on the next bus to Ísafjörður and back on schedule. Peter and Liz hadn't noticed me, but I guess they were only following the Highway Code and the rule concerning disregard for cyclists. I'd seen so few British vehicles that theirs had stuck firmly in my memory. And now, here they were camping on the same site in the far north of The Faroes ..... passengers on the same ferry and stopover thing. It quickly became clear that we could skip most of the Brits on holiday routine and move to the next level. The pair were involved in a research project, and had spent their time in Iceland investigating climatic change over long periods. To this end they had travelled the length and breadth of the country, taking samples of peat for analysis. With a background in education, and a keen interest in the issues at stake, together we covered a good deal of ground in a short period of time, including the nature of a fellow that cycles in difficult places for no other reason than that they are there. All three of us agreed that our times in Iceland, and the short stay in The Faroes had been a rare privilege ..... a single glance from my tent would have been sufficient if ever proof was required ..... a seascape broken up by mountainous islands as far as the eye could see.

35

Narrow streets. Old world charm. Coloured timber buildings clinging to the steep sided valley. Gjógv is home to just sixty. A well mannered stream divided the village. Upstream from the diminutive bridge, steep green hills swept skywards on each side. Below, the tiny natural harbour, a beach of sorts. And gentle surf breaking on smooth, horizontal rock. How different it would be, I conjectured, on a stormy autumn day. Lured on by all of this, it was some time before dragging myself away to start a last ride. Only one thing remained ..... the dipping of fingers in the sea routine. That done, I'd gone no more than a few yards and they caught me red-handed taking a photograph. Despite the fact that it was a dull day with a little low cloud I was rapt by the view from the bridge. They insisted on me being in the frame and we did the camera swapping thing. Otto & Lisbet, Swedish musicians, worked in London at the time but had performed all over the world. The Dutch musician I had met four days earlier worked in Reykjavik. The message is clear: if you want to

Climbing away from Funningsfjørdur on gradients so steep the front wheel lifted with each stroke of the pedals.

Gjógv ..... home to just sixty. Narrow streets, Old world charm. A well mannered stream.

see the world, join an orchestra. Safer than the armed forces, though I guess there are hazards to be faced. In the wrong place, at the wrong time, and hit by a stray note ..... the consequences don't bear thinking about. Quickly recovering after being knocked out by my venture, the pair were pleased to have a little low-down on Iceland as they had considered visiting the country one day. Like the couple I had met only the previous day, their home was in Malmo. It occurred to me that a visit to The Faroes might just be compulsory for its townsfolk, much the same as those whose home is in the North of England are compelled to visit Blackpool Illuminations and eat fish and chips afterwards.

It was just forty miles back to Tórshavn, where I would camp before boarding the Norrona next morning. Not a big ride but this time my head really had got the idea it was all over. Climbing out of the deep valley was hard. That said it is a good feeling ..... knowing that it has to be all downhill from there. Realistically, in a country like The Faroes, that was never going to be the case. And there would be many more steep climbs and descents before cruising gently beside long fjords. Otto and Lisbet stopped in their hire car and like old friends we exchanged more pleasantries before saying final farewells. The fast descent had gone on for ever, but like the good tourist I stopped to take a peek. Through my spyglass it became a good deal clearer. Just offshore from the great lump of rock that is the peninsula called Kollur are two tall stacks. Turned to stone for their attempts to steal The Faroes some time ago, there to this day stand the giant and the witch.

Vast bleak upland, sweeping valleys with fjords at the bottom ..... where you'd expect them ..... gravity being what it is. Colourful villages tucked in there, seemingly in danger of tumbling into the water. Those are my firmest memories of a short stay. But there's always one that bucks the trend. I'd stopped to check how hot the rims were. Having blown patches off earlier owing to hot brakes, I was anxious to avoid a repeat performance. And there below, set on a narrow strip of low lying land between the bulk of Kollur and a mainland that swept down on the other, spread the village of Eiði. Home to six hundred, translated, the town's name points to the difference and describes a flat isthmus. The result is a more scattered community ..... quite unlike so many that huddle together for fear of falling. That was my impression as I ate lunch sheltered in a hollow on the hillside above. Situated at the mouth of Sundini, the narrow strip of water that divides Eysturoy from Streymoy, like so many places, the large harbour was plainly of huge importance to the town. Home to a variety of craft, being Sunday most were tied up, their crew nowhere to be seen and the place appeared deserted. I would have liked to have spent time there but a late start and the steep hills meant that in real terms I had covered little distance. Hot coffee brewed in a sheltered hollow ..... that was my compensation. The rest of the journey was uneventful, if a little tedious. Those unused to cycling might be forgiven for considering that a route that hugged the shore for 25 of the remaining 32 miles to Tórshavn would be a breeze. This is almost never the case. That journey was no exception, as time after time an endless series of deceptively steep hills found me taking off layers of clothing, only to put them on again for swift descents back to sea level. The temperature varied almost by the minute, one moment scudding clouds and cold ..... the next, watery sunshine. And calm. All of this, added to a head that already had me relaxing in a city bar with an expensive beer or three. If ever I needed proof for my hypothesis that what a body is capable of starts in the head, then this was it. Back in Iceland it had me half way up mountain passes before I'd even started, on opposite banks of fast moving rivers before dipping a toe in the water. But that 40 mile stretch to journey's end went down like a lead balloon. Over the huge bridge that leaps between the islands, back on Streymoy and riding down the western shore of Sundini. Then south west along the banks of Kollafjørður ..... that has given its name to the small town of 900 at its mouth. The tunnel is described in the guidebook as unsafe for cycling. Having taken the precaution of learning this only after my passage through it, once more with head torch and cycle lamps ablaze I sallied forth on a two mile subterranean mission, emerging to a hero's welcome. Dreaming on beside Kaldbaksfjørður, somewhat late in the proceedings my legs had got the message. A fine time, but better late than never. Together we sprinted those last seven miles, and in no time at all my tent was on active service once more.

Peter & Liz had beaten me to it, but we agreed to meet up later for a beer or two. He'd already checked them out. Camped close by, the Italian claimed to have been travelling for 4 years. To describe our dialogue as strange is to understate its content. The fellow wanted a woman. And within moments of setting it up he had been over to check out the contents of my tent. Realising that I was in no position to oblige either, he moved on to the next best thing. And for the second time in almost as many days I found myself involved in the fortunes of Manchester United. The reader might not be unaware by now of my competence in this area ..... and my scant resources for anything more than the most casual encounter. It was with not a little difficulty that I extracted myself from a one sided debate on the merits of players about whom I knew nothing. And no, I really didn't know where he might find a suitable woman ..... most, I learned, to his chagrin, turning up as half of a couple. On my own. And old enough to have been his father. Disappointment indeed! Like flies round a dung heap, the fellow had been difficult to shift. But it wasn't fibbing. By comparison, that awful dried risotto meal out of a packet ..... the last of my camp food ..... was interesting. And I really did need that shower.

A brisk 20 minute walk took us into the capital. Short on garish neon, Tórshavn is a charming city with a purposeful ambience. Old properties, narrow lanes and passages, steps to different levels. All this, plus the trappings of a modern city that has it all. Albeit, not entirely unexpectedly, on a small scale. Only three days had passed since rolling out of the ferry suffering from severe traveller's haze. Back, following a distilled tour of the country, having absorbed just a little of what the Faroes has to offer, it occurred to me that I was right back where I started. And Tiganes, the small peninsula that currently separates the international part, the Eastern harbour from the "domestic flights" Western harbour, is where The Faroes started. Here are buildings best described as vernacular ..... classic painted timber structures with roof profiles to match. And set to beguiling narrow streets. Settled in the early 9th century, Tiganes was established as the site of The Faroes earliest parliament ..... the Alþing ..... the People's Assembly, not unlike that in Iceland. And like the latter, it would have been here that disputes were settled, rules made and punishments inflicted on transgressors. It was here that Christianity was introduced to the islands around the first millennium. The advent of Norwegian power shortly afterwards saw a reduced role for the assembly. Danish rule from 1380 saw all its powers extinguished, to become little more then a royal court. And a Danish one at that. The Danes kept a tight grip on The Faroes throughout most of the period of their rule. Oppressive monopolies linked to the mainland shackled the economy. The third decade of the 16th century saw its population dragged through a Scandinavian edition of The Reformation ..... that saw the dissolution of a religious order and all its trappings.

With a monastery dissolution service well established back in the UK, all they had to do was ask. Handy hints on procedure. How to handle the media. What to do with dissenters. Henry would know just what to do. Notices advising that "the service from this monastery will be withdrawn" would be displayed. Others concerned with public safety would advise that "the path to righteousness had been re directed," and point out exciting ways of staying alive. Thus relieved of the Catholic Church, over a period of several years the islanders took on board the Protestant Lutheran Church, and Danish replaced Latin in matters ecclesiastical.

"The Colonist's Companion," a rough guide for those wishing to exploit the less fortunate. An early, and fanciful, publication, the rules were clear, unequivocal. Chapter one is simple and concerns itself with fortifications, defence. Safeguarded against Johnny Foreigner, the book goes on to discuss issues in detail. Solutions on land clearance. How to deal with its former owners. Remedies for shortage of labour back in the homeland. These, plus a whole raft of handy hints set standards that remain the bedrock of unpleasant (and others that ought to know better) administrations the world over. Monopolies. That's the key to it all. Get that right. Tell the locals there's only one outfit to deal with and you're laughing all the way to the bank. Nothing changes. Commercial exploitation by multinational corporation and supermarket alike ensures that the sweatshops of the world are alive and well. See the results of their efforts in a shop near you.

Taken over by no less a figure than the King of Denmark himself ..... from 1709 it became the Royal Trade Monopoly. That's the way it was. And only in 1856 did restrictions cease ..... when traders could, at last, deal on a level playing field. Since that time, the Faroese have developed as a trading nation in their own right. Home rule in 1948 was the final step on a path (or perhaps a sea lane) to current prosperity on the back of the fishing industry. And oil exploration ..... the new kid on the block ..... is a definite maybe at the time of writing.

Black tarred timber, brightly painted timber, turf roofs, corrugated metal roofs, concrete, glass. Ancient and modern. Set to the music of a bright green hillside that tumbles all around. It's all there side by side ..... a microcosm of all that makes a capital city. Conference facilities, theatre, sports facilities, quality restaurants. And more. But all we wanted was a beer or two. Like me, Peter and Liz were sighted out. And anyway I'd done the walkabout when the Norrona briefly tied up here a little short of five weeks past. But seemingly a lifetime. The café Natur, within a whisker of the harbour, sounded just the ticket. With few bars to choose from we liked the sound of it. Occasional live music, simple, tasteful. Expensive beer. What better way to wind up travel experiences that would forever be memories. Blow by blow reports are the stuff of personal diaries. Suffice, then with the fact that despite age difference, never was an evening better spent. Iceland, careers, ambitions, hopes for the future. All this and more. While between us we unloaded a mighty £35, the price of just three Foroya Bjors (beers) each.

Towards life in the fast lane

"Here, we spoke the same language, but the text didn't match. Like they were reading out loud and I had the wrong page."

36

Once I get the idea that it's home time I can't wait. It is said that we are products of our childhood, no matter how we deny it. I have wonderful memories of times at the seaside, of steep sandy tracks through tall bracken leading from the beach back to the caravan. And cliff top evening walks to Borth y Gest for an ice cream. With not an adult in sight. Happy days, yet I couldn't wait to get back home so that I could "get on". There were streams to be blocked, models to be made, trains to spot, dens to be built and camp fires to be lit outside them. Nothing has changed. Five weeks and some of the most exciting sights and challenges ever, but pub lunches, my lovely home, friends, projects and, of course, my wife and son. All were leeching at my spirits. The pub lunch, a pint of warm beer tomorrow. But the rest would have to wait. Realising that I was up against it, I vowed to have words with those in charge of ungrateful thoughts. The voyage, The Shetlands, The Orkney Islands, the train journey home ..... a holiday in its own right for many. And there was I wishing them away. These thoughts, and many others, had occupied my mind while going off to sleep the previous night. Waking far too early I gave them no further consideration. Nevertheless, it was a pensive traveller who finally rolled up the tent, loaded up the bike and rode into the city for a last look around the streets of Tórshavn before joining the ferry.

It's a thoroughly British thing to do. But it irritated the hell out of me. They knew perfectly well where the one and only bike would go. Yet had me waiting till last ..... standing there like a lemon while the cars went on board. If ever there was an award for the daftest rule, then this one would be in there with a chance. I am not the sort of fellow to go against the grain, but found myself sidling on to the loading bay and tying my bike to the side, exactly where it had been on previous legs of the journey. Then he saw me. Clearly in breach of the regulations, and outside again at the back of the queue, there I waited ..... only to be motioned back to exactly the same spot. The loading doors were clanking shut as I secured my bike with the blue plastic rope provided. Red tape, I sniggered, would have been more fitting. That vehicles should be positioned in disembarkation order is plain common sense. But I have yet to work out a reason for the bikes last on rule. That done, and just as quickly forgotten, I dashed up to the rear deck for the departure thing.

Bright, cold, blustery. And I wouldn't have missed it for the world. Green slopes provided the backdrop as buildings became blobs, cars turned into dots. The same fate befell the islands as they, too, turned to specs on the horizon. It might have been film running in reverse. Sixteen A5 size Yellow Pages take care of everything the country has to offer. Yet as our churning slipstream turned a nation into memories it occurred to me that I had barely got beyond the first entry.

It really was too cold to be out there, but it had become a sort of competition as to who would be the last to wimp out, go for the hot coffee option. It might have been the pier on a windy weekend. Sitting low enough it was just possible to keep out of the worst of it. Which is where deck chairs come in handy ..... if there's someone who knows how to handle one. With less than an ounce of acumen between us, it was some time, and a good deal of laughter, before we could relax. No one wanted to be the first with the knotted handkerchief. And in any case, the "News Chronicle" had been out of print for years. Some things are best left between the pages of family photograph albums. The Faroes had disappeared before the weather got the better of us. Then there was just me and a bunch of Norwegians. Who would be used to that sort of thing. Like so many I had come across, we were able to do the holiday routine ..... where we had been, where we would like to go if money was not an issue, where we live. And finally ..... what we do for a living and how could a young chap like me take six weeks out. The fellow had listened to me describing the fact that I run a part time business. Running a business. Now that's an odd concept ..... "isn't running some kind of leg-powered rapid transit?" By the time we abandoned the outside thing I had straightened out enough nuances with the English language to keep him in dinner-table banter for weeks. So, if you ever find yourself at dinner with a drunken fellow from Bergen who, Manuel from Barcelona like, tells you "I rrun a business", then you know where he was that day in July.

That done, the sticky bun and coffee went down a treat. But relaxing in the warmth of the caféteria I realised just how tired I was. My body was still coming to terms with the work it had done and I went off to my (day) cabin for a sleep. I had read of a Faroese diet that includes little or no vegetables, but the reality was worse. Late for the set caféteria lunch, the soup was fine. But beef served with rice, potatoes, and a non-descript sauce left much to be desired. Two carbohydrates and not a vegetable in sight. It was a Faroese ship after all.

I have said it before ..... the reality of sea travel is time to talk. And thirteen hours at sea allows for a deal of it. With the most surprising companions. The Australian had been staying with friends when the call went out. The Brits do a nice queue. Everything in the USA is bigger than it needs to be. The Italians drive too fast. But the Faroese have the edge on the rest of the world where it is concerned. International convention bans it. The Japanese call it scientific research. The Faroese call it culture. And on the back of that seven letter word, take it upon themselves to wreak violence on migrating pilot whales unaware of its wider interpretation in these parts. On hearing the call, an entire neighbourhood, drops whatever they are doing and takes to sea in boats. Surrounded, the pod of whales is driven ashore to be killed in shallow water, seemingly with anything that comes to hand: knives, hooks, harpoons. Dragged ashore from water red with blood, dozens of bodies are butchered for distribution amongst all who took part. With whale meat forming a substantial proportion of the Faroese diet, they do a nice culture and chips. International rules on mousing would, no doubt, make an exemption for cats. A worldwide ban on present-giving would, doubtless, do the same for the fellow in red that pops down the chimney once each year. So it goes on. And I had found myself talking to someone who had taken part in one. I could hardly believe my ears when he told me he'd eaten no vegetables for a week.

Swiftly moving on, it was with great pleasure that I discovered Danish money lurking in the bottom of my bum bag: sufficient for a visit to the bridge, and enough left over for a beer afterwards. No bearded fellow wrestling with a large wooden wheel. No demands for more power barked into tubes leading to the engine room. No film crew flinging buckets of water over the windows. It might have been the next door neighbour's front room where everyone had been invited to see the new double glazing: that much drama as 12,000 tons of the Norrona, her cargo of passengers, their vehicles, and my bike ploughed steadily towards Shetland. Only towards the end of the crossing did our paths cross. It was on the final approach to Lerwick that we said final farewells: Peter and Liz had been interesting company.

Fanfares were off. Lack of demand, it had been claimed. Time was that arrival at any old port up and down the country, and you couldn't move for trumpets. Foreign parts used to be the preserve of toffs. Signs everywhere shouted "no riff raff". Now, just about every Tom, Dick or Harry jets off, with no regard for the consequences. And they'd all come back with funny ideas as to what's to go in salad if Nora Batty was to be believed. There I was, back in the land of my birth. And not a soul to care. Beyond doubt, standards have fallen. But thoroughly British, though, was my ten o'clock in the evening arrival. Cool and blustery up there on deck to watch thoroughly British seaside pebbledash drift by while concrete and stone huddled side by side for warmth. Typically, mid-July and someone had turned the weather off. Harbour installations smiled weakly, apologetic almost, in a drabness that contrasted with brightly coloured buildings and stage sets of vivid green that I had left behind. Or was it simply my expectations ..... and reality back in Lerwick unchanged. That would explain it. And no, the oil workers accommodation barges hadn't been given a coat of extra dullness. It was me ..... touchy, senses finely honed. And wildly expecting things to be different. Then common sense chipped in ..... quietly at first as I trooped off the car deck and out through customs where, reassuringly, I had my passport scrutinised and someone in a uniform asked a question or two. Thoroughly British. Damn fine! By the time I'd got to the Youth Hostel, having ridden on the left, the sense of permanence that stone buildings engender had washed over me and I began to appreciate the place for what it was. That's the travel thing: it concerns contrasts. If everywhere was the same, no matter how delightful, the world would be less appealing by far.

Doubts crept in the moment I entered the Youth Hostel dormitory. Bunk beds for ten did not auger well. But back downstairs it was time to give consideration to food. The pub meal notion would not go away, but at ten thirty in the evening it was not an option. The other thing I had missed was spicy food. The hottest meal on the menu was what I asked for at the Indian Takeaway. Together with rice and a Nan bread, the softest, squishiest in the world, never was a meal and its porcelain plate more appreciated as the sweat rolled off my temples. Fast food, locking things up, chairs, tables, a washing machine, and TV: back to life in the fast lane. But broken down at the roadside and turning over every five minutes, the fellow in the bed above snored loudly in French, while the large bulge in the bed next to me grunted with an American accent. Service stations were plainly open 24/7. And didn't I just know it. Ten men in one room is a constant stream of visitors to the toilets.

37

It's one of the rules of engagement. Life in the fast lane life demands clean clothes. It would be four days before arriving home. There was no option. That done, having taken advice on how to get the most from my full day on Shetland it was to be Sumburgh, a little over twenty miles away. Windy and threatening rain. I'd been there, done that, seen the movie ..... so took the bus south. It didn't feel like I was cheating. With the main event well and truly in the bag, the Sumburgh Hotel, with a good reputation for bar meals and beer sounded just the ticket. Close by, the Iron Age settlement of Jarlshof would complete a grand day out. Streets with stone houses and their walled gardens, shops, offices. Common enough, you might say. But all these, and more ..... even traffic back on the left, demanded full attention as I walked into town. Dependent on others and dressed in civvies, contrasts with my self powered nomadic life of the past five weeks were brought into sharp focus as I waited at the *Viking* bus station. It was so easy. With fare handed over, a glittering whirl of pre-selector gearbox and mighty diesel engine roared into action to speed us through the countryside in a blur that was Gulberwick, Sandwick, Levenwick, and more. Scattered settlements, the remnants of crofting communities. And exciting coastal vistas that opened up beyond struggling green and moorland. Briefed on my mission, the driver pointed to the hotel. Two coaches had just discharged their cargo. Sharing a table, travellers each and every one of us, but I might have dropped in from outer space as I learned of their encounters and they, mine. I was reminded of the café a couple of days out from Reykjavik where I had been unable to share a word. Here, we spoke the same language, but the text didn't match. Like they were reading out loud and I had the wrong page. This hotel, that hotel. The time they stopped for a meal and it was cold. They'd had an hour here, a couple more there. And time to look in the shops. A million miles from my recent experiences, it was not easy concentrating on tales as exciting as this. But warm beer and roast beef with a double portion of vegetables makes an effective antidote for any amount of hotel talk.

Amongst English speakers once more, it was interesting to pick up accents. The couple from Hull didn't do it on purpose: it was that four letter word. There before I could stop it, an instant flashback had me on Manchester Victoria railway station ..... roughly twelve years old and listening to the nose pinched tone of station announcements. Passengers for wherever were to proceed to platform whatever, but hearing of destinations that included 'Uddersfield, 'Ull, 'Alifax, and 'Arrogate made me smile then. And nothing has changed. But I am easily amused: a single mention of a Hampshire address is all it takes for me to be reminded that in 'Ertford, 'Ereford and 'Ampshire, 'Urricanes 'ardly 'appen; and how kind it was to let me come! I guess I could have it treated. But I'd have to go private.

It would have been easy to dismiss those who, for whatever reason, choose to travel in bubble wrapped security as unadventurous. But everyone deserves the luxury of choice. The American family had chosen it because they would meet other people. And driving on the left would have been an issue. Some simply liked the idea that just for a week no decisions were required of them. Others, I know, choose it for the camaraderie, the company: a jolly group facing the finest that travel can throw at them. But make sure to be back on the bus by three! The scale of our differing demands was monumental. The surprise must be that they all shelter under a single umbrella called travel. Why I choose to do what I do, I will never know. It is madness. I know that.

Jarlshof, the Bronze Age settlement next to the beach, just a short walk away, was an eye opener. There I had to leave the travel mode for a while to appreciate the feeling that sites so ancient generate within me. Forgotten for centuries, only when gales blew away sand dune cover in the late 19th century was the importance of the site revealed. Today's visitors see grassed mounds, holes in the ground that reveal once-occupied chambers and a series of interconnecting passages. Layers of evidence of occupation by later generations are there for all to see. But most complete is the hulk of 16th century Old House of Sumburgh, once home to the local laird. Awesome is the expression that came to mind as I set eyes on structures that sheltered people three thousand years ago, stepped on floors they would have walked on. I could have spent

Jarlshof ..... Shetland Isles. Where I had to leave travel mode for a while.

Arrival in Stromness (Orkneys) ..... a town huddled together for warmth.

days investigating the ancient history of these parts. I ought to have spent time just up the road at the Old Scatness project, where another ancient site was being excavated. A strange combination of ancient and modern rubbed shoulders. Right behind, just a stones throw from the beach is Shetland's airport. Planes took off and landed while I was there. Provocative is the word that came to mind, 21st century technology flying just yards above that three-thousand-year-old site.

I ought to have spent time looking at any one of the bays, cliffs, beaches and settlements that surround Sumburgh. But the bus was due in half an hour. Besides, somewhere inside my head was the notion that I had seen enough for a time, and that the journey was over. Truth of the matter was that the hedonist in me sought simpler pastimes. And with this in mind set out for a short walk on the beach. It was good to see "proper" sand after so much black volcanic stuff. The wet-suited fellow out there was having a terrific time. An enthusiastic (and incredibly poor) surfer myself, the kite / sail attached to his harness fascinated me as the wind took him scudding through the waves. But like the grown up that stops all the fun and confiscates the ball, it literally, took the wind out of his sails. The official from the airport stopped him. I guess, though that it just might have been a problem for the authorities there. It might even have blown away, got caught in some vital installation in a worst case scenario. The fact that just one official came clambering over the sand dunes, I found reassuring. Thoroughly British, I considered, visualising a whole posse of armed, helmeted security staff that might all too easily have been the response in some parts of the world. With just time for a brief chat with the fellow I learned a little of the sport that he regards as a variant on surfing; another of his delights. Then the bus came.

Back in Lerwick I took a turn round the town. Not much of a shopper, nevertheless I did appreciate the pleasant ambience of a town with a sense of purpose. And a fish and chip shop. For £3.20 I was able to sit on the harbour and do the seaside thing. Only the boat drew me like a magnet and they were almost cold by the time I got round to eating them. He had built it himself to a 1902 design, a classic that had caught my practical eye. Standing close by one minute: invited aboard and discussing construction techniques with her Norwegian owner / builder the next. Timber built throughout, with good deal of laminated work for the shaped and heavier sections, I delighted in the company of so much craftsmanship. Following a potted account of her construction I learned that together with his wife and another couple they had just sailed her from Bergen, and were about to leave for the return trip via Stavanger, a little further south.

Not sure of my plans for next day, I bought a couple of days' worth of food before returning to the hostel. My ferry for Orkney left at 12 midday for the 8 hour crossing to Stromness and I didn't want to waste the morning in supermarkets. I had picked up a leaflet somewhere on my travels in Shetland, and tonight was the night. Tuesday at the *Douglas Arms* for free "Traditional Unplugged Shetland music," the advert stated. Unmissable. But would it be worth hanging around in a smoke filled bar? The reality was worse. It might have been a railway tunnel in the steam age. With headlines that shouted lung disease, a stinking blue fog lay thick over the proceedings. And the band was late ..... weren't coming at all, it turned out. But with that, a couple of chaps that had brought instruments along for a bash with the band played on their own. With the real band unplugged, just as the advert had claimed, the accordion and guitar was the closest we got. But it did round off the Shetland thing nicely. Full to capacity with oil workers and almost as many accents, before succumbing to the smoke I spoke with a group of them about a way of life that was a million miles from my own. In a somewhat disjointed conversation I learned of a lifestyle that involves a free flight home every three weeks, of hard physical work in between. And living quarters shared with men on opposite shifts. Regular travellers, each and every one of us. But worlds apart, I concluded. Try as I might, a handle on their world was difficult to grasp. But I got the feeling that mine was just as hard for them. It makes you think. It should. Looking back, there had been two kinds of reaction to my venture. The "wow, bet it was hard", exciting, eyes wide open: that sort. And the blank nod, like they haven't heard, don't know how to respond. Or perhaps, have no conception, no association, nothing in memory bank that enables them to log on to a rationale that make a fellow push himself so hard for no other reason than the fact that out there is a challenge. A kind of out-of-control part of one's nature. Back at the chalk face, my report on the evening might well be as follows: "Works hard all the time, but really does need to look beyond his immediate surroundings if he is to take in the broader picture". It is my firm belief that the whole of one's life should be regarded as a learning experience ..... an experience that should spread beyond the rantings and bigotry of the tabloid press.

A bunch of ferry passengers arrived at two a.m. Being a considerate lot, they rustled quietly in Danish. Nonetheless, hostel life is home to all sorts of advantages. And I had made full use of them. Including watching the TV news and "East Enders." But having been so far removed from both reality and soap, neither connected. I was already anticipating the personal, if small, space that would be a full night's sleep back in my tent ..... somewhere on Orkney.

"Back in the frame, that feeling of what happens next had injected fresh spirit into those last few days before arriving home."

38

One of the advantages of a sleepless night ..... just about the only one, apart from the prospect of passionate encounter, is the fact that a whole lot of issues get an airing. Not unreasonably, one of the topics covered was my imminent journey home. And how to get the most from it. Scheduled to arrive in Stromness on Orkney at eight o clock next evening and leaving a couple of days later for the overnight crossing back to Aberdeen, I had a train ticket home on the Saturday. Never one for out and back trips, the notion that I might sail to the north coast of mainland Scotland at Scrabster bubbled to the surface. That was as far as it had got. Disturbed nights so often score a double whammy that results in waking ridiculously early as well, unable to settle. But it afforded an opportunity to straighten out a couple of issues, a brief visit to Bressay being one of them.

With time only for a brief exploration of Lerwick, I was drawn back to Commercial Street. Seriously unromantic by name, I discovered that it extended south; paved, still, with stone slabs, it plays host to numerous interesting buildings, together with vistas over Bressay Sound and the island beyond. And in a mild outbreak of "been there, done that" tourism I boarded the ferry for the five minute trip there. The shortest of rides afforded vistas of the Sound, this time with Lerwick as the backdrop. Seven miles by three, currently home to roughly 400, Bressay is far removed from the soft bustle just minutes away over the water where most of its population work. Boats nodded gently at their moorings as I pedalled beside quiet inlets from the sea and the scattered communities they had spawned. Despite the fact that it was a seriously ordinary dull kind of day, I got just a hint of island life. The guide book tells of wildlife a plenty, gently rounded hills, dramatic sea cliffs and caves. I saw little of these attractions and, furtively avoiding the Heritage Centre, the brevity of my visit went unnoticed.

Riding back to the main ferry terminal was different. Just how or why, I wasn't sure. In reality it was just another in a whole series of doing this, that or the other for the last time: it is the thing called travel. But it had been these streets that I had ridden late that night at the start of my adventure. And approaching the harbour it felt like the whole thing was folding in. Emotions like that can only fester in the vacuum of uncertainty. Getting organised for what comes next occasions their spontaneous evaporation. Check in procedure and boarding pass sorted, I could finally get to grips with the re-scheduling that had been my disturbed night in the hostel. And in one of those "it was meant to be" moments I learned of a ferry route that would turn a simple sightseeing visit into part of the journey. A passengers-only ferry from the southern tip of South Ronaldsay crosses the Pentland Firth and docks at John o'Groats, mainland Scotland's most northerly town, a mere twenty miles from Britain's most northerly railway station in Thurso. From there I would travel to Aberdeen, and pick up the train home. A fine way to round off my North Atlantic travels. Quite why I hadn't thought of it first I would never understand. But the fact was that out of nowhere my journey had been rejuvenated, it had come alive again. The couple had just completed the Land's End to John o'Groats trip on their tandem. They had allowed themselves twenty days, but having completed it in eighteen, crossed to Orkney, then Shetland just so they could let a fellow know about the Pentland Firth crossing! The young German cyclist had sailed from Bergen to the Shetlands. Like me, he had just learned of it and would ride south on Orkney for the start of a long trip that would take in much of mainland Northern Scotland. Age, we agreed did not enter the equation. Retired, like me, the couple regarded life as a journey. But journeys can be very different, the route can vary enormously. You only get something out of those journeys if you put something in to them. Life, we agreed is much the same. And to hear someone less than half our age say much the same was encouragement indeed. Like me, the others had coped with breakdowns: they come as part of the package. Cyclists must be amongst a minority of travellers these days who still carry tools and have the skills to use them for roadside repairs. Certainly, although ever more reliable, with modern cars this is increasingly difficult, near impossible as high tech takes over from carburettors, distributors and the like that could be fixed with basic knowledge and equipment. A spirit, a certain camaraderie joins cyclists. I was reminded of something my travelling companion back in the Western Fjords of Iceland had mentioned. Cycling in Norway, a bad puncture had wrecked his tyre, but in no time he had bought a spare from another cyclist who had taken the trouble to stop. Helpful, practical chap that I am, time was when I would stop to help out stranded motorists. Is it something I'd do in the twenty-first century? Dam right, it's not. Goodness only knows what I might be accused of in a society whose media delights in turning up the heat on otherwise innocuous situations, on the back of increased sales.

Having watched yet another flotilla of islands turn into specks on the horizon before finally disappearing, I settled down for the rest of the eight hour crossing. Maps are the essential ingredient without which travel becomes a game of chance. But for the touring cyclist, their added bulk is just one more item that needs carrying. With only couple of days each on Shetland and Orkney I had settled for lightweight maps, given free of charge by the tourist authorities but, at best, limited in what they can show. Pouring over detailed maps, the Italian and his wife were planning an itinerary for their stay on Orkney. After discussing routes and respective immediate plans we went on to discuss travel in general. Once again, the confines of sea travel turned out to be the vehicle, the catalyst for deep(ish) and meaningful conversation. Through the "what do you do" routine in a flash, a mining engineer by trade, he was attracted, like me, to the cooler countries.   How we got there, I never knew, apart from the fact that the nature of people interested both of us, and I knew little enough of Italy and its people. A voyage of discovery, then, we landed first on finance. The lira, like the other European Union currencies, with one notable exception, was in its death throes. Five months, and the Euro would come marching in but Italy, I learned, was offering little resistance and looking forward to the trading advantages a common currency would bring. Quizzed on the reasons for the UK sticking with Sterling, the obvious next port of call was politics. Forming an orderly queue is a thoroughly British notion. Those who seek solace in that quaint concept will be disappointed in Italy. Where orderly queues are notable by their absence. It is an unnatural concept for Italians. Skiers amongst you will bring to mind the disorganised scramble that precedes Poma or Chairlift. This philosophy, a reflection of human nature, apparently spills over into politics. And in the rush, an incredible number of parties have been known to throw themselves into the contest that is an election. As electoral procedure at differing levels was explained to me I could well believe it. Thoroughly democratic in principle, the subject of recent reform, yet he concluded that the ski lift queue analogy summed it all up nicely. All of this, allied to my somewhat limited hypotheses on the British political scene kept us deep in conversation for some time. I guess that there were inaccuracies on both sides. That is one of the perils of illuminating, if transient encounters. I don't recall how we wound it up, but guess that one of us wanted to go up on deck, go for a drink, or something. But I had appreciated hearing about the scene from the shop floor, so to speak, as opposed some political commentator in the media.

Almost everyone else had one. Reading is one of life's luxuries, and I had missed having books with me. In a week's time I would be in the Channel Islands ..... staying in a hotel with my wife. Where I would read like it was going out of fashion. And it might even be warm! The contrast with my life for the past six weeks would be near-unimaginable.

In jaunty fashion that had shades of Pathé News the film presentation on The Orkneys told of attractions unlimited, most of which I would miss. But it did put me in the picture, so to speak, for at best, travelling can only hope to give the briefest insight on the world of others. Seven hours into the crossing I found the non-smoking lounge. Away from the pernicious smell that some regard as their right, I was able to appreciate our approach to Orkney in comfort.

The weather had deteriorated. By early evening we were ploughing through heavy swell. Up on deck strong wind and squally rain was my first impression of Orkney as the main island drifted by to port and we made final approaches to Stromness. Departure and arrival are focal points of sea travel and, for me, particular joys. In between, there is time to draw a veil over things past. And time to anticipate what is to come. Shetland had disappeared as specks off the radar screen. Appearing as from nowhere The Orkneys had developed form, become the scattered island home for roughly 20,000. At its extreme limits are North Ronaldsay and South Ronaldsay. Lying somewhere between them is Mainland, the largest island, where most of the population live. And washing its southern shore, further sheltered by the islands of Hoy, Flotta and Burray lies evocative Scapa Flow.

In Stromness, relatives and friends were waiting. After meeting up with their folks they would be whisked away, have meals placed before them. Later they would sit in front of fires on a cool, stormy evening to share tales of what happened when they were away. Or how long it had been since they last stayed. In contrast, I saw a town huddled together for warmth under a sky that looked as though it was about to fall in on us all. Wet stone buildings spoke of warmth within while in the harbour increasing wind played on the surface of the water. People wore hats, had hoods over their heads, drew themselves in against the weather.

After cancelling my crossing back to Aberdeen I rode away from the harbour, taking directions for the camp site. Back out in the weather it didn't seem anything like as bad. With an immediate goal in mind I was back in charge and no longer prey to negative emotions. Just one block from the sea front the road seemingly went on for ever. It reminded me of the narrow winding streets of Cornwall's fishing communities. Paved, like Lerwick's main street, in large stone slabs and lined on both sides with solid buildings, it could have been a scene from a hundred, maybe two hundred years ago. Between the buildings passages led down to the sea, where fishing gear was stacked, or someone had turned their yard into a walled garden. Beyond were boats of every shape and size at their moorings and green hills sweeping down beyond. Fascinated by all of this, the weather quite forgotten, it was with some surprise that I left the shelter of the town to find myself on a very exposed camp site next to the sea shore. I could have put my tent up behind the wall. I should have put my tent up behind the wall. But it would be much more exciting sleeping at the water's edge. Raised above the sea, much as the ha ha lifts a formal garden above its surroundings, it had all the potential for an interesting night. The view and accompanying soundtrack did it. To cook my evening meal while the wind and rain lashed down outside. To settle down and record my thoughts with the gentle hiss and flicker of my stove for company. To hear the sea swilling against the wall just a few feet away. All this, plus the luxury of uncontested sleep: it was good to have my own space again. Reflection time again ..... and from the warmth of my sleeping bag, while considering a *résumé* on the whole of my life to date, it occurred to me that quality rather than quantity might be more suited to the occasion. A short reflection, perhaps no more than a glance in the mirror concerning the last couple of days promised moments of endless fun. But seconds into the exercise it occurred to me that I would almost certainly fall asleep before the end. And then what would people say? Putting the tent up earlier had been interesting:

that's where I would start the reflection. And if I was still awake, then I'd give tomorrow's agenda some consideration. Wind rushed along the shoreline. There had never been any doubt as to how to position it. So, with flysheet unrolled and flapping on mown grass, the immediate task was to peg it down at the stern, allow it to blow downwind from there. With poles inserted and wind in its tail, it became three dimensional at a stroke and tugging to break free. Working under pressure, in moments I had the outer tent anchored down, kit thrown under cover. Quickly clambering in behind, in no time the inner tent was pegged out and suspended from the poles. It is always a good moment. With outer zips pulled shut, that moment when I unzip the inner tent and, with wet outer clothing tossed into the storage area, clamber in to unpack and play house. At a stroke, all that weather is out there. That had been hours before. The storm had got worse since then. A strong, low mountain tent firmly pegged down is a wonderful place to be on night such as that. Simple things take on new meaning in a tiny space that passes for home. It is an invitation to contemplate, a time to savour. The crossing back to Aberdeen cancelled, to an extent I was out on a limb again and thriving on that hint of uncertainty. Unexpectedly, the last part of the trip had turned into a journey again. Back in the frame, that feeling of what happens next had injected fresh spirit into those last few days before arriving home. And, still something of a novelty, I could go for a pee under the cover of darkness. Then slept to the sound of wind, rain and thrashing sea.

And a little culture

"It was some time before I made it inside. Before doing that, I needed to soak in that aura, that special feeling radiated by and exclusive to ancient buildings representing so much effort and skill."

39

Having slept amazingly well through the storm it was still pouring down. Taking rather longer than usual before getting on the road paid off, for coasting back through Stromness the rain, too, had eased. The harbour, once again, drew me like a magnet. Railway stations have the same effect. I guess it's their association with travel, the atmosphere, that sense of anticipation that such places engender. Fantasy facilitators. A hang over from childhood. Perhaps? A ferry across the Pentland Firth at 5.15 that evening meant a relaxed rest-of-the-day, and a little under 45 miles riding. Often enough, all I feel the need to do is to walk amongst the streets of a place, to absorb the sights and sounds, to take on board an aura. And that is exactly what I did, but not before locking my bike firmly to a lamp post. For me, no amount of tourist trinkets or media experience comes close to this. And it's a whole lot cheaper. Neither was I drawn to lip-pouting fresh coffee. Or flaunted cleavage that is a sticky bun. But these are assessed separately and it was down to pure good fortune that my wallet remained closed. I don't do temptation at all well, and with that in mind it wasn't long before pedalling out of town.

Short on trees, Orkney makes up for the deficit with rolling green hills, prehistoric antiquities, rare birds. And coastline. 570 miles of it surround just 376 square miles of islands. A mere 20 miles off the Scottish mainland, where the North Sea meets the Atlantic, some 70 islands, 18 of which are inhabited, make up the group. Evidence of occupation from the 4th millennium BC can be seen. Small communities from mainland Scotland are thought to have been the islands' first inhabitants, later developing into tribal units, with all the baggage that follows. Traces of development through Bronze and Iron ages are to be found, evidenced by ancient food preparation debris, the remains of stone buildings, burial chambers. And more. By 600 BC, massive fortified round towers, now known as brochs, were appearing. Tribes were plainly developing skills that would provide endless hours of fun 2000 years later. Only the name has changed. They call it football these days, so I guess all that practice in tribalism still comes in handy. And it's always best to plan well ahead.

It is thought that descendents of those responsible for constructing the brochs were the northern branch of the Picts, that unruly band, the rationale behind Emperor Hadrian's massive erection. Twenty feet high in its heyday, and extending from the Solway Firth to the Tyne estuary, it was designed to keep out those pillaging Picts. The Romans plainly considered the Picts to be a bad lot. Even today, almost two thousand years on, the wall remains a powerful feature on the landscape, a reminder of the regard that opposing factions felt for one another. Similar technology, forts and all, was applied in 1961 as Germany felt the breath of the Cold War. A similarly powerful and symbolic reality it, too, outlived its usefulness to be removed thirty years later in the re-unification exercise that followed the demise of the communist bloc of Eastern Europe. Orkney remained a wall-free zone. The Romans never made it that far north. That honour fell to the Vikings, who began to colonise the islands in the 8th century. On the sea route from Norway to Ireland, like Shetland the Orkneys saw considerable change. Pagan Vikings arrived on islands that had only relatively recently taken Christianity on board. Little hard evidence can be found concerning those early days of colonisation. Historians have postulated on the possibility that the Picts were annihilated, brutally disposed of to make way for a new order. Certainly, there are few signs that the two factions lived in harmony, and some speculate on the possibility that vanquished Picts were enslaved by their victors. A great many more signs point to a complete take over. Those signs can be found without recourse to archaeology. For, almost without exception, Orcadian place names can be traced back to Norse roots. Christianity caught up with the islands again around the first millennium, and Scandinavian rule persisted until 1468 when, like Shetland, they passed to the Scottish crown as part of the marriage settlement between James III of Scotland and Margaret, the daughter of King Christian I of Norway and Denmark.

I enjoyed the ride to Kirkwall immensely. Up and down rolling green hills, the roadside, a riot of wild flowers, the like of which I had not seen for weeks. It all reminded me of home, apart from the certain knowledge that the sea lay just beyond the horizon which ever direction I cared to look. And approaching Finstown, having crossed the island from west to east, there it was, shining in the morning sun. Then it rained. A special kind of rain reserved for small islands when there is nothing to prevent sudden squalls rushing in from the sea. A bus shelter comes in very handy at times like these. After drying up as quickly as it came, I cruised along the coast road that would take me to the capital, Kirkwall, and a pub lunch.

Heavy traffic built up on fast dual carriageways that ducked and dived on a series of concrete underpasses and flyovers. Major junctions, multi lane roundabouts, electronic lane control from overhead gantries meant that I had to keep a sharp eye on road signs. A wrong lane would have placed me miles off beam before being able to turn round and try again. Following signs for the city centre, successfully through suburbia, with traffic intensifying, towering office blocks every which way, then suddenly, the flashing neon glitz of a thriving city that is going places. I could go on to describe a city brimming with big name shops. I could describe a city alive with trendy bars, a reputation for racy nightlife, a chic city where people like to be seen. Fact is that like all that nonsense about suburbia, it would be untrue.

The reality of the situation was a gentle ride through semi-rural suburbs that quickly found me overlooking the crescent that is Kirkwall's sea front and harbour. Backed by solid looking stone buildings that looked like they could withstand a storm or two, like other island settlements I had come across, this was a settlement that plainly looked to the sea for much of its livelihood. First, a walk on the harbour. Fishing boats, ferries linking with outer islands. And a lifeboat that shouted "come take a look!" It bristled with technology, was self-righting, fitted with propeller guards, plus all the knobs and whistles. The kind of machine that almost makes a fellow's eyes water. If you can begin to appreciate emotions like that. It still amazes me when I am reminded that lifeboats are manned by volunteer crews. But that said, I can get my head round the business of being a volunteer, so guess I'm less amazed already.

The ferry was just leaving for one of the smaller islands. To watch boats is to dream. In moments I had it. Rocky shore, sandy beach, small harbour. And behind, in the tiny village, white painted houses with corrugated metal roofs set against the weather. The real world caught up with me before getting any further into the fantasy. But so far from the shops my wife wouldn't have liked it anyway.

Kirkwall is a tiny city and royal burgh. Together with its population of around 6000, it is the administrative centre for the Orkneys. Being an island economy the port is kept busy with the necessities of life, agricultural exports and, like Shetland, the oil industry. But it was the cathedral I wanted to see. Not much of a city person, not much of a culture vulture at all. But I miss it when it's not there. Once more it put me in mind of the year spent teaching in Tasmania, Australia's island state.

A wonderful experience, summed up, to an extent, by the fact that my surf board lived on the roof rack of our car so that, at a moment's notice, after work I could pop down to the beach to ride Pacific surf. In the boot we carried a plough disc. Set up between a couple of rocks down at the beach, a fire beneath. An instant barbeque. An enviable lifestyle in a year that included surfing in Bali and skiing in New Zealand. But perhaps the highlight, the grand finale that remains with me almost as much as all the rest put together was our visit to China on the way home. All of us had the most amazing year, a year when I would pinch myself to make sure it wasn't a dream. That it really was me watching a performance at the Sydney opera house. That I did swim in New Zealand's naturally heated pools. That I surfed from Kuta beach. Childhood had taught me that these were things reserved for other people. And folks like us didn't do that sort of thing.

But to take the train from Hong Kong for Guangzhou. To fly out to Xian, to walk into a covered arena that housed the Terracotta Warriors, excavated for all to see. That is an experience I will never forget. Besides building the Great Wall, Emperor Shi Huang unified China, had three quarters of a million conscripts working for 36 years on his tomb. In death he demanded to be guarded. His ancestors had insisted on being entombed with live slaves, warriors, horses, weapons. The higher the rank, the more would be required to make the ultimate sacrifice. Humanitarian Emperor Qin Shi settled for life size clay replicas. Re-discovered in 1974, many have been restored and stand, once more, in battle formation under a canopy the size of a football stadium. More than 2000 years old, the figures are truly remarkably in their accuracy and their sheer presence, right down to individual expressions. After so long away from anything approaching that level of antiquity or culture, it is an experience that I will cherish for all time.

Stepping inside St. Magnus Cathedral after the empty vastness of Iceland and all that had followed, I was keenly aware of the contrast it offered. Memories of seeing the Terracotta warriors. And their contrast with anything the previous year had offered. Approaching that ancient building on stone paved streets that set the shop fronts off beautifully, the analogy had seemingly sprung out of nowhere. Suddenly it was there, right in front of me. Possessing an aura that might have been borrowed from York or, perhaps Ely, it took me by surprise. Island culture had grown to mean small, vernacular, craggy seascapes, beaches. But here, just yards away from all of that, a magnificent building that might have been there for ever. Dating back to 1137, one could be forgiven for thinking that it has. It was some time before I made it inside. Before doing that, I needed to soak in that aura, that special feeling radiated by and exclusive to ancient buildings representing so much effort and skill. A mass of timber staging. Ropes on wooden pulleys. Hundreds of chisel-wielding workers swarming over the site. A stream of horses bringing endless supplies. My mind had gone into overdrive producing those images. But to step inside was to enter another world. Peaceful beyond words, I sat down and allowed the silence inside my head. It is probably unfair to make comparisons, but to see such craftsmanship, such attention to detail, such devotion to the pursuit of belief and worship was to invite them. The closest I got was icebergs, I conjectured, as images of their natural presence and raw, untamed beauty flashed through my mind. And what a privilege to have witnessed both on the same journey. I had to remind myself where I was. Some would contend that such magnificence could only be found at the heart of Europe's finest ancient cities. But perhaps it is, I argued!

Back outside it was lunch time. Sitting beside a coal fire in "The Bothy Bar", on the right side of roast beef with all the trimmings and hand-pulled beer, the world was, indeed, a wonderful place. An un-prepossessing place to look at, I would never have considered it. But a little local recommendation goes a long way. Try it when you travel. It has the edge on any guide book. Several more pints of that wonderfully smooth ale would have gone down a treat, but my legs don't work too well after alcohol. So it was with regret that I left it all behind for the road south. If I'd stayed behind long enough there was to be a band. "Rocking in the Isles," the evening was billed. I'm a sucker for play on word, double meanings, unspoken innuendo. And it made me smile.

Time, now, for nothing more than a parting perambulation amongst all that stone. Small, but perfectly formed, a certain confidence, an air not so much of the trendy place for the chap about town, neither market town full of farmers stocking up for the week. But somewhere in between. The capital. All things to all people. It wasn't late, neither was there time to spare, but I couldn't leave before another look at the harbour. And twenty-five miles was going to be a long way if there were a lot of hills. The whisky distillery was offering tours. But no, there really wasn't time. And with that I swept (slowly) out of town, heading south.

I knew about Scapa Flow. Who doesn't? Something to do with the war. But just how much of a something, I was about to find out. My first glimpse was from the headland south of Kirkwall. There it was. Seemingly enclosed on all sides. Accessible only through narrow passages between islands. An important base for allied shipping in both world wars, the Vikings, too, knew about Scapa Flow ..... a vast natural harbour that has been used for centuries. The Germans knew about it too. And early on in the First World War, a U- boat managed to evade its defences. As a result of this, decrepit ships were scuttled at strategic points and anti submarine nets positioned. It was from Scapa Flow that the Grand Fleet sailed in 1916 to engage the German High Seas Fleet in the Battle of Jutland. An inconclusive result at the time saw thousands lost, and a German fleet that never again witnessed active service, only to return for internment after the November 1918 armistice. Ten months later in June 1919, with surrender terms irrevocable, under orders from the German officer in command at Scapa Flow, the entire fleet was scuttled, with further loss of life. Most of the ships were eventually salvaged, but death and destruction did not end there. In 1939, in the first month of World War 11, a German U boat penetrated defences once again, to sink HMS Royal Oak and drown over 800. The submarine had slipped through Holme Sound, the gap between Orkney Mainland and Burray. This resulted in further defences and more blockships, but the final piece in the jigsaw was a series of causeways linking the island chain, and finally cutting off eastern access to the strategically placed harbour. Those causeways are the modern road. And I was riding on it. I have commented before on the fact that places that are witness to high drama, to human suffering on a monumental scale have an aura that never leaves. Tasmania's (it was known as Van Diemens Land then) Port Arthur, its genteel parkland and crumbling ruins, Is thin disguise for the personal tragedy of convicts unfortunate enough to wind up there so many years before. Beautifully tended military cemeteries of Northern France tell their own tale. Royal Oak is a designated war grave, too. Rusting remains of scuttled shipping broke the surface of the water like the arm of a drowning man, a stark reminder of what people are capable of doing to fellow human beings. The futility that is war. Call it what you will. Call them ghosts. Think of it as a feeling that leaks to the surface ..... still. But riding gently past the remnants of violent times on that cool, grey afternoon was an uncanny experience. The chapel at Lamb Holm was odd in a different kind of way; constructed within a Nissen hut, its worshippers were Italian prisoners of war. The visitor could be forgiven for thinking that he or she had stepped inside from an Italian village, such is the transformation, the ambience, the feeling of tranquillity. Ingeniously conceived and carried out with whatever materials came to hand, the illusion, the stage set appears real enough. Contrasting sixty years on with the reality outside, the rest was for my mind to create. Neighbouring huts, a rail network, security fencing, and the rest ..... for what was, essentially a labour camp and industrial site for the causeway construction project.

Technically, islands no more, almost five miles of causeway found me on South Ronaldsay and just ten miles from the John o'Groats ferry at Burwick on the southern tip. Waiting to leave from St Margaret's Hope was another ferry that I had learned of only the previous day. A vehicle and passenger vessel, for £12 it would have deposited me at Gills bay, just a short distance west of John o'Groats, and well placed for Thurso. It would have saved almost fifteen miles of riding and have me arriving in Thurso earlier than anticipated. But I'd never been to John o'Groats, and it is mainland Britain's most northerly town, or realistically speaking, cluster of buildings. And it's the sort of thing I do.

We had both decided to cross the Pentland Firth in order to see John o'Groats. I guess that the operators see it as a niche market and charge accordingly. He had dismissed the service from St Margaret's Hope for the same reason as me, and now we were part of a captive audience, along with passengers from the bus. I could scarcely believe a £19 fare for the forty minute crossing but, with no alternative available, handed over the cash. Tim, from Hamburg, too, was knocked out by the fare. It was here that, with nothing more than an address and a promise, I lent money to a complete stranger who hadn't bargained for costs on such a scale. The fact that we were cyclists had meant instant camaraderie.

Tim and I had met briefly while waiting to board the ferry from Shetland to Orkney. It had been that meeting with the couple on the tandem that brought us to the Pentland Firth crossing. The Pentland Firth, I knew, had a reputation for strong currents. Friends of mine, the same friends that took me through the Menai Straits all those years past had canoed there as well. Frightening in that tiny craft: it would be closer to fascinating than from the deck of a ferry that coped with them daily. Only neap tides meant it was flat calm, dull even, and with Orkney slipping into the distance we sat in the bus-like cabin. Young enough to be my son, the cycling, the travel thing meant a good deal in common, and we were able to share experiences easily. A popular attraction despite a fare of almost £1.00 per mile, I was back on deck to witness arrival at the tiny harbour. Bleak, with a scattered community that clung to the hillside was my first impression. To the east, Duncansby Head, the real north easterly tip of mainland Britain climbs steeply away from the settlement, where a lighthouse sits on cliff tops. Most visitors miss the best bits because it means walking. I, too, missed the Stacks of Duncansby, a spectacular rock arch and series of jagged columns rising straight from the sea just a short distance to the south, and visible from the cliff top path. But Guinness needed drinking: there was pizza to get through as well and, afterwards, a 20 miles ride to Thurso. I walked rapidly through the Last House shop and Museum where an odd photograph of times past caught my eye. But without so much as a stick of rock my wallet had stayed firmly shut.

John o'Groats takes its name from Dutchman, Jan de Groot. In 1496, King James IV granted him the ferry franchise to Orkney, then a relatively new part of Scotland. To prevent exploitation of the market, fares were set by the authorities. Some speculate on the possibility that this spawned the name for the silver coin, the Groat. The Royal Mint will, no doubt, have current charges in their sights, so I guess it will only be a matter of time before a £19 coin called the Rip-off hits the tills. Someone took my photograph by the signpost ..... that signpost. The one that says it is 874 miles to Lands End. With beer and food to get through, something had to go. Sadly, it was to be the audio visual experience. Neither would I make it to the craft workshops, despite the obvious attraction of novelty candles, knitwear, and more. Jan de Groot is reputed to have lived in an octagonal house. The John o'Groats hotel is reputed to reflect its style. Part of the disused hotel complex, the bar had the appearance of an attraction about to follow suit. Three years before, I had rounded off my 1000 mile ride round Tasmania with a drink in Devonport, where I would join the ferry to cross the Bass Straits for Melbourne. The young barmaid had been interested to hear of my journey. We spoke for some time, shared our travel experiences. I was a valued customer. If there's one thing the Australians are good at, its travel. And cricket. But I guess that travellers are two-a-penny in John o'Groats. And most of them will have walked or cycled from Lands End. The comfortable lounge bar of that beautifully restored colonial style Australian Irish pub contrasted vividly with surroundings that made the prospect of eating in a bus station café seem appealing. I don't suppose the barman would have been interested if I'd hopped all the way, or done it head over heels. Iceland eh? That much interest. Pizza out of the freezer. It might rhyme. It might have come from "Iceland," the shop, but there the novelty ended. For that is all there was to eat. With a strong lead already, the bus station café notched up another point. I had heard rumours about the background to the situation. Certainly, something wasn't working. At the end of mainland UK, such decrepitude might have been the end of the world. Maybe a little beyond.

Leaving the octagonal experience behind, vowing never to return, it was well into a grey, blustery evening that threatened rain. But with the bit firmly between my teeth ..... after all, this really was the home straight, I set off into the wind. Four miles on, the jetty looked like it belonged in some major international harbour. It needed to be big: the vehicle ferry, Pentalina B had recently started its new Orkney service from there, so I guess that the operators had scoured the land for redundant harbours and dropped their bargain into tiny Gills Bay where I found it, apparently still short of the finishing touches that would transform the area. "Gills bay week," when yachties of the world would cruise the Pentland Firth. Their womenfolk would vie with each other for the finest in fashion. It could only be a matter of time before that sparkle in the eye of local entrepreneurs would become the reality of a thriving marina to rival the world's finest. Not confined to maritime pursuits, the competitive spirit is alive and well in claims made for the proximity of almost everything in that northern corner. The dullest pub, the most expensive ferry, the most spurious claims. But whatever else it might or might not have, John o'Groats does have the most curious attraction and, like me, the punters will keep rolling in. Just to say they've been there. The Queen Mother must have been curiously attracted as well. Just a couple of miles down the road is Castle Mey ..... the royal mum's holiday cottage in the village of that name. Dunnet Head, the most northerly point on mainland Britain is the genuine article and I ought to have pedalled the mile and a half just to say I'd done it. But from teashop to tussocky headland, I missed them all. And the view that extends (on a good day) to Cape Wrath, that north western tip. But the evening was closing in and it had been a long day. The easier option was to walk on the beach at Dunnet Bay. There, with gentle surf sweeping on to smooth golden sand that extends for over two miles, I did the finger dipping in the sea routine that confirmed arrival back on the mainland. And Dunnet Head was clearly visible. The surprise was no sign informing visitors that they were on the beach nearest to that most northerly point in mainland Britain, and I had just seen the most northerly wave to wash up there. Though, doubtless, like the tale of the hole in the road, this one is being looked into.

Sharing a name with its splendid river, Thurso was the biggest town I had seen for some time. Believed to be derived from the Viking "Thor's-a," meaning river of the god Thor, 8500 live there in Scotland's far north. Much of the town is based round ample Georgian streets. But it was well into the evening before pedalling gently through those streets between solid stone buildings simply re-acclimatising, getting used to the idea of traffic, people and the like. Not unexpectedly I was called out to take a peek at the beach. The surfers had all left, but spectacular waves that bring the punters rolling in continued to crash in on the evening scene. Not quite Sydney's Bondi beach: in fact classier by far, as I recalled the disappointment of reality that was dingy concrete surroundings and less than clean, surprisingly cool water. But still, to be in a position to make judgements, comparisons like that I regard as privilege indeed. Having cruised the streets, got a fix on the place, I wanted to know about train times for my journey south the following day. It had been years since visiting Inverness, self-proclaimed capital of the Highlands. I would travel there next day, spend the night in a Bed and Breakfast, and pick up another train to Aberdeen the following morning. That decision had simply crept up on me when I wasn't looking. I would sleep in a bed. I would walk beside the river Ness, take a peek at the Caledonian Canal. And eat a fine restaurant meal. All of these decisions fell into place as I logged back on to life on the mainland, a life that was busier already.

About to re join the real world, and Thurso was the introductory offer. Certainly, it felt like a town, it had all the features that, by definition a town must possess. Shops, offices, industry, employment, and a selection of housing that appeared to cater for all ranks.

Britain does a good rank. Done it for years. And nothing changes. Serfs, they used to be called. At the beck and call of the local lord. In a society dominated by the aristocracy, few had a say on how the country was run. William the Conqueror had distributed land in return for favours done, battles won: and nothing much changed for centuries as titles and the privileges that went with them were handed down through the generations. Peasants did as they were told, and later, as the industrial age overtook Britain they left the rural areas behind to become factory fodder for the workshop of the world as a new brand of exploitation hit the shelves. But where to store these operatives between shifts at the factory? That problem was solved as swathes of terraced houses became the industrial towns and cities that are a familiar sight today.

Factory owners set themselves up as new gentry, making rapid strides in establishing camp and taking on the airs and graces of those with inherited money. Thus, Britain got a second tranche of grand houses and estates, this time built on industrial as opposed to the well established rural sweatshops.

The landed gentry, the ruling class, had it all stitched up. They alone, were eligible to be members of parliament, and had the right to vote. As late as 1830, out of a population of 24 million, only 440,000 could vote. Only in 1832 did parliamentary reforms begin to make a dent on the situation: that first bill brought male property owners, professional people, and traders into politics. But it was almost a hundred years and the reform bill of 1928 before every man or woman over the age of 21 felt the breath of democracy, gained the right to vote.

The ruling class had seen increased mobility brought by the railway age as a threat, for the labouring class could then take their efforts elsewhere and make unreasonable demands on their employers. But, confined to tied cottages, they could still be kept down as combinations, an early attempt at trade unions were outlawed by employers who fought the idea of rights for employees. It took the First World War, and the wiping out of so many young men, to initiate the breakdown many of the taboos that existed between the classes. The Second World War saw the end of so many preconceptions concerning God-given rights, and a whole lot of awkward questions were asked. By the 1950's ordinary people wanted bathrooms in their houses. Soon it would be central heating, cars, and foreign holidays. Where would it end? The toffs wrestled with uncertainty, and the possibility that no one cared any longer to touch their forelocks as they passed.

With the great houses either wrecked by dry rot and demolished, or there for Joe Public and his next-door neighbour to visit as tourist attractions, all that is left is to build your smart house behind a large wall amongst a bunch of others, call it an executive estate and put "The" in front of the name. The rest of the population can put double glazing and plastic windows in their terraces and have the latest registration, paid for on the never-never, parked outside, while those in between might manage a tidy semi on a nice estate. That, then is the new social order, laid out for all to see. Complete with icing, candles and ribbons, Council homes, Terraces, Victorian villas, the new estates, and those walled wonders with twiddly bits stuck on. All shout what level their owners are at, while the latest Audi or Tonka truck titillates the neighbours. And that is what hit me on re-entry to a Britain that has grown up since my childhood. That is just one of the things that travel does: it opens my eyes wide.

By the time I had toured the town, and contemplated all that history, it was pouring with rain. And the notion of a whisky or three got the better of me. The scene inside caught me off guard, peeling off layers of wet clothing and settling into the noisy bar.   The latest hits blared from the juke box and young people drew heavily on cigarettes. I had to choose my seat carefully to avoid the worst of the blue cloud of smoke. Able, for just a few minutes, to appreciate the scene for the total contrast it presented, I could only wonder at the long term health prospects for those youngsters, and many more like them, so plainly hooked up to cigarettes. No longer the interesting traveller, now a balding fellow in a sea of youth out on the beer and smoke experience. Our differences screamed loudly as it became clear that we inhabited different worlds. This, then was re-entry to the real world, and it was with just a little sadness that I stepped out into the rain and made my way to the cliff top campsite.

Thurso ..... The surfers had all left.

Caledonian Canal, Inverness ..... Couldn't have been more different.

It's all over, now

"Back amongst travellers who kept their noses in their books ..... travellers with a small t ..... travellers who read magazines on trains and do their nails."

40

I slept to the sound of surf breaking on the cliff below, but slipped away before six the following morning to catch the early morning train south. At that time of the morning, there is always someone out with a dog. That delivery truck discharging its contents into a shop. And traffic lights that take for ever to go green because nothing comes along to change them. But, after a short ride through empty streets, I wound up at the railway station with time to soak in the atmosphere and anticipate the journey. I have said it before ..... and nothing changed my opinion on the effectiveness of a railway station for its anticipatory and reflective powers. Thurso has had a train service since 1874, when the line south was completed. Despite threats of closure it remains a link, a lifeline by which the town can claim connection with the outside world. That, in my opinion, is what a rail service, even in the motor age, does for a region. It imparts a special confidence that buses and cars cannot deliver. Throughout both world wars, the line was of strategic importance, as nearby Scapa Flow was an important naval base and personnel and equipment were ferried up there regularly. So much did the navy depend upon the connection that for two years, starting in February 1917, in addition to normal and exceptional wartime traffic, a 14 vehicle special through train, complete with officers' sleeping compartments and prison cells for those who had fallen foul of regulations, left London and Thurso daily for the 717 mile, 22 hour journey.

Homeland by the rocks, the Vikings named Scarbolster, and sheltered their longboats there. Scrabster, two miles from Thurso was, and remains the port of embarkation but plans to extend the railway there never materialised. Construction of the harbour began only in 1841, and fifteen years later a ferry service to Stromness, on the Orkney Islands was started. Extended in 1897, and at the time of writing, the subject of further extensive works, Scrabster is the gateway to the northern Scottish Islands, Scandinavia, and the Faroes.

Like the cat that has its claws stuck to clothing when you try to put it out, Thurso clung to me. Gone are the days of Guard's Vans on all routes, the result being limited space for large luggage, cycles and the like. With four bikes on board already the conductor, although sympathetic to my cause, had to turn me away with the hope that there would be room on the next service south in four hours. Thus becalmed, travel plans for the day went out of the window as I watched the train leave. The problem, I realised, was the Lands End to John o'Groats thing and a resultant stream of satiated walkers, runners, hoppers, skippers and cyclists all making their way south after 874 miles under their own steam.

Twenty miles of lush countryside took me to Wick with a clear determination to get on the next train south at its starting point. In 1589 it became a royal burgh. In 1862 over 1100 boats fished out of the harbour. In 1937, the town crowned its first herring queen. Today it is the administrative centre for Caithness, that northern region. But none of this interested me as I briefly toured the streets. I had other things on my mind. Willing something to happen is a complicated business. Eating the most amazing breakfast of bacon, eggs, sausage, tomatoes, toast and marmalade, together with gallons of coffee is an important part of procedure. A difficult concept for those not directly concerned but it does have a remarkable effect on the spirits of those who find themselves short on sleep and left behind in the race south.

I had a reservation all the way home from Aberdeen but not wishing to leave anything else to chance I booked my bike on an early train out of Inverness the following morning to meet up with it. But it would be down to the discretion of the conductor as to whether I could get it to Inverness. Incredible as it might sound, a (road) luggage van follows the afternoon train south, and if all else failed I could get it on that. So I was left with willing and sweet talking if we were to make it south together.

Arriving on the train, the two young men were hoping to cycle to Land's End in eight days. Unlike me, they would ride light and would use guest houses.   Flown over from California specially to do the ride, his third, the American had cycled from Land's End to John O'Groats in eleven days ..... and his flight home left London on the next. Despite the fact that he'd dismantled his bike and packed it into a bag, he'd got on the wrong side of the conductor and almost been turned away. More conciliatory by far, I engaged the woman in conversation. Where I'd been, what my plans were ..... and wasn't it a difficult job she had. But it worked and like New York, the song, so good they named it twice,

Thurso was so good I visited a second time as the train headed back there before finally setting off south for Inverness, and a real bed. Tom and I spent a deal of time talking challenges and experiences. Despite quite different journeys, the similarities were surprising. I thought it was just the insecure bit of me but Tom, the confident Californian, does it as well. Constantly checking that things are where I think they are. Ensuring that bags and panniers are secure, that wallet and documents were where they were an hour ago. The final check that nothing has been left behind after stopping. Pausing to examine the route ahead. Mental preparation before tackling difficult hills. The coffee thing half-way through the morning. And the sheer luxury of evening meals and a beer or two after a hard day at the pedals. These, and more, were our common experiences on the road.

It was an odd thing to have someone else in the driving seat, for the countryside to flash past, to stop only where others decided. To see it all through glass. Tidy, deserted stations in the middle of nowhere came and went. Mountain, moorland, river and loch ..... There one moment, gone the next. And beyond Helmsdale, coastal vistas with deserted golden sandy beaches, as we hugged the shore through Brora, Golspie and once-privately owned Dunrobin station shouting, still, that forelock touching landlord thing from its mock Tudor buildings. The modern A9 road strides across Dornoch Firth, but we turned inland to follow its wooded shores. On through Tain, to skirt Cromarty Firth with Dingwall at its head, still a junction for the line to Kyle of Localsh and the Isle of Skye on the west coast. All too soon we were coasting alongside Beauly Firth, then slowing down to cross the swing bridge over the Caledonian Canal, passage for coast to coast sea going vessels since 1822, and drawing to a halt in a city terminus. I had been up since five in the morning, cycled twenty miles to Wick, and in four hours on the train been back to Thurso and travelled a hundred and eighty miles. By road it is 110 miles ..... a journey that would have kept me busy at the pedals for most of the day. Thrashing rivers, surf on sand, moorland, woodland, oil rigs, naval installations, rural hamlets, small towns, urban landscapes ..... then I was locking my bike to a lamp post in a busy city centre. For me, travel often concerns contrasts. That day they came thick and fast as I compared rapidly changing scenes with a daily routine that had seen me battling with stinging wind and rain, grinding up mountain passes for hours on end. Or both.

The Welsh would have called it Aberness, the English, plain Nessmouth, the French, a romantic sounding Bouche de Ness. But Inverness, where the river Ness joins the sea reflects its surroundings beautifully. Nothing else would have worked, given that delightful accent with which the locals pronounce it. And what of that big fellow just a little upstream. Imagine a Lake Ness monster, or a (well, it sounds French!) Monstre du Lac de Ness. Names like that cannot match the raw impact of that yarn-inducing lonely soul who tantalises, titillates and draws the punters year after year. Despite being round the clock several times there's a lot of mileage left in the tank before that creature of the deep is traded in for the latest model. Inverness entertained me as, eyes wide open, I briefly walked the streets and mingled with the crowds. A city only since the millennium, the regional capital, home to 50,000, it is the only centre in the Highlands with a population in excess of 10,000. All so different to empty places that had been my companion for so long.

A whole room to myself. A bathroom as well. And I could turn the TV on when I liked. My B&B felt odd, yet strangely familiar as I logged on to buildings again. Chairs to sit in, tables to sit at, doors to open. At variance with domestic life that was crouched on the floor of a small tent ..... the great outdoors my partner. I did watch TV ..... mindless early evening stuff. Then strolled into the city for a meal. To have waiters hovering as I decided what to eat, and "would sir like a drink?" The stuff of dreams not long before. So normal for couples talking quietly in the softly lit surroundings. Strangely alone, a feeling amplified, perhaps, by the knowledge that in less than twenty four hours I, too, would re-join the couples thing. This was a last gasp for my independent journey.

Pleased by the hot spicy Thai meal, unconcerned by its cost, I stepped out on to the bustling evening street scene and walked again. With senses finely tuned to my surroundings, I noted graceful old houses, hotels, glass fronted shops and offices, the castle. Built as late as 1835 on the site of an earlier fortress, overlooking the river it currently houses the sheriff's court. Theatre, museum, galleries ..... I missed them all. But what I did see pleased me enormously as I took in gardens, lawns, colourful displays of flowers and strolled along manicured tree lined banks of the wide river that, spanned by fine bridges, swept deliciously alongside. All of these man-made features told of nature so elegantly tamed that is this city. I remembered crossing glacial run-off rivers in Iceland where man, at the mercy of nature, only just manages to keep the lid on it.

James Watt was involved in a scheme as early as 1773, but it was almost thirty years before anything more took place. Travel isn't just a modern phenomenon. Thomas Telford got about a bit, for in 1802 he was involved in surveying work for it. But twenty years elapsed before it was completed, just four years before his famous suspension bridge joined Anglesey to mainland Wales. Widened in the 1840's to allow the passage of larger vessels it was, and remains, an East-West passage for sea going vessels wishing to avoid the long trip round the north coast and the hazardous Pentland Firth. Leaving the city centre behind, I walked out to the Caledonian Canal that strides across the Highland region, linking Fort William on the West coast to Inverness on the East. Loch Lochy, Loch Ness, and Loch Oich, 22 miles of man-made canal and 29 canal lochs separate the two, making 60 miles in total. Moored up for the night was "Lord of the Glens". Chartered by an American tour company the enormous cruise ship also regularly visited Oban and the Western Isles. White uniformed crew and staff attended each and every whim. Passengers sipped at the bar, peered from the decks over still water. Hyper-sensitive to my surroundings after seeing so much, it couldn't have been more different to those rivers. Those freezing cold rivers and wide expanses of gravel strewn water that tumble towards the sea as they dash away from the ice.

At some point on my perambulations it occurred to me that, for the first time in more than a long while, I had left my backpack behind in a locked room. That bloody bag had hardly left my side for almost six weeks. It is one of the down sides of a nomadic life ..... for lose those vital bits of kit, those plastic cards, passport, wallet, camera, and the whole event goes belly up. For that reason, if for no other it would be good to stop. Coincidentally, that is precisely what I had in mind, as I phoned home with a progress report. Television was quite impossible. It had been a long day and my eyes just wouldn't take notice of instructions to stay open.

41

Waking up in a room of my own was odd. A tiny tent is one thing ..... the company of several others, that is Youth Hostelling ..... quite another. Toothpaste and brush were where I had left them in the bathroom. And somewhere to pee without looking to see if there was an audience. It was, after all, my bathroom. If only for a night. But it was a notion I could get used to. If I worked at it. Thurso had been the introductory offer to towns. Inverness found me appreciating simple home comforts that would go unnoticed by most. Go on ..... ask yourself if finding the toothpaste where you left it the night before might be construed as odd?

After breakfast I set off to travel more than 400 miles home. A final ride through the city streets and beside the river ..... reflecting, once again, on the contrasts with "nature rules OK," that had been my companion for so long. Then, with just minutes to spare and almost no time to anticipate the journey I wheeled my bike into the guard's van and settled into my seat for the hundred-plus miles to Aberdeen. Nairn, Elgin, Keith and more. Bungalowland, Detatchedville, Mortgagestown, Unkempstown, Rentedflatsville. There for those who care to look, they all came and went as we drew into tidy stations, well patronised by shopping bags and their feminine minders. It was, after all, Saturday. They had plainly seen a bright star shining over the big city. Realising that the authorities demanded more taxes, they would buy new clothes, fill lunchtime restaurants with exhausted wallets and their hungry keepers before a triumphal return, import duty and VAT paid. The gods would be satisfied for a further week.

Green fields flashed past. Trees, walls, fences, towns, villages, hamlets, roads. I saw them all. And the hares dancing that special dance on their hind legs. That prelude to further delights that so afflicts the human race as well. All of this beyond glass ..... and passed in a jiffy. I wondered how many others had noticed. Back amongst people and the places they live. Back amongst travellers who kept their noses in their books ..... travellers with a small t ..... travellers who read magazines on trains and do their nails. All such a change from where I'd been. Where everyone stopped to speak, to share experiences. The young woman sitting opposite was reading a magazine. On my travels in foreign parts it would have been so natural to chatter, exchange stories, but not here. And what would I say to someone so heavily immersed in a subject like that? Seven steps to great sex flashed across its cover. But just imagine, one hand busy with those scrumptious straps and clips ..... counting to five on the other ..... then missing out on those last two consummating moves because you ran out of fingers. "Fun with numbers," the solution might shout. "You can count on great sex," others might screech. Encouragement indeed for those struggling with literacy and numeracy as Miss Pringle distributes those handouts, smiling a knowing smile behind horn rimmed glasses.

As far as the eye could see things were growing. Trees, crops, grass, shrubs, weeds. Colours, greens of every shade, a tranquil river or two, stone buildings. Beyond doubt, man had been here. Alive to all of this and finely tuned in to my surroundings, I didn't want to miss a thing. The telephone wires on poles went up and down as we progressed ..... just like they used to. Then more manicured still, a golf course. And not a corrugated roof in sight.

Picture the ten year olds in forty years time as they re-live their childhood. Smell the ancient preserved High Speed Train throbbing and belching out toxic blue fumes as grandchildren are told of happy days waiting for its late arrival at a station smelling like the maintenance pit of a bus garage that's about to go out of business. I don't think it will catch on. Not like the flies round the cow-dung-heap scene that is today's fathers wisely unravelling the mystery of the fire in its tummy. And why there's no face on the front. To pushchair-sized people who would probably rather be playing computer games. Undeterred, their charges almost asleep, they speak of delicious rods, cylinders, levers, dials, and not to be frightened when it blows off steam. Of course they're going to scream. Who wouldn't when something with the manners of Puff the Magic Dragon in a temper roars his fearless roar beside you ..... when travel means a child seat in the back of the people carrier. But it will be some years yet before we end our national affair with the nectar that is live, raw energy ..... the tamed, leaping wild animal that is a steam locomotive.

Back from that short visit to the future, my train was drawing in, noisy engines beneath each carriage doing the blue toxic fume thing nicely. Back gardens, back yards, back streets, tattered pink curtains, derelict vehicles. And more. See Britain by train, the adverts implore us. But travel to the depths of almost any city in the land by this means and it becomes a viewing platform for the bits that are hidden away from most. Aberdeen was no exception as the detritus of the fourth largest economy in the world drifted past before accelerating towards Bungalowland and a much easier on the eye coast. For the first time on the entire journey I was retracing my steps as we tripped south beside dune, beach, surf and soft agricultural pasture. On through industrial Dundee ..... over that bridge, next to the remains of the one that collapsed all those years past ..... that snaking two mile crossing high above the Tay estuary.

The woman opposite had finished with it and "would I like to read it?" The first newspaper I'd picked up in a long while and, not unreasonably, it told of gloom and doom. What this footballer, that politician was doing, and who they might be doing it with. Gripping stuff that had me on the edge of my seat. And looking for somewhere to throw up. But the travel section made it all worthwhile as I read a reprint of advice from 1792. Grand tourists of the day could be forgiven for not knowing quite what kit to take with them for their adventure in foreign parts. Rough Guides, Lonely Planet publications. And the rest. They would come along later. But in the meantime it was advisable to take the following, wrote Mariana Starke: pistols & knives, silver table spoons, sugar tongs, cork or double soled shoes & boots, which are absolutely needful in order to resist the chill of brick and marble floors, a rhubarb grater, liquid laudanum, vitriolic acid, pure opium. Additionally, two bedside cases, towels, table cloths, napkins, a cot, so it could be transferred into a sofa bed, two large, thick leather sheets, two pillows, two blankets and a silver or plated teapot would be required.

And there was me with just a bike and what I could carry on it. If only I'd seen that feature first, I reflected, as we sped past fishing village, small town, and densely populated urban area alike. All of it a wild dream for those offspring of aristocrats on their pampered perambulations. On between those enormous painted steel tubes that punctuate the breathtaking vista from the Forth Bridge. And then the back yards of Edinburgh where the topless tourist buses don't go.

Changing platforms had been a mad scramble of luggage and its owners. The woman had two small children, a pushchair and large suitcase. Between us we got all of this, and my bike, past impossible stairs. The American family had plainly read that feature before they left home. But what with pistols and knives not being allowed on the plane, I guess they were down on that one. The rest near-filled the guards van for the journey south. Then, with back yards left behind and no diesel engine beneath we cruised along quietly just like trains used to do. It still felt odd. After hundreds of miles that would have taken days by bike the bungalows and back yards came into view once more. Moments later, with Carlisle's red stone far behind we whirled up Shap amongst bleak moorland and flew past motorists on the M6. I must have dozed a little, for Preston ..... and a long wait for my final connection ..... appeared out of nowhere.

The Danish pastry had come out of a plastic bag, and "would I like regular or large?" the fellow asked when I requested coffee. It's the sort of response I'd expect in a beachside café on the West Coast of the USA ..... and about to ride the surf. But sitting with another sticky bun and coffee waiting for the train from hell was about as different as it is possible to get from that American fancy ..... and those Icelandic filling station cafés where I had fled to escape wind and stinging rain.

With a roar that might reflect its dinosaur status, the dilapidated train tumbled on to the branch line, then called at roughly a hundred stations as it lurched and groaned in an easterly direction. Most people would do anything to avoid this service. But not me, anticipating arriving home after so long away. People ignored each other. No one cared where I had been, where I was going. Back home now. Almost. Then the sun came out for the first time all day, and the fields shone bright green. The grey mill towns and their terraced homes were fascinating after so long away. New perspective on old sights. Travel has the power to inspire.

Beyond the conurbation that is much of East Lancashire I had planned to ride on the canal bank in anticipation of home and all that it meant to me. But she had checked the timetable, and stood on the platform to meet me. The tears well up in my eyes as I record that moment. Later, walking round our garden hand in hand, taking in the hills and moorland beyond, I started the process of logging on to a life temporarily left behind. A life richer for the experience.

Appendix

Some facts
The following is a list of what went with me:

KHS Montana Pro twenty-one gear mountain bike; equipped with rack mounted rear panniers; handlebar mounted front carrier box; three water bottles, total capacity a shade over two litres.
Phoenix Phreak tent,
Down sleeping bag,
Sleeping mat,
Trangia stove, methylated spirits & matches,
2 plastic plates, 1 bowl, 1 mug,
2 knives, 2 forks, 2 spoons, tin-opener,
Windproof fleece,
Kagoule,
3 tee shirts,
2 long sleeve tops,
1 short & 1 Long sleeve shirt,
Pair cycling leggings (proofed),
Pair lightweight casual trousers,
Pair shorts, 8 pairs pants
3 pairs socks,
Wool hat,
All terrain, multi purpose shoes,
Flip flop sandals,
Head torch & spare batteries,
Cycling helmet,
Front / rear cycle lamps & spare batteries,
Cycle tools, puncture kit, spare tyre (folding variety) & lock,
Toilet paper, 4 dried meals for emergency use,
Muesli, coffee, dried milk,
4 bungee cords (for securing tent, sleeping mat, shopping, clothing)
Numerous polythene bags, elastic bands,
Camera, 6 films, Psion computer, spare batteries, mobile phone, travel documents,
Guide book, maps.
Travel towel (15"x 12"!), soap, toothbrush & paste, tea tree oil, plasters, sun block.

Some statistics

Distances in my head are in miles. Road signs are in kilometres. Five miles are roughly eight kilometres.

Visited: Iceland, Shetland, Faroe, Orkney Isles.

Distance travelled by train:	1000 miles
Distance travelled on ferries:	1800 miles
Distance travelled by bus:	400 miles
Distance travelled by car:	300 miles
Distance travelled by bike:	1500 miles
Total distance travelled:	**5000 miles**

Number of nights at sea:	4
Number of nights camping:	28
Number of night spent in Youth Hostels:	7
Nights spent in B&B:	1
Total number of nights:	**40**

Place names explained:

a:	river
baer:	small hill or ridge
bjarg:	cliff
borg:	outcrop
breid:	broad
bru:	bridge
dalur:	valley
ey:	island
eyri:	spit
fjall:	mountain
fjörður:	fjord
floi:	gulf
foss:	waterfall
gigur:	crater
hlid:	slope
Höfn:	harbour
holmur:	islet
hver:	hot spring of fumerole
jokull:	glacier
jokulsa:	glacial river
mork:	woods
nes:	peninsula
sandur:	sandy delta
skard:	mountain pass
vatn:	lake
vik:	bay
vollur:	plain or field

Some Faroese variations:

brekka:	slope
fjallaskard:	mountain pass
Gjógv:	ravine
havn:	harbour
oy:	island
vagur:	bay

Acknowledgements

For all sorts of reasons, my thanks to so many individuals and organisations .....

First and foremost, my parents ..... for ensuring that I was born in time to take early retirement from teaching before the rules of engagement changed ..... and unwittingly allowing me to take a bash at a second career.

Chris, my son ..... who, at the age of eleven, took me on my first cycle camping trip. That was just the start. And it's gone on from there. Together with his ongoing support and practical help concerning my feeble efforts on the computer.

My wife, Pam ..... for being at the end of a telephone line when I take off for several weeks at a time. Together with her steadfast support throughout the journey that was writing *Arctic Cycle*, and seeing it through to publication.

Pam Lister, School Secretary ..... who, remarkably, was able to decipher my spectacularly untidy notes and transform them into presentable paperwork that, as Head of Department, I was required to generate. Pam typed out all of this ..... and maintained that something about my style always made her smile. Encouragement indeed. And the catalyst for my writing ..... that I have come to regard as a new angle on creativity. Which has been my life and career.

My sister in law Pidge Wood, together with friends Liz Holmes and Eric Smalley ..... all of whom read my early ramblings and made encouraging suggestions.

TV Presenter, Nicholas Owen ..... who, having read the final draft, urged others to enjoy *Arctic Cycle*.

Friends/colleagues Derek Jennings, Roy St Pierre, Peter Smith, Pat Hustler, Judith Moorhouse ..... together with local library staff Joanna Cummings and Johanne Hartley ..... and Jo Watson of Colne Bookshop ..... for their much valued comments on cover design.

Proof readers ..... friends David Turner, David Handley, Pat Hustler and Liz Holmes.

The memory of my uncle ..... Leonard Barker ..... whose legacy was the catalyst for this journey.

Friend and fellow writer Keith Hill ..... for his amazing faith in my work, and unfailing conviction that it deserved publication. Sadly, Keith passed away before seeing *Arctic Cycle* completed. He is not forgotten.

Pendle and Barnoldswick writing groups ..... for taking me beyond my (writer's) comfort zone.

The Icelandic Embassy in London ..... who answered many questions when I was planning the journey.

The *Lonely Planet Guide ..... Iceland, Greenland & the Faroe Islands* ..... my companion throughout the journey ..... and the outpouring it spawned.

Countless websites that I used whilst researching for *Arctic Cycle*.

The more than several publishers who turned me down with the most delightfully (and sometimes less so) worded knock-backs. All of them combined to make me ever more determined to see *Arctic Cycle* published.

Keith and Fiona Pearson ..... who put me in touch with Kennedy & Boyd Publishers.

With the exception of Alice, Wonderland ..... and my own flights of fancy ..... everything you read of in the book is real. As are the countless people I met on that journey who, inadvertently, contributed to Arctic Cycle. Only their names are changed as it has not been possible to contact them all for permission to mention them.

Andy Shackleton
July 2006

About the Author

An avid traveller, runner, skier, cyclist ..... and unbelievably poor surfer .... Andy is no stranger to physical challenges. It is only natural that his first book should concern the biggest challenge of his life. A regular marathon runner, he freely admits that cycling round Iceland was the hardest thing he has ever done.

Designing and making has been Andy Shackleton's life. For over thirty years he taught those skills to others. In his spare time he has tackled anything from simple DIY to major house and classic car renovation.

Following early retirement he sought further creative challenges. And added writing to well known skills with wood, metal, stone, and more.

Young on the inside, married for more years than he cares to consider, family grown up ..... Andy's home is on the Lancashire/Yorkshire border, where he regularly drops over the garden wall to run on the hills.

Index

A

Aberdeen 18-21, 26, 225, 226, 229, 240, 245, 249, 250
Akranes 98, 102
Akureyri 36, 66, 68, 69, 70, 76, 94
Alþing 105, 108, 119, 212
Alþingishus 122
Arnarson 119

B

Bakkafjörður 43, 44, 45
Bakkaflói 43
Bergen 13, 26, 27, 140, 216, 223, 226
Berufjörður 161
Berwick 20
Birds 45, 51, 56, 82, 122, 231
Bjargtangar 84
Blönduós 69, 73
Blue Lagoon 16, 101, 104, 115, 120
Books 43, 228
Bordeyri 70, 77
Borgafjörður 102
Borgarnes 97
Borðoy 188, 194, 199
Borðoyarvík 199
Boulders 53, 56, 57, 134, 147
Breiðafjörður 77, 81, 83
Breiðdalsvík 165-167
Bressay 23, 225
Bretison 204
Brjánslækur 81
Bru 75, 76, 81, 91
Brunel 72, 185
Búðardalur 80, 81, 94, 207
Buðir 167
Buses 43, 76, 78, 84, 86, 93, 96, 115, 136, 143, 165 187, 219, 222
Butter Mountain 37

C

Caledonian Canal 240, 243, 246, 248
campsite 71, 196, 242
Carlsberg 49
Cars 102
Christianity 65, 108, 110, 204, 212, 232
Cornwall 23, 229
Cyclist 42, 43, 55, 66, 83, 106, 113, 157, 159, 180, 182, 184, 193, 226, 227

D

Denmark 26, 33, 55, 108, 136, 206, 213, 232
Dettifoss 52, 55, 114
Dicuil 105
Djúpivogur 160, 161, 163
Duncansby Head 238
Dursley Pedersen 55
Dyrhólaey 138

E

Edinburgh 20, 196, 251
Egilsstaðir 35, 126, 139, 169, 173, 175, 176
Eiði 210
Eyjafjörður 66
Eysturoy 186, 199, 210

F

Farming 64
Faroes 16, 27, 28, 33, 157, 162, 169, 177, 178, 180-182, 186-188, 197, 200, 203, 204, 207, 208, 210, 212, 216, 244
Fáskrúðsfjörður 167, 168, 170
Faxaflói 100
Ferries 20, 26, 83, 180, 185, 195, 215, 226, 238
Finnbogadóttir 177
Fishing 68, 160, 194, 233
Fjords 74, 75, 130, 159, 165, 167, 207, 227
Flatey 83
Fógetinn 121
Football 20, 187, 212

Forth 20, 251
Fuglafjørdur. 202
Funningsfjørdur 207, 209

G

Gaelic 200
Galleries 21, 69, 122
Geysers 16, 21, 69, 111
Geysir 104, 110, 111, 113
Gigjökull 132, 134, 136
Gjógv 199, 202, 207-209
Glaciers 16, 53, 69, 128, 131, 134, 140, 142
Godafoss 65
Gota 204
Grimsey 39
Grímsstaðir 53, 56
Grindavik 115
Gullfoss 104, 114-117

H

Harald 26, 105, 108
Hartsholm 204
Heating 36, 204, 242
Heriot 99
Hjartarson 177
Hlíðarfjall 68
Höfn 142, 143, 147, 155, 156, 160
Hólmavík 92, 93
Hostels 104, 178, 254
Hrútafjörður 75, 77, 80
Hummer 65
Húsavík 36, 52
Hut 35, 39, 48, 77, 92, 96, 134, 237
Hvalfjörður 97, 102, 107
Hvammsfjörður 80
Hvammstangi 74, 80
Hver 58
Hveragerði 104, 126
Hverfell 61

I

Icebergs 15, 153, 171
Inverness 240-249
Ísafjarðardjúp 87
Ísafjörður 75-77, 81, 84, 86, 90, 93, 94, 208

J
Jarlshof 219, 220, 221
John O'Groats 226, 238, 239, 245
Jökulsárgljúfur 52
Jökulsárlón 147-151
Jökulsá á Dal 37

K
Kaldbaksfjordur 211
Keflavik 52
Kirkjubæjarklaustur 139
Kirkwall 232, 233, 234, 236
Klaksvík 185, 188, 191, 194-199
Kollafjörður 211
Kollur 210
Kópasker 51
Krafla 59
Krossa 134

L
Lava 61, 62, 116
Lebanon 61
Leirvík 191, 194, 199, 200
Lerwick 13, 18, 21, 23, 24, 26, 105, 218, 222, 225, 229
Le Corbusier 69
Ljósavatn 65
Lögberg 108
Lögurinn 35
Lupins 40, 123, 180

M
Mablik Endar 45, 174
Mainland 228, 236
Meccano 54
Melrakkaslétta 39
Midge Lake 52, 62
Moraine 59
Morsárjökull 146, 147
Museums 122
Mýrdalsjökull 131
Mývatn 52, 58, 59, 62, 65, 66

N
Námafjall 58
Námaskarð 58
Narvik 13, 140

Newcastle 19
New Zealand 21, 43, 131, 142, 196, 234
Norðragøta 203, 206
Norrona 13, 105, 180, 210, 213, 217
Northumberland 19, 20
North Ronaldsay 228
Norway 13, 16, 23, 26, 35, 67, 76, 98, 105, 110, 119, 140, 192, 193, 200, 227, 232

O
Olfusa 126
Orkney 13, 17, 22, 169, 215, 221, 223-239, 244
Oxara 108

P
Palestine 61
Panniers 18, 42, 62
Parliament Plains 105, 112
Partick Thistle 20
Pentland Firth 226, 231, 237, 238, 239, 248
Pyrenees 88
Pytheus 105

R
Railway 147, 166, 231
Raufarhöfn 36, 48
Repairs 53, 68, 97, 140, 159
Reykjahlíð 59, 63
Reykjanes 100, 115
Reykjavik 16, 52, 57, 58, 68, 69, 72, 74, 76-84, 91, 93, 96-108, 115, 117-132, 136, 138, 139, 145, 147, 177, 182, 208, 219
Reyðarfjörður 159, 168, 169
Rivers 15, 16, 35, 37, 43, 57, 73, 108, 114, 132, 134, 146, 155, 167, 195, 240, 247, 248
Route 1 28, 36, 57, 80
Runavík 188

S
Saga 109, 110
Saladt 81
Scandinavia 26, 29, 200, 202, 244
Scapa Flow 228, 236, 244
Scotland 20-22, 26, 68, 225, 226, 231, 232, 238, 240
Scrabster 206, 225, 244
Scree 92
Selfoss 126
Seljalandsfoss 129, 133, 135, 138
Seyðisfjörður 15, 30, 32, 33, 34, 37, 80, 162, 169, 175-178, 180, 181, 206
Sheep 56, 92, 94, 194, 195, 200, 202, 203
Shetland 13, 17, 18, 21, 23, 25-28, 105, 169, 218-228, 232, 234, 238
Sigridarstofa 114
Skaftafell 142, 143, 145
Skaftafellsjökull 145
Skálafjørdur 186, 206
Skeiðarársandur 140
Skipton 19
Skógafoss 138
Skútustaðir 64
Smjörfjöll 37
Smoky Bay 119
Snaefellsnes 82, 100
Snow 13, 32, 35, 37, 40, 45, 55, 90, 132, 164, 185
South Ronaldsay 226, 228, 237
Spokes 54, 71, 97, 145
Springs 36, 113, 119
Steingrímsfjörður 93
Streymoy 186, 210, 211
Strokkur 112, 113
Stromness 221, 223, 225, 228, 231, 244
Stykkishólmur 80-84, 122
Sumburgh 219, 220, 222
Sundini 210, 211
Supermarkets 25, 33, 49, 72, 100, 128, 165, 179, 213
Surface 36, 43, 45, 86,

111, 130, 157, 161, 174,
Suðureyri 86
Swellies 32
Switzerland 42

T
Tangafjordur 186
Tasmania 21, 43, 142, 172, 234, 236, 239
Tay 20, 251
Teacher 22, 27, 59, 79, 146, 156, 206
Tent 15, 18, 35, 36, 43, 67, 71, 79, 87, 137, 153, 164, 171, 229, 230
Þingvallavatn 105
Þingvellir 104-110, 112
Þorshöfn 46, 47
Þórsmörk 128-130, 134, 139, 146, 147, 159
Thule 105
Thurso 226, 237-246, 249
Tiganes 212
Tjörnin 12, 124
Toftir 185-189, 206
Tomasson 114
Tonka 81, 98, 101, 128, 165, 178, 207, 242
Tórshavn 28, 29, 181, 183, 185, 186, 189, 197, 204, 210, 211, 212, 215
Trees 45, 64, 69, 76, 106, 123, 175, 194, 204, 231, 249
Trolls 76, 132, 133
Trondur i Gotu 204
Tunnels 16, 86, 97-102, 119, 168, 185, 192-194, 202, 211, 223
Turf roofs 16, 29, 191, 203, 204, 207, 213
Tyres 16, 18, 46, 55, 71, 72, 74, 77, 79, 82, 84, 97, 120, 130, 139, 142, 143, 147, 156, 227

U
Unsealed Roads 40, 46, 82

V
Varmahlíð 71, 73, 80
Vatnajökull 35, 140, 142
Vegetation 33, 35, 53, 56
Vik 138, 141
Vikings 25, 26, 81, 175, 200, 204, 232, 236, 240
Vopnafjörður 40, 41, 44

W
Washing 31, 39, 43, 45, 55, 56, 77, 143, 161, 165, 178
Waterfalls 55, 65, 69, 86, 129, 133, 165
Waterfall of the Gods 65
Weather 16, 25, 29, 36, 57, 84, 97, 164, 173, 228, 230
Western Fjords 74, 75, 130, 227
Wheels 16, 18, 54, 71, 77, 98, 105, 193
Wick 245, 246
Y
Youth Hostel 26, 67, 68, 100, 104, 169, 196, 207, 218

Printed in the United Kingdom
by Lightning Source UK Ltd.
112787UKS00002B/61-318